Law and Religion in a Global Context

Volume 4

Series Editor

Frank S. Ravitch, College of Law, Rm 315, Michigan State University, East Lansing, MI, USA

Law and Religion in a Global Context will focus on law and religion issues from a global perspective at a time when that field is of increasing importance and relevance around the world. Designed to be broad, the scope allows for books on the relationship between religion and government as well as on religious law. Focus will be placed on comparative law issues, but also on issues within single countries. Representative areas of focus will be:

- the relationship between government and religion ranging from laicete to theocracy
- religious freedom in pluralistic societies
- the relationship between religious freedom and other freedoms such as freedom of speech and sexual freedom
- regulation of religion by government
- original contributions on religious law

The series seeks to highlight up and coming voices in the field alongside those of established scholars. We encourage scholars from a wide range of geographic perspectives to apply. Purely doctrinal analysis of law and religion is not preferred. Nor is analysis of religious law issues without any original contribution or insights. The only exception to this rule might be books on legal doctrine from a region that has been under analyzed in English language literature.

Paula Montero • Camila Nicácio •
Henrique Fernandes Antunes
Editors

Religious Pluralism and Law in Contemporary Brazil

Springer

Editors
Paula Montero
Department of Anthropology
University of São Paulo
São Paulo, Brazil

Camila Nicácio
Law School
Federal University of Minas Gerais (UFMG)
Belo Horizonte, Brazil

Henrique Fernandes Antunes
Brazilian Center of Analysis and Planning
São Paulo, Brazil

ISSN 2946-5931 ISSN 2946-594X (electronic)
Law and Religion in a Global Context
ISBN 978-3-031-41980-5 ISBN 978-3-031-41981-2 (eBook)
https://doi.org/10.1007/978-3-031-41981-2

This Springer imprint is published by the registered company Springer Nature Switzerland AG
The registered company address is: Gewerbestrasse 11, 6330 Cham, Switzerland

Paper in this product is recyclable.

Acknowledgment

This book would have been impossible without the support of the São Paulo Research Foundation (FAPESP-Brazil, n° 21/08955-6).

Contents

List of Contributors

Cleto Junior Pinto de Abreu Center for Historical Research, HSE University, Saint-Petersburg, Russia

Olivia A. Barbosa University of São Paulo, São Paulo, Brazil

Paula Bortolin State University of Campinas – UNICAMP, Campinas, Brazil

Sabrina Soares D'Almeida Brazilian Center of Analysis and Planning, São Paulo, Brazil

Henrique Fernandes Antunes Brazilian Center of Analysis and Planning, São Paulo, Brazil

Dirceu André Gerardi Law School, Getúlio Vargas Foundation (FGV), São Paulo, Brazil

Paula Montero Department of Anthropology, University of São Paulo, São Paulo, Brazil
Brazilian Center of Analysis and Planning, São Paulo, Brazil

Helena de Morais Manfrinato Othman Brazilian Center of Analysis and Planning, São Paulo, Brazil

Renata Nagamine Brazilian Center of Analysis and Planning, São Paulo, Brazil

Camila Nicácio Law School, Federal University of Minas Gerais (UFMG), Belo Horizonte, Brazil

Rafael Quintanilha Department of Anthropology, University of São Paulo, São Paulo, Brazil

Lilian Sales Federal University of São Paulo, Unifesp, Guarulhos, SP, Brazil

Aramis Luis Silva Federal University of São Paulo, São Paulo, Brazil

Introduction: Religious Pluralism and Law in Contemporary Brazil

Paula Montero, Camila Nicácio, and Henrique Fernandes Antunes

This book is the result of collective research that focuses on analyzing the way in which the framework of pluralism, whose legal reference is the Constitution of 1988, gave rise to conflicts surrounding the classic notion of secularism. This framework, in force until very recently in Brazil, prescribes the formal separation between the State and religions and the State's neutrality in the face of religious practices. This collection of studies indicates that attempts of regulating religion anchored in this framework became the object of growing tensions and disputes from the 1990s onwards. In particular, the right to religious freedom has become especially controversial topic when it comes to religious organizations actions in the public arena. The same can be said about the principle of "tolerance", understood as a normative ethos of the relations among religions, which grants religious groups their autonomy to self-regulate.

By instituting pluralism as a constitutional principle, the Charter gave rise to the gradual emergence of new political agendas focused on diversity issues. Concomitantly, it allowed for the recognition of new subjects of rights engaged in defending these new agendas, as well as the creation of new institutional frames and devices

---

The texts that comprise this collection are the result of the project "Religion, Law and Secularism", coordinated by Paula Montero and financed by São Paulo Research Foundation (FAPESP) (2015/024975). We would like to thank FAPESP for the funding.

P. Montero (✉)
Department of Anthropology, University of São Paulo, São Paulo, Brazil
e-mail: pmontero@usp.br

C. Nicácio
Law School, Federal University of Minas Gerais (UFMG), Belo Horizonte, Brazil
e-mail: cnicacio@ufmg.br

H. Fernandes Antunes
Brazilian Center of Analysis and Planning, São Paulo, Brazil
e-mail: henrique.antunes@cebrap.org.br

P. Montero et al. (eds.), *Religious Pluralism and Law in Contemporary Brazil*, Law and Religion in a Global Context 4, https://doi.org/10.1007/978-3-031-41981-2_1

capable of implementing them. The articles in this collection describe the new configurations of some of these agendas that, from the 2000s onwards, emerged in disputes on secularism, tolerance, religious freedom, human rights, the family and cultural heritage. They also map the actors that emerge in these disputes: they are state representatives, religious leaders, parliamentarians, researchers, scholars, and activists, among others. One can see, therefore, that it is a matter of observing actors located in very unequal positions of power, who have different skills and competences and who relate with others to promote and/or contest rights and how they are interpreted. The studies developed here highlight that, given the emergence of this institutional and legal context associated with pluralism, the actors are compelled to develop new mobilization strategies and different specific skills that enable them to debate in the most different public arenas (Cefai 2017).[1] How and by whom these actors are trained to do so was also a subject of our interest in this volume. In particular, we noted that mastering the language of rights and managing its tools becomes crucial to control the categories and interpretations of the rights that are circulated and that shape the disputes consolidating the advance of its agendas. Human rights gain centrality in these disputes as a language in which actors constitute themselves as subjects of rights and form activism network, boosting their demands by modeling ways of expressing themselves in public. How the actors appropriate this language, which specific rights are constituted from it and in which scenes these disputes develop and can be empirically observed, were some of the questions that guided our work.

1 The Legal-Administrative Changes of the Post-Constituent Pluralist State

The Brazilian Constitution promulgated in 1988 marks the adoption of a new perspective in law, known for what is conventionally called modern constitutional law or new constitutional law. Grounded on the ideas of the hierarchy of norms and the supremacy of the Constitution, neoconstitutionalism proposes that the norms of constitutionalized human rights, also referred to as fundamental rights, have a higher

[1] Cefai (2017, p. 200) defines public arena as a social arena in which actors "define their problems as public and feel, act and speak accordingly". Inspired by this concept that aims to overcome the limitations implicit in the theoretical models that treat religious pluralism as a "market," as in the utilitarian view, or as a "field" in the approach that emphasizes the relations of power and domination between religious groups, we use this term in the articles presented here to describe the variety of scenes in which the actors interact in the name of something defined as a subject of public interest. The arenas can be of a legal nature (such as public hearings, meetings of jurists, police stations counters), political (such as parliamentary debates, public policies, guardianship councils) or civil (network of religious activists, religious rituals, civil associations). We emphasize that this approach, by privileging relationships and not established groups, enables us to observe connections between different social and institutional worlds.

status than other rights and that their interpretation is informed by the former. The idea of constitutional supremacy has appeared in the literature at least since the 1930s. However, it took on another form in the post-World War II period, proposing the supremacy of fundamental rights and, consequently, the material hierarchy of law. This conception gained ground in several democracies during the same period. In this framework, human rights and the principle of human dignity, of Christian origin and recognized in Brazil as one of the foundations of the Republic, became central to the operationalization of law and legal institutions. In this process, they became part of growing pluralism in Brazilian society and in disputes that intensified involving the authority of the Judiciary as arbiter of social conflicts. According to this understanding, beyond a mere "political charter" between the State and citizens, the Constitution is considered a legal norm of fundamental importance, whose plexus of values and principles must inspire and be respected by infra-constitutional norms, under penalty of control and review. In Brazil, this constitutional framework was strongly observed in the context of regulating private relations, historically marked by individualism and patrimonialism, and by the passage from individuality to sociality, in which notions such as contract and property must fulfill a social function. On the other hand, in the wake of a long dictatorial regime, and in the name of the principles of freedom, equality, autonomy and non-discrimination, the 1988 Constitution intended to promote a pluralist society, open to the diversity of life projects, whether related to religion, ethnicity, or what we currently call gender and sexual orientation. In other words, the Constitution projects a pluralist society in the very act of declaring it as if it existed beforehand, and in this society respect for diversity appears as a guideline and, therefore, as a reference for implementing public policies and making laws and judicial decisions.

In order to establish more favorable conditions for constructing this plural society, the new Charter and subsequent laws established new rights and also new legal instruments aimed at expanding the population's participation in the justice distribution system. As a result, they expanded the role of those entitled to participate. Instruments such as the *Ação Direta de Inconstitucionalidade*—ADIn (Direct Action of Unconstitutionality), *Ações Declaratórias de Constitucionalidade*—ADC (Declaratory Action of Constitutionality) and *Ações de Descumprimento de Preceito Fundamental*—ADPF (Actions that Breach Fundamental Precepts)[2] no longer belong only to legal-judicial jargon. They comprise the grammar of various social agents and institutions, allowing them to challenge the constitutionality of laws and normative acts enacted by Parliament or government bodies. In addition to expanding the list of actors legitimized to propose such actions, the 1988 Constitution and subsequent legislation opened up the possibility of civil society taking part in discussions of pressing issues through public hearings, held in the Judiciary and in the Legislative. Especially in the Judiciary, the resort to the *amicus curiae*, or "friend of the Court", has been consolidated as a possibility of listening to diversity and social polyphony, in the antechamber of decisions to be taken by the Federal

[2]Lawsuits that comprise the control of constitutionality in the Brazilian legal system.

Supreme Court. Based on the criterion of the subjective pertinence of the representation, actors are accredited to participate, making contributions to the Court that are likely to broaden and diversify the reference frameworks that guide the definition of the legal norm. These contributions often consist of antagonistic views of a wide range of issues that dispute the attention of judges and parliamentarians. Using this type of tool can be considered an indicator of how fracturing these issues are for the broader society. Through these legal devices, discussions about the definition and circumscription of the notion of family, the relevance of criminalizing homophobia or even the coherence between religious education in public schools and secular regimes pass through the mediation of social and institutional representation and enter parliament and the courts vocalizing social pluralism.

Nevertheless, the levels of judicial decisions and law-making are not the only targets of these new forms of participation and claims. Some of the studies in this collection show that, in addition to the Judiciary and the Legislative Power, similar channels and tools are open in the administrative area, based on hearings, public consultations and the possibility of representation, instruments with which public policies and State bureaucracy are equally disputed to promote and/or question rights.

Indeed, successive post-Constitution democratic governments have expanded tools for civil society participation in public management. To this end, they have developed a policy to create and implement management councils in areas considered strategic. As a result of this institutional novelty, the presence of civil, religious and non-religious associations was expanded in implementing rights, with access by these organizations to public funds.

Religious organizations found a favorable field to act in a wide range of arenas in this new administrative format of cooperation with the State to promote a rights agenda. An important enabling element of this model of cooperation between the State and civil society was the 2014 Legal Framework for Civil Society Organizations (Law 13,019), which proposed legal and institutional solutions aiming to normalize this relationship. Before this law was approved, the parameter for this cooperation was the Budget Guidelines Law, which, due to its scope and lack of clear rules, led to legal uncertainty and continuous criminalization of social organizations. The legal framework defined three types of partnership—promotion, term of collaboration and cooperation agreement –, the rules of accountability and established a public notice to select the social organization that will enter into the partnership. In addition, it began to require organizations competing for the public notice to present their statute in which they describe their social objectives and to demonstrate previous experience, and technical and operational capacities.

This new management context focusing on civil organizations encourages the internal reorganization of religious institutions.[3] Although the Legal Framework has

[3]The Civil Code of 2002 (Law 10,406) had already changed the legal personality of churches, making them equivalent, regardless of their constitutions or internal forms of government, to civil associations governed by private law. Through Law 10,825 enacted the following year, they were,

exempted churches from specifying their social purposes in their statutes, in practice, religious organizations that associate with the State for the exercise of some activity subsidized by it must present the public relevance and effectiveness of the service they provide to society. In this process, those responsible are obliged to incorporate the grammar of rights and abandon the ecclesial infrastructure as a support for social work. Thus, as missionary agencies or administrators of "goods of salvation" in the classic Weberian expression, characteristic of the juridical-legal format of the church type, these organizations had to evolve into a multiplicity of different civil entities to be able to be incorporated, as partners of the State, in implementing rights.

2 Religious Activism and Rights

The growing role of religious organizations both in terms of producing laws and in terms of managing and implementing social rights has impacted the design and conduct of public policies in several areas. One of the effects of this action by religious organizations is the expansion of the role of religious actors in framing pluralism, either by regulating or recognizing differences. Carried out in the form of social movements, law, more than religion or morality, gains centrality as a resource in social action, both for mobilization and in litigation, playing a strategic role in processes in which the analysis of articles in this volume address. There are growing networks of religious activists who conceive law no longer as a "reason" or "reference" immanent in a normative act or discourse, but as a resource (Commaille 2015), some will say "weapon" (Isarel 2009), available in the social game, where new actors, new procedures and new rights emerge. This volume does not, therefore, deal with the relationship between religion and the law from an externalist point of view to one and the other, that is, taking religion and law as distinct fields, although subject to theoretical articulation. We question the relationship between religion and law by observing the practices of the actors, which led us to consider how they have used legal language and judicial instances to contest the law, to affirm it, or even to resignify it. The courts were also the focus of our attention when they became the object of political dispute and they began to be perceived by religious segments as antagonists to their agenda, that is, parties in conflicts rather than arbiters. Finally, it also seemed important to us to turn our analysis to legal documents and rhetoric to provide a repertoire of the reasons given for interpreting a certain norm by the lawmakers.

The perspective outlined above clarifies why we place the legal field as a privileged place to observe lines of force that dispute the ideological, political and

however, differentiated from political parties and other civil societies and associations. Defined as "religious organizations", they gained autonomy to manage themselves. This legal personality, which recognizes churches as associations, makes them able to enter into partnerships with the public administration. For a good example of how these changes are expressed in evangelical organizations, please see Cleto Abreu (2021).

social transformations of Brazilian society from the 2000s onwards. In fact, the opening to pluralism established by the 1988 Constitution already allowed us to foresee this nexus insofar as it sends religious and non-religious actors back to an indeterminate and permanent process of defining rights, in which tensions are established inside and outside the legal field, constituting, thus, this arena.

We have edited this volume into two thematically separate but connected parts. The first part is dedicated to case studies on minority rights and their impacts on the debate surrounding secularism and the limits of religious freedom. These works show how the expansion and legal recognition of religious, gender and racial pluralism strains the requirements for the protection of freedom and religious tolerance. In the second part, the focus shifts to case studies that analyze the narratives that dispute the language of human rights. These studies show that disputes concerning the content of human rights refer, *par excellence*, to the indeterminacy regarding this permanent redefinition of rights and serve as a parameter for the inscription, at any time and under certain conditions, of possible consensus in laws, judicial decisions and public policies.

The dissensions, present in all the cases analyzed here, mobilize a wide range of actors—religious leaders, civil society members and State representatives –, who are engaged in expanding or refraining the recognition of the rights of gender, religious and racial minorities and in the effort to redefine the limits of what can be understood as religious freedom and human rights. The chapters analyze these disputes in different public arenas (Cefai 2002) as mentioned above: *legal* ones such as the Public Hearings in the Federal Supreme Court examined by Montero et al., Sales and Almeida, *political*, such as the parliamentary debates explored by Bortolin, *administrative*, as in the cases of the chapters by Nicácio and Antunes that focus on the way in which state bureaucracies formalize, respectively, "religious intolerance" complaints and the demands for recognizing religious practices as cultural heritage; and, finally, the arena of *civil organizations*, examined in the chapters by Abreu, Manfrinato and Silva et al., respectively, exploring how the concept of religious freedom is dealt with by evangelical law-makers, and the use of the language of human rights by the institutional leaders of Muslim and transgender organizations to portray and control their public image.

The notion of public arenas, therefore, enabled us to compose, based on well-circumscribed empirical cases, a multidimensional and rhizomatic panorama of the tensions that correlate actors and institutions without obliging us to treat religions as corporate groups and to think about political legal, religious and civil spheres as separate, homogeneous or self-contained. The data collected by the research in this collection transform the routine image that one has of religious actors as simple congregants in a community of believers and practitioners of a religion. Thus, the studies carried out by Abreu show that these actors are also organized in networks of activists who engage in communication and mobilization structures. From the cases at hand, we observed that the rapid diffusion through information networks produced by these agents has a great effect on the national political culture, spreading a certain understanding about the moral value of diversity. The interconnection between the different experiences takes place, in practice, through discursive networks that articulate different actors, iterations of arguments and categories, and the connection of different networks via trajectories and displacements of successful strategies from one case to another. In order to understand this phenomenon, our analysis examined the dynamics of actors' engagement in different arenas, their discursive and performative resources, their forms of categorization and their strategies for addressing and producing audiences. Finally, the articles also aim to demonstrate the complexity of the processes that enable these actors to exist in the legal-State arenas.

3 Part 1. Pluralism: Minority Rights, Religious Freedom and Secularism

Recognizing religious, racial and gender diversity as an object of protection at the legal level, but also as a social experience, has made "religion" and the defense of its freedom an object of continuous legal controversy. The set of cases examined here enables us to observe that the agenda of respect for diversity highlights, often dramatically, the crisis of the republican principles of "tolerance" and "religious freedom," whose scope seemed settled for a long time. Furthermore, these studies also address the primacy of State devices, and their forms of regulation, in the configuration of disputes to redefine these principles. Indeed, as the studies conducted by Nicácio; Bortolin; Antunes; Montero et al. show, it is in the competition for access and management of governmental legal-administrative devices that actors dispute the understanding and limits of these categories. This does not mean that actors necessarily have legal competence to use these concepts. In fact, most of the time, it is not what one sees. Due to this, the studies presented here also set out to examine why, in what way and in what context the actors resort to these normative judgments.

The results of these confrontations in the different arenas are quite complex and contradictory and cannot be anticipated as a simple imposition of the power of influence of religious actors' views on non-religious or secular perspectives. The studies in the first part show that government devices and arenas work as true filters that guide the *mise en forme* of the debate, to use Nicácio's expression more widely, modifying the terms of the problem to be solved. Furthermore, the institutional engineering developed over the last two decades to incorporate the recognition and respect for diversity into the State agenda has significantly altered the way of defining religion: in the case analyzed by Antunes, for example, the very process of regulating religious use of ayahuasca, sanctioned in the 1980s, rooted the conception in the administrative imagination and public opinion that these religions constitute an Afro-indigenous legacy that deserves to be preserved also as part of the cultural heritage of a plural society. Progressively including indigenous ethnicities in this process generated new dissents and classifications, reconfiguring this public debate. The disputes around the patrimonialization of the religious use of ayahuasca resulted in debates about the proper uses of the brew and the nature of the relationship between the state and ayahuasca groups, as well as in the questioning of the notions of tradition, Indigenous peoples, heritage, cultural rights, the right to diversity and diffuse rights. Such disputes resulted in the emergence of new forms of claiming collective rights and affirmative policies regarding the State. The racialization of a religious practice, particularly Afro-Brazilian ones, constitutes a long-term historical phenomenon in Brazil. However, the expansion of recognizing religious pluralism from the 2000s onwards gave rise to an inversion that led to the ethnification or culturalization of indigenous religion, as demonstrated by Antunes, on the one hand, but also to the racialization of religious intolerance as pointed out by Nicácio, on the other hand.

In addition to racial diversity, disputes over the recognition of gender diversity also conflagrated the issue of religious freedom. The study conducted by Abreu shows how, as a result of these disputes, the issue of religious freedom moves from Parliament to the Judiciary, supported by the National Association of Evangelical Jurists (ANAJURE). Through the legal principle of conscientious objection, ANAJURE has been establishing legal strategies to counter the guidelines of criminalizing homophobia and decriminalizing abortion in the name of civil and religious freedom.

Recognizing diversity also opposed the principles of secularism and religious freedom in the case of offering religious education in public schools. The study conducted by Montero et al. demonstrates that in the legal process of resolving the aporia of offering Religious Education as a school subject and respecting, at the same time, the secularity of the State and the principle of diversity, the understanding of the nature and purpose of this type of teaching was altered. From a catechetical and doctrinal instrument, it became an object of academic knowledge (of history, anthropology or philosophy of religion) and an instrument for the moral education of children, becoming a means of teaching them to respect differences.

4 Part 2. Human Rights as Language

According to authors such as Lefort (2011), Luciano Oliveira (1992) and Moyn (2010), among others, in the 1970s, human rights became vernacular and emerged as an anti-totalitarian framework. Nevertheless, issues related to minority identities from a social point of view only appear as a norm in the 1990s, at the end of the Cold War. This change has transformed human rights into what Moyn calls a maximalist framework.

In the long historiographical debate on the topic addressed by Silva et al., authors such as Moyn (2010) recognize the 1970s as a significant turning point. With the decline of nationalist, socialist and communist utopias, human rights became popular on a global scale, becoming a *lingua franca*.

In the Brazilian case, human rights became vernacular, at this time, as a language of justice in the fight against the military regime, in a process in which Catholic actors and the Church's network were fundamental. Catholic institutions defended the expansion of social and civil rights, especially during the military dictatorship (1964–1985), contributing to the constitution and defense of a "culture of rights" (Sales and Mariano 2019). However, with the advent of the democratic regime, there was a progressive shift from the anti-totalitarian and anti-torture platform to an agenda of promoting minority rights, consolidated by the promulgation of the 1988 Constitution.

In this new national context, the interpretation itself and the prevailing meanings of human rights became the object of dispute. Its defense by the Catholic Church reached a milestone in the 1990s, when the state agenda of sexual and reproductive rights was drawn up more clearly and, in the following decades, increasingly efficient tools for implementing these policies were created. The Human Rights Secretariat, created in 1997, adheres to the diversity rights policy, based on dialogues established with the demands of movements dedicated to gender, feminist, black, and indigenous diversity. Over the years, there was a boom in public policies aimed at broadening the paradigm of inclusion that considers society from a wide range of differences—ethnic and racial, gender and beliefs. In this scenario, universalist policies lose their prominence in favor of prioritizing differentialist public policies. As a result, the notion of human rights undergoes a change in meaning, shifting away from the grammar of political persecution and social rights to incorporate the defense of the rights of ethnic and racial minorities. The 2013 National Human Rights Action Plan definitively detaches the protection of human rights from the scope of the Catholic Church to the State, as shown by the analyses carried out in the chapters by Bortolin and Sales, respectively. The studies presented here show that the Catholic Church led the opposition in relation to sexual and reproductive rights. However, in terms of the rights of ethnic minorities, such as Indigenous peoples, blacks and *quilombolas*, and also in terms of these populations land rights, it still maintains, on the contrary, the monopoly and legitimacy of its protagonism (see Almeida).

In the case of evangelicals, nevertheless, the avatars of human rights follow a more recent path of their own. The new paradigm of political activism of some evangelical segments, following the previous public culture inaugurated by Catholic groups to confront the demands of sexual and reproductive rights, mobilizes above all the right to religious freedom. From an instrument to defend the public presence of Protestants in the twentieth century, religious freedom has become, at the same time, for some Pentecostal evangelical sectors, an instrument to obstruct demands for sexual and reproductive rights and to expand the privileges and legal protections granted by the State to the religious organizations. Moreover, in marginal segments of evangelism, self-proclaimed as inclusive churches, human rights are operated in processes of recognition of sexual minorities either as subjects of rights or as religious subjects. In their ethnography of the ordination of the first transgender evangelical pastor in Latin America, Silva, Barbosa and Nagamine describe how the language and enactment of human rights are no longer a rhetorical formula of legal connotation, becoming a liturgy and a ritual that make abstract notions of law and justice tangible. Through the iteration of oaths, declarations and appeals, the ceremony mobilizes the imagination and experience of those present around the value of human rights, evoking a constellation of codes, such as love, dignity, suffering and resilience, which are projected in the proposition of other family units.

As Talal Asad (2011) stressed, contemporary ways of conceptualizing human suffering have repeatedly come into conflict with liberal democratic values, such as the right to freedom of conscience, as behaviors carried out in the name of individual beliefs also claim the right to resist the permanent expansion of new segments protected by the State. These tensions become increasingly evident when constructing humanist discourses and in Christian interpretations of human rights. The fight against suffering, injustice and the desire to impose moral standards of respect for human dignity are also at the basis of many reformist discourses, both religious and non-religious, in defense of heterosexual marriage and in opposition to abortion. This contradiction becomes increasingly evident insofar as human rights form a public language within which different confrontations take place and as these disputes rapidly expand, becoming a compelling element of an imaginary present in social mobilization. The dispute for the shaping of this ethical (and aesthetic) device formulated in the language of human rights is, therefore, one of the guiding themes of this work. This edited volume aims, therefore, to contribute to a greater understanding of the new dynamics established under the aegis of pluralism, which mobilize the recent tensions around religious freedom and human rights in Brazil.

References

Abreu C (2021) Os pobres, os públicos e o reino de Deus: uma sociologia do engajamento de organizações evangélicas na arena dos direitos sociais. Tese de Doutoramento FFLCH

Asad T (2011) Reflexões sobre a crueldade e a tortura. Revista Pensata 1(1):160–187

Cefai D (2002) Qu' est ce qu' une arène publique?. In: Issac Joseph, L' Héritage du Pragmatisme. La Tour D' Aiges de l' Aube

Cefai D (2017) Públicos, problemas públicos, arenas públicas: O que nos ensina o pragmatismo (Parte 1). Novos Estudos Cebrap 36(1):187–213

Commaille J (2015) À quoi nous sert le droit? Gallimard, coll. « Folio essais », Paris

Isarel L (2009) L'arme du droit, Paris, Les Presses de Sciences Po, coll. « Contester »

Lefort C (2011) Direitos do homem e política. In: *A invenção democrática: os limites da dominação totalitária*. 3ª ed. Tradução de Isabel Loureiro et al. Autêntica, Belo Horizonte

Moyn S (2010) The Last Utopia: Human Rights History. Belknap Press of Harvard University Press, Cambridge

Oliveira L (1992) Direitos humanos e cultura política de esquerda. Lua Nova 27:149–165

Sales L, Mariano R (2019) Ativismo político de grupos religiosos e luta por direitos. Religião e Sociedade 39(02):9–27

Part I
Pluralism: Minority Rights, Religious Freedom and Secularism

Religion and Laicity in Dispute: Two Categories Under Construction in Brazil's Legal Debate on Religious Education in Public Schools

Paula Montero, Dirceu André Gerardi, and Rafael Quintanilha

Abstract The main object of analysis in this chapter is the debate on the constitutionality of Religious Education in public schools held at the Public Hearing organized by the Supreme Federal Court (SFC) in 2015. Thirty-two representatives from religious and non-religious entities presented their points of view on the topic. We demonstrate that the discursive configurations observed in this scene are doubly modulated: on the one hand, by addressing the problem and the rules of the game prevailing in this legal arena, and on the other hand, by the actors' repertoire, the type of organization they represent and the networks to which they are connected. In the first part of the chapter, we propose to reconstitute the main moments of the controversies regarding Religious Education regulations in public schools to identify the configurations and changes throughout the twentieth century. Then, we will map the categories and forms of argumentation put forward at this event by representatives of governmental organizations and civil society (religious and non-religious) present at the event. We construct the hypothesis that the systematic description of how these categories were articulated in this legal arena by these actors (in the sense of the term attributed by Daniel Cefaï) sheds light on the configurations and meanings attributed to the religious and non-religious in the current post-constituent context.

P. Montero (✉)
Department of Anthropology, University of São Paulo, São Paulo, Brazil

Brazilian Center of Analysis and Planning, São Paulo, Brazil
e-mail: pmontero@usp.br

D. A. Gerardi
Department of Anthropology, University of São Paulo, São Paulo, Brazil

Law School, Getúlio Vargas Foundation (FGV), São Paulo, Brazil
e-mail: andregerardi3@usp.br

R. Quintanilha
Department of Anthropology, University of São Paulo, São Paulo, Brazil

P. Montero et al. (eds.), *Religious Pluralism and Law in Contemporary Brazil*, Law and Religion in a Global Context 4, https://doi.org/10.1007/978-3-031-41981-2_2

1 Introduction

The issue of Religious Education in public schools in Brazil has already led to numerous studies (LIMA 1978; Cunha et al. 2003; Cunha 2005, 2006; Giumbelli and Carneiro 2007, 2010; Oliveira 2014; Santos 2016), as controversies concerning the laicity of the state are the background, which arouse the interest of these authors. Taking this debate as a reference, the objective of the chapter is twofold: first, to reconstitute the main moments of the controversy on Religious Education in Brazil throughout the twentieth century. Based on the existing literature on this topic, we propose to recompose, in broad terms, the disputes concerning regulations to understand in what terms and for whom religion is a public problem (Cefai 2017); second, to make new configurations and meanings visible of the main categories of this debate in the post-constituent context, which incorporated pluralism as a civic virtue. From documentary records collected for the study, we will examine in this chapter the debates on the constitutionality of Religious Education in public schools developed at the hearing convened by the Supreme Federal Court in 2015.

Our contribution is based on the evidence that laicity as a concept is insufficient to characterize the relationship between religions and the State in the contemporary world. In the vast body of literature on the subject, even if the institutional separation of Church/State is one of the basic principles of the configuration of the secular State (Asad 2003; Taylor 2007; Esquivel 2008; Modood 2009; Portier and Lagrée 2010; Casanova 2011; Calhoun 2012; Connolly 1999, 2011; Baubérot 2016), many forms of collaboration and alliance between these two institutions remain in modern democracies, and many new ways of cooperation and consortium are recreated. In this chapter, we analyze this relationship and its tensions by examining actors' presentations at the Public Hearing organized by the Supreme Federal Court in 2015. The introduction of pluralism into the legal framework of the 1988 Constitution significantly changes the terms of controversy regarding Religious Education and, consequently, laicity. Returning to the historical genealogy of the construction of this public problem, we will demonstrate how, throughout these debates, the notion of religion as a school subject loses its clerical nature to be modulated as part of the civic formation of the student, as it is progressively perceived as the equivalent to spiritual and moral values.

Analyzing this controversy in a recent legal arena sheds light on the aporia that the 1988 Constitution evoked by inscribing in it the respect for religious pluralism as a novelty and, at the same time, maintaining previous legislation that included providing Religious Education in public schools as an element that was "indispensable for fostering citizenship." In this chapter, we will formulate the following hypothesis: debates in the Public Hearing examined here shed light on an innovative way to reconcile the antinomy between the laicity of education and the mandatory provision of this school subject. The actors have disputed over the definition of the category of religion, which separates it into two distinct forms: religion as *confession* (dogma, belief, having faith) and religion as *tradition* (culture, history, heritage, patrimony).

The empirical basis of the research on this debate derived from data collection from news media, documentation on the Direct Action of Unconstitutionality (ADIN - 4439) and Public Hearing transcriptions since the outset of the action in 2010. After classifying the speech of 32 participating speakers and the judge-rapporteur, we coded data using the Atlas.Ti software to describe the rules that organize the scene, identified the actors and their networks, determined the terms of the dispute, and systematized the actors' arguments and positions.

2 Religious Education as a Public Issue in a Historical Perspective

The issue of Religious Education in Brazilian public schools refers to a long-term political debate, which, since the end of the nineteenth century, has been a matter of great controversy, opposing liberals, Protestants, atheists, agnostics, socialists and traditionalist Catholics, intellectuals and humanist lawyers (Oliveira 2014). Therefore, since the beginning of the Republic in 1889 until today, public schools have been a field of disputes in which the notions of laicity and religion are defined. Let us now look in more detail at how and for whom religion became a public problem throughout disputes in the twentieth century.

2.1 Religious Education in Republican Constitutions

Promulgated in 1891, the first republican Constitution of Brazil explicitly mentions the lay nature of public schools in article 72, item 6, not making an exception to any kind of Religious Education. According to Gustavo Gilson de Oliveira (2014), this understanding of the liberal current, according to which the introduction of religion as a school subject in public schools offends the principle of separation between the Catholic Church and State, prevailed until the 1930s. However, from the Vargas era, the agreement that teaching religion "is essential for the spiritual, moral and ethical formation of citizens and human beings" was consolidated in the political and legal disputes on the topic (2014:43).

The political importance of the subject was reiterated in 1931 when, by decree 19.941, Getúlio Vargas instituted Religious Education throughout elementary to high school courses, making it optional only for students whose parents or guardians expressly required it. In this formulation, this school subject has lost its elective character.

Educators such as Anísio Teixeira, Fernando de Azevedo and Lourenço Filho were harshly critical of this decree. Exponents of the *Movimento da Escola Nova (New School Movement)*, the inaugural milestone of the project to renew public, secular, compulsory, and free education in the country, considered that laicity should "[place] the school environment above religious beliefs and disputes" to protect it from the "disturbing pressure" of those who aim to use the school "as an instrument of propaganda for sects and doctrines" (Cunha et al. 2003, p. 132). The reform movement was a target of intense opposition from the Catholic hierarchy, which, at that juncture, held a monopoly of a significant number of private schools and saw the State as a strong competitor in its expectations of controlling the population's means of education. In 1932, Archbishop D. Sebastião Leme, who led the *Liga Eleitoral Católica*—LEC (Catholic Electoral League), elected the majority of deputies who supported the National Constituent Assembly (Mainwaring 1989, p. 48), and demonized educational reformers, accusing them of being "communists" and of despising the action of the Church and the role of the family in education (Cury 1984).

This tense equilibrium of forces is reaffirmed in the 1934 Constitution, which, according to the will of most constituents, reiterates Religious Education as mandatory in public schools' curriculums "given in accordance with the principles of a student's religious confession manifested by parents or guardians [...]" and attendance by the student is optional (Art.153). Guaranteed by law, Religious Education began to be provided in public schools, not according to the student's religious confession but based on the well-known and traditional catechetical model of parish schools. Very influential Catholic intellectuals at the time, such as the Jesuit Leonel Franca, a member of the National Education Council and vice-president of the *Colégio Santo Inácio* in Rio de Janeiro, were convinced that school without God "is necessarily antisocial." According to liberal leaders, such as the Methodist, Guaracy Silveira, a São Paulo constituent of the Brazilian Socialist Party elected in 1933, the norm was defined as the imposition of "Catholic catechesis in the classroom" (Santos 2016, p. 40).

In a game of forces that developed around this issue, in 1937, liberals had a minor victory when the authoritarian Constitution of the *Estado Novo* (New State) paradoxically imposed a strong secularizing turn. It removed the mandatory introduction and compulsory school attendance from Article 133. However, this suppression did not last a decade. The situation was again reversed in the 1946 Constitution, as the wording of Article 168 returned to the status quo of 1934. Religious Education was therefore once again mandatory in public school curriculums and had to be taught in accordance with student confessions and providing for optional enrollment.

The 1988 Constitution is as an important milestone in the recent configuration of this debate. Interestingly, although self-proclaimed a "Citizen Constitution," its constituent deputies did not exclude the obligation to introduce Religious Education in the curriculum of public schools. Perhaps this is due to the Catholic Church, strengthened by the role it played in mobilizations against the military regime in the 1970s and an important ally of the social movements in the constituent debates, that galvanized enough political forces to lead several Christian associations,[1] in favor of this permanence.

In the final wording of the Constitution (Art. 210),[2] Religious Education, the only school subject mentioned in the law as necessary to ensure primary education, was maintained in the public education curriculum. The document assumes that learning a religion is necessary to encourage citizenship, understood now as a regulated and peaceful coexistence of differences. On the other hand, political forces opposed to this thesis managed to ensure, that this subject would be restricted to elementary education and that enrollment would be optional. Considering this arrangement, the legislators understood that, as it is optional, Religious Education would not hinder either the laicity or the principle of freedom of conscience. We will now see how the attempts to implement this rule over the next decade took place amid a new debate concerning which professionals should be legitimate teachers of this school subject, and what content should be introduced in the curriculum.

The social and political situation in which this post-constituent debate took place is no longer the same. After all, inspired by the international law agenda of the 1980s, the new Constitution incorporated a notion of citizenship that, unprecedentedly, articulated the protection of diversity, cultural rights, and ethnic minorities. In the domestic sphere, the evident decline of Catholic hegemony made palpable in the 1991 Census figures, placed the rights of equality and equity inherent in pluralism on religious actors´ political agenda. This new perspective modified the context in which the format of Religious Education in the curriculum of public schools was discussed. Emphasis on respect for religious diversity as a right, by enunciating the possibility of access to Religious Education for all 147 religions listed in the *Instituto Brasileiro de Geografia e Estatistica—IBGE* (Brazilian Institute of Geography and Statistics), highlights the arbitrary monopoly of the Catholic Church on this subject in public education, thus introducing a new element into this debate. We saw that ensuring the conditions of students´ free choice was the core of the argument concerning safeguarding laicity. However, in light of such a wide range of possible choices, the electiveness of this school subject is no longer an operational

[1]The Interfaith Education Association of Curitiba (ASSINTEC), the Council of Churches for Religious Education of Santa Catarina (CLER), the Regional Pastoral Institute (MG IRPAMAT), the National Conference of Bishops (CNBB), the Association of Catholic Education in Brazil (AEC) and the Brazilian Association of Catholic Schools (ABESC) were some of the Christian organizations that acted on the Constituent Assembly's Education Commission (Santos 2016, p. 45). According to Cunha (2005), evangelical deputies who, at first, formed an alliance with liberals and socialists against Religious Education in public schools, changed their position, benefiting from Catholic support for their demands to legalize the control of the mass media by churches.

[2]1988 Constitution. Art. 210. "Minimum contents will be set for elementary education to ensure common basic education and respect for national and regional cultural and artistic values. § 1 Religious Education, with optional enrollment, will be a school subject in the normal hours of public elementary schools. § 2 Regular elementary education will be taught in Portuguese, whereby indigenous communities will also be guaranteed the use of their mother tongues and their own learning processes".

precautionary criterion. In terms of equating the regulation of this matter, the tension between the demands related to the laicity of education (protection of the principle of freedom of choice) and the concern regarding the rights to equity and religious equality (introduction of the entire spectrum of existing religious diversity), generated a heated debate over the next decade. It focused, as we shall see below, on the dispute of defining what should be understood as religious in terms of this school subject and on the problem of how to equate introducing religious and non-religious diversity.

2.2 Religious Education Regulations in the National Education Guidelines and Framework Law of 1961, 1996 and 1997

The first *Lei de Diretrizes e Bases*—LDB (National Education *Guidelines* and Framework *Law)* was created in 1961 to regulate education based on the framework defined by the Constitution. In debates when it was being drawn up, which began in 1947, the Church managed to maintain Religious Education in the curriculum of public schools, but its opponents ensured as a safeguard that it did not impose "onus on public authorities" (Lima 1978). In those 15 years that separated the promulgation of the 1946 Constitution and the regulation of this school subject in 1961, the State's monopoly on education was in dispute. Defended by Gustavo Capanema, who wrote an article on education in the 1946 Constitution, this exclusivity was disputed, on the one hand, by the New School Movement, which defended the decentralization and flexibility of curricula, and, on the other, by representatives of Catholic Church interests, such as Tristão de Ataíde and also deputy Carlos Lacerda, who fought against state interference in educational business and the standardization of secular education, perceived as lacking in spirituality. Ensuring that Religious Education would remain in the curriculum of public schools and preventing, in the name of freedom, secular public education from prevailing over the network of Catholic confessional schools were, as Montalvão observed, "the two great political battles of Catholic educators in the 20th century" (Montalvão 2010, pp. 32–35).

In disputes about regulating this school subject, divergences emerged as to the best way to preserve students' freedom of choice: should its introduction into the curriculum be mandatory or elective? Should student attendance be compulsory or optional? Should the content of this school subject be Catholic or vary according to the parents' confession?

The 1961 National Education *Guidelines* and the Framework *Law* maintained Religious Education on an optional basis to protect public schools' laicity. It announced the criterion "student's religious confession" to define which religion would be taught, thus reinforcing the idea that taking this subject would be a personal choice of the student. Along the same lines, the course would be given free of charge to the State and teacher training and hiring would be the responsibility of the religious authorities.

The 1988 Constitution makes the previous National Education *Guidelines* and Framework *Law* obsolete, such as the one in 1961, as well as its revised version in 1971, during the military regime which, in its dispute with the Catholic Church, introduced this school subject called "Moral and Civic Education." Since the proclamation of the new Constitution, there were 8 years of debates to present the final text of the new National Education *Guidelines* and Framework *Law*, approved in 1996. The main divergence in this debate was still related to the weight of the role reserved for the State in controlling the education system. In its final version, the document agrees with the parties in dispute, declaring that education is a duty of the family and the State (Art. 2).[3]

Religious Education remains optional, introduced into the elementary school curriculum, offered free of public charge, and according to the students or their guardians' preferences. Two new features appear in this version of the National Education *Guidelines* and Framework *Law*. Although the respective religious authorities still controlled programs and teachers, for the first time, out of respect for diversity, the content of Religious Education was split into two possible formats legally named as: confessional (given by religious advisors) and interfaith (a program developed in collaboration with several religious entities).[4] Non-Catholic organizations were authorized to qualify to teach this school subject, ensuring the State was not involved. Under strong pressure from the Catholic bench, these innovations, however, did not last long. The following year, a new bill was approved, sent to Congress by the Ministry of Education and Culture (MEC), which proposed suppressing the reference "without the onus to the State" and the mention of interfaith as an "expressly recognized modality of Religious Education".[5] We cannot determine how the debate and the correlation of forces that led to this change

[3]LDBEN- Art. Education, a duty of the family and the State, inspired by the principles of freedom and ideals of human solidarity, aims at full student development, their preparation for exercising citizenship and professional qualifications.

[4]LDB. Art. 33. "Religious Education, with optional enrollment, is a school subject in the public elementary school curricula, free of charge to the public coffers, according to the preferences expressed by the students or their guardians, in: I – confessional, according to the religious option of the student or guardian, given by teachers or religious advisors prepared and accredited by the respective churches or religious entities; or II – interfaith, resulting from an agreement between the various religious entities, which will be responsible for preparing the respective program." (1996).

The literature on religious literacy sometimes distinguishes between "education about religion" and "religious education." They both refer to the content of this school subject. We are using here the legal distinction that was negotiated between religious actors. We will see later that religion and confession will not be understood by the actors as necessarily equivalent terms.

[5]According to Luiz Antônio Cunha (2005) a bill proposed by the Minister of Education determined a change in the article. Submitted to Congress, it merged with two other proposals in progress. The bill's rapporteur, Father Roque from the Workers' Party, obtained its approval (law 9.475/97) by changing the wording of article 33 of the LDB (9394/96). In addition to the suppression of the reference to "no onus to the State", this new wording also suppresses interfaith as an "expressly recognized modality of Religious Education" (2005:142–143)

in the National Education *Guidelines* and Framework *Law* took place in such a short time. However, in Cunha's assessment (2005:143) it weakens the lay position of secularism. If in the previous version, the positions were established around confessionalism vs. secularism, in the new version, the dispute shifted to the opposition of confessionalism vs. interconfessionalism, obliterating the possibility of confronting religion at school. In our perception, by suppressing the word "confession" from the text and prohibiting proselytism, the 1997 version shifts the debate to another level.

At this point, the controversy had already taken on a different shape: it was no longer a question of deciding whether or not Religious Education would be part of the curriculum of public schools, issue that had already been addressed in the new Constitution. The requirement to respect "Brazil's religious cultural diversity" shifted the problem of how to manage this school subject to the State: it needed to offer the means to guarantee equal treatment of religious diversity and be concerned with monitoring the contents and the form of this education to prohibit proselytism. As previously mentioned, the new wording of Article 33 (Law 9.475 of 1997) of the National Education *Guidelines* and Framework *Law* reiterated the Constitutional inscription according to which "Religious Education is an integral part of citizen education". An ideal that conceived the moral formation of nationality associated with Christian values had endured. However, the novelty introduced in the 1997 version, by suppressing the mention of the confessional/interconfessional character of religious education, delegates this regulation to regional secretariats, prohibits proselytism and transfers the debate on laicity from individual guarantees of "free choice" to collective guarantees of "respect for diversity".

The new formulation of this law shifted the power to define the contents of this school subject to government agencies, state or even municipal education systems, which now have the authority to "regulate the procedures for defining the contents of this education and to establish standards for qualifying and admitting teachers" (lei 97/9475 art 1). Furthermore, the explicit prohibition of "proselytism" in the norm radically modifies, in our view, the student's status, who can no longer be treated as a proselyte or adept. The rule also transforms the minister's status, who goes from being a preacher to a specialist in a field of knowledge. This nuance changes the nature of this education, by instilling in the student's position a perception of the conditionality of the phenomenon to be studied, and the nature of what can be taught: neither doctrines to be memorized nor truths validated only by testimony.

This mutation shifts the center of the dispute, which is the content of this school subject and the definition of those who will be authorized to define it. By explicitly ensuring the protection of diversity, qualified as religious cultural diversity and non-confessional diversity, the new wording of the norm is restricted to the regulation of procedures: content and teacher qualifications were left to the regional education systems, that should listen to the civil society, "constituted by different religious denominations" (lei 97/9475 art 2). It is noteworthy that this civil society design removes the indifferent and non-religious advisors from the dispute.

Therefore, the 1997 National Education *Guidelines* and Framework *Law* summarize, the main phantoms that, at this point, were already perceived by non-religious political forces as pernicious consequences of Religious Education when offered under State tutelage. First, the dangers of proselytism, when incorporated into the doctrinal contents of this school subject: this model would violate the principle of publicity by disrespecting the student's freedom of choice; second, the persistence of the Catholic monopoly on public education conspiring against the protection of religious diversity; thirdly, by leaving the decision of the contents to those directly involved in the transaction, that is, the professionals responsible for administrating regional education systems, after hearing the different religious denominations, the arena of conflict is transferred to the level of local policies, at the risk of generating a profound dispersion of the curriculum and formats that compromise with the interests of their oligarchies.

Some effects of this shift can already be seen. Over the next decade, state systems joined various political forces to define their models. For their part, the religious forces are organized under the leadership of Catholics, who created the *Fórum Nacional Permanente do Ensino Religioso* (Permanent National Forum of Religious Education - FONAPER) in 1995, aiming to produce supra-religious consensuses, as well as helping to define curriculum parameters, let alone train teachers. Local governments such as the State of Rio de Janeiro, for example, passed a law in the 2000s that instituted the confessional format to Religious Education for elementary, and middle schools. Four years later, there was a public exam to fill these positions and the power to accredit those approved was delegated to religious entities. In São Paulo, alliances were made with the University. In 2001, the São Paulo Department of Education requested the assistance of historians Eliane Moura and Leandro Karnal from the University of Campinas to draw up a proposal focusing on the history of religions. The conflicts and results of these regional regulations are already starting to be the object of interest in some academic studies (Lui 2006; Giumbelli and Carneiro 2006, 2007, 2010; Braga 2008; Santos 2016). Although we will not address them in this chapter, these regional disputes prepared the ground for Lula's government agreement with the *Santa Sé* (Holy See), which had been in the making since 2006.

2.3 Religious Education Regulations in the Agreement Between the Holy See and Brazil

In November 2008, the Agreement between the Holy See and Brazil on the Juridical Statute of the Catholic Church in Brazil was promulgated. The document comprises 20 articles, which reaffirm the Church's juridical personality, autonomy, and traditional privileges. Processing the Agreement in Parliament rekindled the debate on Religious Education and its implications for the secular nature of the State.

Authors such as Luiz A. Cunha (2009, p. 272) argue that the international agreement between Brazil and the Vatican, negotiated far from public opinion, would alter, in article 11, the understanding of article 33 of the *Guidelines* and

Framework *Law* by mentioning that Religious Education would be confessional. As previously mentioned, the terms "confessional" and "interfaith" were only in the first version of this article 33 and the mention of these categories was removed from the new wording approved in 1997. However, by reintroducing the term confessional, the Agreement was seen as an attempt to reinsert previously deleted categories into legislation. Indeed, this became the main argument of the forces that, in the name of laicity, denounced the Agreement and the unconstitutionality of the article. However, Cunha makes an even more important observation: the Agreement, whose article 11 concerns the guarantee of state neutrality in relation to confessional schools, ventures to discreetly add an article to it that aims to guarantee Religious Education in public schools. This boldness, which Congress silenced when approving the document the following year, signals, on the one hand, the strategic place of public schools in the moralizing project of the Catholic Church and, on the other, the persistence among the cadres of the Parliament of a naturalized framework of the religion conceived as associated with confession or beliefs.

There were many critical reactions to this proposition. Those who perceive the indirect consequences of this decision on the very notion of secularism as disastrous sought to organize themselves, demanding, as Roseli Fischmann did, that Congress should reject the Agreement. Some denounced, as sectors of the Presbyterian segment, the privileges of the *Padroado* that the Agreement would bring back, and even those who criticized the confessional character of the proposal, such as the movement of Religious Education teachers. Scientific societies and students published notes repudiating the initiative, while five of the 28 deputies who constituted the Foreign Affairs Committee of the Chamber of Deputies voted separately against the Agreement.

One of the results of this dispute over the consequences of this Agreement on secularity was the Direct Action of Unconstitutionality (ADI - 4439) filed in 2010 by Deputy Attorney General, Deborah Macedo Duprat de Britto Pereira, accompanied by representations made by Waldemar Zveiter, then Dean of the Rio de Janeiro Court of Justice, and Daniel Sarmiento, then a regional attorney in the state of Rio de Janeiro. Their profiles show that the initiative comes from very well positioned segment in the legal spheres of the state of Rio de Janeiro. Some of them were linked to Freemasonry and maintained a personal relationship with the judge of the Federal Supreme Court, Luís Roberto Barroso, rapporteur of the case. Their professional careers reveal that some of them also extended their political networks to Parliament.

The action proposed by the Prosecution and the Federal Attorney General's Office questions the constitutionality of article 33 of the *Guidelines* and Framework *Law* and paragraphs 1 and 2 and Article 11 of the Agreement with the Vatican, which understands Religious Education in public schools as confessional. Considering the issue as too complex and willing to give greater democratic legitimacy to the future Supreme Federal Court decision, the rapporteur of the action, Roberto Barroso, conveneda Public Hearing,[6] on March 10, 2015.

3 Debates on the Unconstitutionality of Religious Education in the Public Hearing

In the opening words of the Public Hearing, Minister Luís Roberto Barroso defined the role of the Hearing in the contemporary democratic model. According to him, "contemporary democracy is made up of votes, rights, and reasons." In a Habermasian formulation of the function of this arena, Barroso emphasizes its deliberative dimension so that "the best reasons guided and chosen according to public reason prevail in the public space" (ADIN – 4439). We will not dwell here on the criticisms that authors such as Talal Asad (2003) and others have already made of this homogeneous and rationalist public sphere conception. In particular, its assumption, also emphasized by Charles Taylor (2007), is that actors, including religious ones, should only deliberate in the language of reason. This epistemic distinction implicit in Justice Barroso's opening speech, between secular reason and religious languages, would force most religious actors to adopt an argumentative attitude when speaking of their religion, which, as we shall see below, happened only partially.

A Public Hearing does not have decision-making power. It only offers subsidies to technically and representatively substantiate the Supreme Federal Court's decisions, even though many decisions do not consider the arguments put forward there. We will, however, leave the analysis of the vote on this matter at the Supreme Federal Court in 2017 for a future study. Given the specificity of this arena, in this section, we are interested in describing the rules of its operation and its characters. Our purpose is to understand, on the one hand, the genres and specificities of the narratives that enact secularity and religion in this scene and, on the other, the forms of personification of this civil society that the rapporteur identifies in the "public space". The summons to the Hearing, the rapporteur's dispatches, and the opening will be the guiding documents of our analysis.

[6]Law 9868/1999 creates, among others, a new institute in the Brazilian constitutional jurisdiction: the amicus curiae. They aim to hear from representatives of civil society and experts or persons with experience and authority in the matter under discussion. The admission of applications for admission as amicus curiae in a process depends on the rapporteur.

3.1 The Characters and the Game's Rules

In addition to those who registered as participants, the Public Hearing notice already specified, by way of entry, the Institutions to be summoned and those invited to participate as amicus curiae.[7] At the outset, it can be observed that the CNBB, represented by its lawyer, was listed among those present in the capacity of summoned to participate, alongside the President of the Republic (represented by the Federal Attorney General) and the representative of the National Congress. The fact of being summoned reveals that, despite the recent decline of Catholic hegemony in Brazil, the CNBB is still implicitly thought of as a constituent institution of public power and not just a sector of civil society. Along with the summoned bodies, fifteen civil associations appeared as summoned in the official list published in the notice, most represented by their lawyers. They were categorized in the document as representatives of the public education[8] system, religious[9] and non-religious[10] groups and experts with "recognized authority on the subject".[11]

The March 10, 2015 call provided a space of 3 months for the registration of interested parties. According to the rules, at the time of registration, applicants had to present: their qualifications, résumé, and a summary of their positions. Choosing these participants was at the discretion of the rapporteur. In his dispatch of May 15, he informs that he invited ten entities,[12] including Muslim, Baptist, Pentecostal,

[7] The figure of the amicus curiae is an instrument for opening the Federal Supreme Court to popular participation in interpreting and applying the Constitution, in accordance with the terms of art. 138 of the 2015 Code of Civil Procedure.

[8] Permanent National Forum of Religious Education (FONAPER) and the Association of Catholic Education in Brazil (ANECB). Founded in 1995, FONAPER is a civil association of private, confessional and union law that brings together legal entities, mostly churches of all denominations, identified with Religious Education. According to Luiz Cunha (2005, p. 143) FONAPER is hegemonically Catholic and has shown to be efficient including state legislation of "interfaith education, with teachers accredited by religious entities, included in teaching staff through public examinations and paid by the State". ANEC is an entity associated with the CNBB and can be found in all states of the federation and represents Catholic institutions dedicated to education.

[9] *Conferência dos Religiosos do Brasil*—**CRB** (Brazilian Conference of Religious Advisors)

[10] *Grande Loja Maçônica do Estado do Rio de Janeiro*—**GLMERJ** (Masonic Grand Lodge of the State of Rio de Janeiro), *Associação Brasileira de Ateus e Agnósticos*—**ATEA** (Brazilian Association of Atheists and Agnostics) e *Liga Humanista Secular do Brasil*—**LIHS** (Secular Humanist League of Brazil).

[11] ***Ação Educativa*** *Assessoria, Pesquisa e Informação* (Educational Action Advice, Research and Information), ***Conectas*** *Direitos Humanos* (***Conectas*** Human Rights), ***Ecos****-Comunicação em Sexualidade* (Ecos-Communication on Sexuality), *Comitê Latino-Americano e do Caribe para a Defesa dos Direitos da Mulher*—**CLADEM** (Latin American and Caribbean Committee for the Defense of Women's Rights), *Plataforma* ***DHESCA*** *Brasil e Instituto de Bioética* (DHESCA Brazil Platform and Bioethics Institute), Direitos Humanos e Gênero—**ANIS** (Human Rights and Gender). Alongside these institutions associated with Human Rights, there are three organizations linked to Catholic jurists in the states of Rio de Janeiro, Rio Grande do Sul and São Paulo.

[12] *Conselho Nacional de Secretários de Educação*—CONSED (National Council of Education Secretaries); (2) *Confederação Nacional dos Trabalhadores em Educação*—CNTE (National

Spiritualist, Israeli and Buddhist representatives. In addition to the invited entities, the dispatch informs that 227 applications were registered, among which only twenty-one[13] were accepted.

The analysis of the final composition of the Hearing shows that the imaginary map drawn by the organizers regarding which actors would be directly involved in this public issue was divided into the State (representatives of the executive and legislative) and civil society. As can be seen from Table 1 below, "civil society" appears to be made up of thirteen organizations linked to churches and thirteen

---

Confederation of Education Workers); (3) *Confederação Israelita do Brasil*—CONIB (the Brazilian Israelite Confederation); (4) *Conferência Nacional dos Bispos do Brasil*—CNBB (The National Conference of Bishops); (5) *Convenção Batista Brasileira*—CBB (the Brazilian Baptist Convention), (6) *Federação Espírita Brasileira*—FEB (the Brazilian Spiritist Federation) (7) *Federação das Associações Muçulmanas do Brasil*—FAMBRAS (Federation of Muslim Associations of Brazil), (8) *Igreja Assembleia de Deus—Ministério de Belém* (Assembly of God—Ministry of Belem) (9) *Liga Humanista Secular do Brasil*—LIHS (Secular Humanist League of Brazil), and (10) *Sociedade Budista do Brasil*—SBB (Brazil Buddhist Society).

[13](i) *Ação Educativa Assessoria, Pesquisa e Informação* (Educational Assistance, Research and Information Action); (ii) AMICUS DH—*Grupo de Atividade de Cultura e Extensão da Faculdade de Direito da USP* (Culture and Extension Group at the USP Law School); (iii) Anis—*Instituto de Bioética, Direitos Humanos e Gênero* (Institute of Bioethics, Human Rights and Gender); (iv) ANAJUBI—*Associação Nacional de Advogados e Juristas Brasil-Israel* (Brazilian Association of Jewish Lawyers and Jurists); (v) *Arquidiocese do Rio de Janeiro (*Archdiocese of Rio de Janeiro); (vi) ASSINTEC—*Associação Inter-Religiosa de Educação e Cultura* (*Interfaith Association of Education and Culture)*; (vii) *Associação Nacional dos Programas de Pós-Graduação e Pesquisa em Teologia e Ciências da Religião*—ANPTECRE (*National Association of Graduate* Studies and *Research* in *Theology* and *Science* of *Religion*; (viii) *Centro de Raja Yoga Brahma Kumaris* (Raja Yoga Brahma Kumaris Center); (ix) *Clínica de Direitos Fundamentais da Faculdade de Direito da UERJ*; (*Fundamental Rights Clinic* of the State University of Rio de Janeiro *Law* School (x) *Comissão de Direitos Humanos e Minorias da Câmara dos Deputados* (Commission on Human Rights and Minorities at the Chamber of Deputies); (xi) *Comissão Permanente de Combate às Discriminações e Preconceitos de Cor, Raça, Etnia, Religiões e Procedência Nacional* (Permanent Commission to Combat Discrimination and Prejudice of Color, Race, Ethnicity, Religions and National Origin); (xii) *Comitê Nacional de Respeito à Diversidade Religiosa da Secretaria de Direitos Humanos da Presidência da República* (National Committee for Respect for Religious Diversity of the Secretariat for Human Rights of the Presidency of the Republic); (xiii) *Conectas Direitos Humanos* (Conectas Human Rights); (xiv) *Conselho Nacional de Educação do Ministério da Educação* (National Education Council of the Ministry of Education); (xv) *Convenção Nacional das Assembleias de Deus—Ministério de Madureira* (National Convention of the Assemblies of God—Ministry of Madureira); (xvi) *Federação Nacional do Culto Afro Brasileiro*—FENACAB (National Federation of Afro-Brazilian Cults) with the *Federação de Umbanda e Candomblé de Brasília e Entorno* (Umbanda and Candomblé Federation of Brasília and Surroundings; (xvii) *Fórum Nacional Permanente do Ensino Religioso*—FONAPER (Permanent National Forum for Religious Education); (xviii) *Frente Parlamentar Mista Permanente em Defesa da Família* (Mixed Parliamentary Front in Defense of the Family); (xix) *Igreja Universal do Reino de Deus* (Universal Church of the Kingdom of God); (xx) *Instituto dos Advogados Brasileiros*—IAB (Institute of Brazilian Lawyers); and (xxi) *Observatório da Laicidade na Educação em conjunto com o Centro de Estudos Educação & Sociedade* (Observatory of Secularity in Education in conjunction with the Education & Society Study Center).

Table 1 Institutional affiliation of panelists by linking sector

Sector of representatives	Institutional Origin	Institutional Position	Organization	Freq.
(i) State	Executive And legislative	Government bodies	• CONSED • CNE/MEC • CNRDR/SDH/PR	3
		Representantives in parliament	• Commission on human rights and minorities at the chamber of deputies • Commission to combat discrimination/legislative assembly of Rio de Janeiro (ALERJ) • Mixed parliamentary front in defense of the family	3
(ii) Sociedade Civil	Religious organizations	Religious representatives	Catholics-(CNBB and Archdiocese of Rio), Pentecostals-CONAMAD /Madureira, CGADB/Belém and IURD), Muslims-(FAMBRAS), Afro-(FENACAB and FUCBE), Buddhists-(SBB), Jews-(CONIB), Spiritists-(FEB), yoga-(Brahma Kumaris), Baptists-(CBB)	13
	Non-religious organizations	Legal organizations	• ANAJUBI • IAB • Fundamental rights and gender clinic/UERJ • Amicus DH USP	4
		Activists from pro-secularity and human rights civil organizations	• LHIS • ANIS • Conectas human rights • OLÉ and CEDES	4
		Specialists	• ANPTECRE • Educational action	2
		Religious Education Trade Unions	• ASSINTEC • FONAPER	2
		Teachers trade union	• CNTE	1

Source: the authors (ANAJUBI—*Associação Nacional de Advogados e Juristas Brasil-Israel* (Brazilian Association of Jewish Lawyers and Jurists)
Arquidiocese do Rio de Janeiro (Archdiocese of Rio de Janeiro)
ASSINTEC—*Associação Inter-Religiosa de Educação e Cultura* (Interfaith Association of Education and Culture)
ANPTECRE—*Associação Nacional dos Programas de Pós-Graduação e Pesquisa em Teologia e Ciências da Religião* (National Association of Graduate Studies and Research in Theology and Science of Religion)
AMICUS DH—*Grupo de Atividade de Cultura e Extensão da Faculdade de Direito da USP*
Ação Educativa Assessoria, Pesquisa e Informação (Culture and Extension Group at the USP Law School)
Centro de Raja Yoga Brahma Kumaris (Raja Yoga Brahma Kumaris Center)

(continued)

Clínica de Direitos Fundamentais da Faculdade de Direito da UERJ (Fundamental Rights Clinic of the State University of Rio de Janeiro Law School)
CDHM/CD—*Comissão de Direitos Humanos e Minorias da Câmara dos Deputados* (Commission on Human Rights and Minorities at the Chamber of Deputies)
Comissão Permanente de Combate às Discriminações e Preconceitos de Cor, Raça, Etnia, Religiões e Procedência Nacional da Alerj (Permanent Commission to Combat Discrimination and Prejudice of Color, Race, Ethnicity, Religions and National Origin)
CNRDR/SDH/PR—*Comitê Nacional de Respeito à Diversidade Religiosa da Secretaria de Direitos Humanos da Presidência da República* (National Committee for Respect for Religious Diversity of the Secretariat for Human Rights of the Presidency of the Republic)
Conectas Direitos Humanos (Conectas Human Rights)
CNE/MEC—*Conselho Nacional de Educação do Ministério da Educação* (National Education Council of the Ministry of Education)
CONAMAD—*Convenção Nacional das Assembleias de Deus - Ministério de Madureira* (National Convention of the Assemblies of God - Ministry of Madureira)
CGADB—*Convenção Geral das Assembleias de Deus no Brasil—Ministério de Belém* (General Convention of the Assemblies of God in Brazil—Ministry of Belém)
CONSED—*Conselho Nacional de Secretários de Educação* (National Council of Education Secretaries)
CNTE—*Confederação Nacional dos Trabalhadores em Educação* (National Confederation of Education Workers)
CONIB—*Confederação Israelita do Brasil* (The Brazilian Israelite Confederation)
CNBB—*Conferência Nacional dos Bispos do Brasil* (The National Conference of Bishops)
CBB—*Convenção Batista Brasileira* (The Brazilian Baptist Convention)
FEB—*Federação Espírita Brasileira* (The Brazilian Spiritist Federation)
FAMBRAS—*Federação das Associações Muçulmanas do Brasil* (Federation of Muslim Associations of Brazil)
FENACAB—*Federação Nacional do Culto Afro Brasileiro* (National Federation of Afro-Brazilian Cults)
FUCBE—*Federação de Umbanda e Candomblé de Brasília e Entorno* (Umbanda and Candomblé Federation of Brasília and Surroundings)
FONAPER—*Fórum Nacional Permanente do Ensino Religioso* (Permanent National Forum for Religious Education)
FPMPDF/CD—*Frente Parlamentar Mista Permanente em Defesa da Família* (Mixed Parliamentary Front in Defense of the Family)
Anis—*Instituto de Bioética, Direitos Humanos e Gênero* (Institute of Bioethics, Human Rights and Gender)
LIHS—*Liga Humanista Secular do Brasil* (Secular Humanist League of Brazil)
SBB—*Sociedade Budista do Brasil* (Brazil Buddhist Society)
IURD—*Igreja Universal do Reino de Deus* (Universal Church of the Kingdom of God)
IAB—*Instituto dos Advogados Brasileiros* (Institute of Brazilian Lawyers)
OLÉ e CEDES—*Observatório da Laicidade na Educação em conjunto com o Centro de Estudos Educação & Sociedade* (Observatory of Secularity in Education in conjunction with the Education & Society Study Center))

professional organizations. Interestingly, the latter were chosen among four types of professional classes: jurists, activists, specialists, and union members. In addition, in this choice, the links with the Catholic Church prevailed: it appears as a class representative, as part of specialists and as a group of jurists.

In any case, the twenty-one entries admitted as representatives of civil society gave its final composition a gain in diversity: to the two groups initially invited—

unions and representatives of religious organizations - were added academic experts, jurists, and human rights activists focused on gender and secularism and representatives of parliamentary committees. In this new design, the currents of interest become more complex and less polarized, making it difficult to visualize the lines of force that dominated the debate about secularism. Nevertheless, when we ask ourselves what appears in this arena as civil society, we realize that it is constituted, in more than a third, of representatives associated, in one way or another, with religious organizations.

3.2 The Rules

The thesis of the Attorney General's Office advocated that the only way to reconcile the secular character of the Brazilian State with Religious Education in public schools would be to adopt a non-confessional model of this education. In this model, this school subject should offer doctrines, practices, and histories of different religions as part of its programmatic content, including non-religious positions. It should be taught by teachers not affiliated with churches or religious denominations and prevented from taking sides. By endorsing non-confessional education, the Attorney's Office aimed to safeguard the principle of secularism by shifting the object of this school subject from the "sacred," thought of as a universal fact, to the historicity of beliefs, their unique and contingent configurations. In this proposal, it is not only the content of this school subject that varies, but above all the demarcation of the object and its heuristic conditions.

Using this new framework as a reference to safeguard the secular nature of education, the action aimed to demonstrate that the articles mentioned above (Article 33 of the LDB and Article 11 of the Agreement) would be in disagreement with the Constitution if education were to be offered in a confessional format or even interfaith one.

Furthermore, the rapporteur, Justice Barroso, also stated that the focus of the debate would be to find the form of Religious Education that would best preserve the principle of secularism. Since offering or not this school subject was not under discussion, the debate shifted to criteria that delimit the least onerous model to uphold secularism. Furthermore, considering that this school subject was already being taught in state education systems, the intention was to discuss the impact of these experiences on the public education system, religious confessions, and non-religious positions.

Even before the start of the debate, one can see, therefore, that two basic implicit formulations already overdetermine the possibilities of argumentation. The first one is the assertion that Religious Education in public schools does not violate the principle of the State secularism; the second one assumes that "religion" and "confession" are not necessarily equivalent terms.

Based on this framework, the debate focused on defining the relationship between "religion" and "confession". Let us now move on to analyze arguments and presentations to understand more clearly how the different positions articulate the relationship between these two categories.

3.3 The Debate: Presentations, Categories, Arguments, and Positions

At the Public Hearing, thirty-two speakers took the floor. If we observe their credentials, they can be grouped into eight broad categories referring to the institutional positions they occupied in the debate. To make it easier to analyze, we have grouped these positions into two main areas: (i) State representatives, including members of parliament and state bodies, and (ii) Religious and non-religious civil society representatives, as described in Table 1.

Based on this typology, the analysis below will examine the nature of the arguments, their different configurations, the main categories that arise in the debate and the nature of the presentations. Furthermore, taking into account that the speakers represent organizations, we ask ourselves if and how this institutional representation affects the debate concerning the two main areas suggested by the rapporteur, namely: how to reconcile the principle of secularism offering Religious Education and which type of offer would be the least onerous for the secularity of the State. Of course, although our map of positions considers the implicit assumption that religious and non-religious representations produce contrasting arguments and decisions, in practice, the boundaries between them are sometimes barely discernible, either because the same person speaks on behalf of different entities, or because in their trajectories multiple belongings are juxtaposed. All the more so, given that these people were invited to speak on behalf of a group or organization, when analyzing what the person says, there is a risk of taking what they say as an expression of the "world view" or "cosmology" of that group as a whole, particularly in the case of religious representatives. We know these groups and their alliances are plural and dynamic in real life. Thus, the speeches will not be analyzed to portray what these actors "think" or "believe," but to understand how the controversy is shaped and transformed due to such interactions.

3.4 Presentations of Executive and Legislative Representatives

As can be seen in Table 2, the Executive and Legislative powers comprised six presentations.

Table 2 Frequency of distributing presentations by State representatives per category

Sector	Institutional representation	Institutional positions of the debaters	Representative presentations				
			Non confessional.	Confessional.	AgainstER	No position	Total
State	Executive and legislative	Government	3	0	0	0	3
		Members of parliament	1	2	0	0	3
Total			4	2	0	0	6

Source: the authors

The three positions of executive body representatives, Carlos Deschamps,[14] President of the National Council of Education Secretaries (CONSED), Luiz Roberto Alves,[15] President of the Ministry of Education (MEC) Basic Education Commission and Gilbraz Aragão,[16] in the dual position of representative of the National Committee for Respect for Religious Diversity of the Secretariat for Human Rights and the National Committee for Respect for Religious Diversity of the Secretariat for Human Rights, followed the rapporteur's position: they considered that Religious Education should be offered in public schools in the non-denominational model, that is, not devoted to teaching doctrines and winning proselytes. In the case of representatives from the legislative power, two deputies were in favor of the confessional Religious Education model: the assembly, **pastor Eurico** (PATRIOTAS/PE ex-PEN), who is a member of the Permanent Mixed Parliamentary Front in Defense of the Family and the Evangelical Parliamentary Front,[17] and the consultant in the Chamber of Deputies **Manuel Morais**, speaking on behalf of the deputy, pastor Marcos Feliciano (PODE/RJ ex-PTN), then member of the Commission on Human Rights and Minorities at the Chamber of Deputies and member of the Evangelical Parliamentary Front. The third deputy comes from the state of Rio de Janeiro. **Carlos Minc** (PT/RJ), who, self-declared as a Jew, and was a member of the Permanent Commission to Combat Discrimination and Prejudice, stood behind the non-confessional model.[18]

[14]PhD in Electrical Engineering from the Federal University of Santa Catarina (UFSC). He was Dean of the Regional University of Blumenau (Furb) and Director of the Technological Research Institute of Blumenau. He was also a member of the Santa Catarina State Development Council (Desenvesc), the Blumenau Business Association Council (Acib) and the Blumenau Regional Development Council.

[15]He obtained a Ph.D. in Language and Literature from the University of São Paulo (1981). He was a professor and principal of the state public school in the Greater ABC region for 24 years and a full professor at the Methodist University. He served as an advisor to social movements in the metropolitan area for public policies on education, culture and social management. He studied at the Hebrew University of Jerusalem (1974–1976). He did his post doctorate at the University La Sapienza, de Roma (1993–1994) and was Erasmus Professor at the Public University of Florence (2006–2007).

[16]Professor of the Postgraduate Programs in Sciences of Religion (PPGCR) and Theology (PPGT) at the Catholic University of Pernambuco, coordinator of the Transdisciplinary Observatory of Religions in Recife, vice president of the *National Association of Graduate* Studies and *Research* in *Theology* and *Science* of *Religion* (ANPTECRE) and member of the Civil Society Representatives of the National Committee for Respect for Religious Diversity (CNRDR), period 2014–2016.

[17]The Parliamentary Fronts are associations of deputies, of a supra-party nature, intended to promote, together with representatives of civil society and similar public bodies, the discussion and improvement of legislation and policies relating to a particular sector.

[18]In 2003, Carlos Minc, PT deputy, joined forces with minority religious groups (Spiritists, Jews, Catholics and Born-again Evangelicals, Afro-Brazilians) to approve a law that suppressed confessional Religious Education in public schools in Rio de Janeiro. This law would overturn Law 3459/2000 sanctioned by Governor A. Garotinho, which extended the obligation to offer Religious Education to secondary and professional education and determined public examinations for this school subject. The law was vetoed by Governor Rosangela Mateus, an evangelical and Garotinho's wife, his predecessor in charge of the State of Rio de Janeiro.

We can see, therefore, that the Executive position proved to be well consolidated in terms of a non-confessional education, but the representatives' manifestations from the congress commissions, in the contrary, were not consensual. In this case, the particularities of these people's trajectories and the political context of that moment seem to make a difference. Representatives from the Executive bodies have had sound academic careers, although two have gone on to teach at confessional universities. In the case of the Legislature, two congressmen who voted for confessional education are also pastors and participate in the "evangelical bench". The strategy developed in recent decades by evangelical churches, in particular, neo-Pentecostal churches, of the massive use of the electoral system to gain their representation in Parliament has already been widely studied. Today pastors occupy 12% of seats in Congress. For these sectors, their presence in the legislative power system would be a way of gaining recognition and power to influence the agendas of interest of their churches, including Religious Education. We saw that in this case, regardless of their party affiliation, but orchestrating themselves in bench coalitions, they took a stand for confessional education, unlike deputy Minc. It is difficult to say whether this demonstration expresses the consensual position of the evangelical bench as a whole or just the particular interest of the churches these deputies lead. We also do not have information on whether the topic was debated in the two Commissions represented there, such as the Human Rights Commission, which Pastor Marco Feliciano had already chaired in 2013 during a controversial term, and the Combat Against Prejudice, chaired by Carlos Minc at ALERJ. In any case, considering the dispersion of religious leaders' positions, we cannot consider confessional education as a unanimous expression of their interests. As we will see later, unlike the evangelical parliamentarians, the nine religious representations associated with other church organizations were divided on this issue, some preferring the non-confessional model and others even being against Religious Education in public schools.

However, before analyzing these positions, let us examine more deeply the justifications that underlie these evangelical parliamentarians' manifestations.

3.5 Arguments of Legislative Representatives

One of the main elements that divided the parliamentarians' positions revolved around understanding the religion category itself. The debate focused on defining the relationship between "religion" and "confession": would they be equivalent and/or inseparable categories, as defended by the CNBB, or would they name distinct phenomena?

The argument of deputy pastor Eurico, representative of the Mixed Parliamentary Front in Defense of the Family, distinguishes the two categories. In defense of "confessional" education, he states that [...] "Religious Education is one thing and the faith that we follow is another [...]" (ADIN – 4439). Parents teach faith at home and at school it is taught "religion in general". According to him, "religion in general" teaches, or should teach, "respect among people and between religions" and, according to him, "the religious denominations themselves are already doing it in their internal meetings". The deputy supports the offer of Religious Education in public schools because it "leads people to learn more about values". According to the pastor, the problem of Religious Education emerges when this "religion in general" comes into conflict or disrespects the "confession", either because it makes mistakes concerning some doctrinal points, or because it intends to "deconstruct faith and belief". These arguments show that, despite speaking out in defense of confessional education, the pastor is attributing a very particular meaning to the concept of "confession". When distinguishing "faith" and "religion in general", his argument attempts to find a definition of "confession" halfway between the idea of "doctrine" and "historical phenomenon". For him, every confession is based on faith, but its doctrinal content may vary. Thus, for the deputy, "religion in general" is "confessional" in a broader sense, because it teaches moral values derived from beliefs. However, at the same time, "religion in general" is secular, as the perspective of variability in the doctrinal content of religions is assumed. However, what cannot be done with Religious Education is to "deconstruct faith", that is, historicize it to the point of making it a contingent condition of the human.

Considering these arguments that modulate the meaning of the "confessional" category, distinguishing it from "doctrine", the congressman claims to agree with the prosecution's propositions when "questioning the confessional Religious Education when linked to a specific religion". He concludes that the Prosecutor General of the Republic (PGR) "defends that Religious Education should be taught in a secular way, approaching the perspective of various religions [...] even because the State is secular, it has no official religion". The pastor also agrees with the PGR in the sense that " Religious Education should have a non-confessional nature", understood here as "prohibition of the admission of teachers as representatives of the religious confessions": the content of the subject "religion in general" must be taught by non-religious professionals as the State cannot have an official religion. The secularity of the State would also be ensured by the secular format of confessional education, guided by the abstract and universal values of "religion in general". In this argument, the deputy pastor introduces a third term in the initial proposition, which opposes "confessional" (doctrinal) to "non-confessional" (non-doctrinal). "Non-religious" Religious Education, according to this version, is perceived as "non-confessional" or secular because it is devoided of beliefs and values or may even be anti-religious.

Feeling awkward about his dual position as pastor and representative of the Mixed Parliamentary Front in Defense of the Family, the deputy sought to defend the paradoxical configuration of "secular and confessional" Religious Education. He distinguishes "faith" and "religion" in the style of many Protestant pastors today. The first is understood as a pious attitude taught in private life by the family (faith and doctrine), and the second, "religion in general" to be taught at school, would correspond to abstract and universal moral values inherent in the various doctrines. This distinction between faith and religion, which modifies the Catholic understanding of confession as a doctrine, would guarantee that Religious Education would not violate the principle of the State secularism.

The other evangelical legislative representative, Manuel Morais, mobilizing the categories specific to the language used in the Commission on Human Rights and Minorities, associated the offer of Religious Education to "promoting an education for citizenship". According to him, the school would not be "proselytizing" when offering "confessional" Religious Education in response to a family demand. This is because, although teaching a doctrine, the child would not be being indoctrinated, that is, "recruited, as he already confesses [. . .] he has already chosen this". Here, the category used to distinguish "doctrine" from "proselytism" was the fact of "choice": the family has already "chosen" the child's faith. Thus, in the logic of Human Rights, the role of law would be to ensure "equality" of the different choices. By offering "confessional" Religious Education, the school would provide a "free service to the poorest families" who cannot afford private religious schools. This "confessional" education, even if doctrinal, would not violate the principle of secularism because it would respect family choices and equal access to this type of education by the poorest.

Speaking on behalf of the Commission to Combat Religious Intolerance and Racism of the Legislative Assembly of Rio de Janeiro, in his speech, Deputy Carlos Minc defended the non-confessional model. According to him, the school material used by Rio's public schools encourages intolerance against non-Christian religions. Doctrinal textbooks, Bible verses, Holy Week commemorative posters, and other teaching materials in everyday use in schools would, in practice, make children who practice other faiths feel uncomfortable. Minc argues that church participation is contrary to the National Education *Guidelines* and Framework *Law* when preparing teaching materials. He criticizes that State Law 3.459/2000 approved by the Rio de Janeiro legislature, which requires prior accreditation by ecclesiastical authorities for a teacher to be accepted in a public examination, and grants churches the power to remove public service professionals. Nevertheless, it recognizes the "humanist and solidary aspect of all religions", citing as examples, the defense of the environment by the former Minister of Environment, the Evangelical Marina Silva (2003–2008), and the defense of Human Rights "common to all the faiths". For this reason, he advocates "absolute religious freedom". However, "having lost two great-grandmothers in Nazi concentration camps" he claims to "know intolerance well". Giving churches the power to select teachers based on their religious convictions and to produce doctrinal teaching material, as in "confessional" religious teaching, would, in his view, constitute an offense to the guarantees of secularity in public education. Consequently, it would characterize a stimulus to religious intolerance.

Three representatives of the Legislative declared their religious convictions as Evangelicals and Jew. This personal convictions modulated their way of arguing. Eurico, representative of the Parliamentary Front in Defense of the Family, claims that "faith is learned at home", with the family and, therefore, faith would be a phenomenon of the private order. Teaching "religion" would be reserved for public education, defined as the transmission of "universal moral values". To a certain extent, Minc's claims are along the same lines when he associates religions with humanism, solidarity and human rights. His disagreement here concerns the possibility that "confessional" education, controlled by ecclesiastical authorities, is capable, in practice, of operating in a non-doctrinal key. When reduced to indoctrination, this teaching model would encourage intolerance and violence against minority religions. Moreover, the representative of the Human Rights Commission, Manuel Morais, guided his speech towards the opposition between "freedom" and "equality". According to him, the guarantees of freedom would be assured considering that the "choice" of faith was made privately, without "undue interference by the State". The State would also guarantee equality by offering the poorest access to religious formation.

It is noteworthy that parliamentary actors, religious or not, mobilize the main categories that form the classic framework of modern liberal secular democracies: freedom, equality, state neutrality, faith as a personal choice, tolerance, etc. What sets them apart is the way these categories are articulated in practice to describe and signify, in this context, their connections with confessional/non-confessional education. We can also see a distinction between these two positions regarding the understanding of who will be held accountable and will have the decision-making power over the provision of Religious Education. The representatives of the executive branch understand that managing and supervising rules is the State's responsibility as it is responsible for preventing favoritism, even though the definition of these contents should be left to religious leaders. On the other hand, representatives of the legislative power associated with evangelical organizations consider that managing school "confessional" education is families´ responsibility under the supervision of ecclesial hierarchies. Therefore, in terms of practices and regulation control, differences in proposition emerge more clearly.

3.6 Presentations and Arguments of Civil Society Representatives

The categories that represent civil society in this arena are quite heterogeneous. For the sake of this analysis, we can group them around the axis of religious organizations and non-religious organizations, as shown in Table 3.

The distinction of these positions in the religious/non-religious axis does not correspond precisely to the division of the "confessional"/"non-confessional" positions. Let us begin our analysis with the largest group and, presumably, the most interested in this issue, the thirteen religious leaders who took the floor.

Table 3 Frequency of manifestation distribution of civil society representatives by category

Sector	Institutional Representation	Institutional positions of the debaters	Representatives' Presentations				Total
			Non-confessional.	Confessional.	Against Religious Education	No position	
Civil society	Religious organization	Religious leaders	3	4	5	1	13
	Non-religious organization	Civil activists for secularity and human rights	3		1		4
		Legal organizations	4				4
		Experts	1		1		2
		Religious education unions	2				2
		Teachers unions	1				1
Total			14	4	7	1	26

Source: the authors

3.7 *Demonstrations by Representatives of Religious Organizations*

The table above shows that religious leaders' presentations on this issue were highly dispersed. Contrary to what one might think at first sight, religious teaching in public schools is not a demand from non-Christian religious leaders and divides the evangelicals´ views. As can be seen, out of a total of thirteen presentations, the referral for "confessional" education teaching was clearly in the minority. The majority took a stand against the offer of this type of education in public schools. How, then, to interpret the meaning of these presentations?

Table 4 presents the distribution of these presentations by the religious leaders. One can see that only the Catholic representatives (CNBB and the Archdiocese of RJ), the Muslim representative, and the president of the Council of Education and Culture of the Assemblies of God were in favor of "confessional" Religious Education. The other nine speakers dispersed into "non-confessional", indifferent, and even anti-religious positions in public schools.

This dispersion, added to the five leaders who sent demonstrations against Religious Education in public schools, an alternative that was not foreseen in the

Table 4 Presentations of participants from religious organizations (freq.)

	Representatives' Presentations			
Institutional representation	Non confessional	Confessional	Against religious education	No position
The Brazilian Spiritist Federation—FEB	1			
National Federation of Afro-Brazilian cults—FENACAB	1			
Raja yoga	1			
CNBB		1		
Archdiocese of Rio de Janeiro		1		
Federation of Muslim Associations of Brazil—FAMBRAS		1		
AD—Council of Education and Culture—CECAD		1		
AD—Ministry of Belém			1	
The Brazilian Israelite Confederation—CONIB			1	
The Brazilian Baptist Convention—CBB			1	
AD—Ministry of Madureira			1	
IURD			1	
Brazil Buddhist Society—SBB				1
Total	03	04	05	01

Source: authors

scope of the debate, is extremely enlightening. It shows that the grammar of Catholic interests completely shaped how the debate was presented insofar as they supported it. Therefore, as we said the decision to withdraw Religious Education from schools was not at stake in the debate. If the offer of this school subject was not under discussion, all that remained was to debate the least onerous model for defending State secularism. Even so, the alternatives put on the table—the "confessional" and the "non-confessional" models—implied a relationship of equivalence between religion and confession only held by representatives from the Catholic Church. For example, the objections raised by representatives from Buddhist and Afro-Brazilian organizations did not fit into this framework. Their explanation about the alternatives on which it was necessary to give an opinion and the rules for enacting them went beyond the issues at stake in this debate as we will see in more detail below.

Let us turn now to the repertoires and categories mobilized in these speeches and to the analysis of how they express the relationships between the notions of "religion", "confession", "moral values", and "secularism".

Analyzing the arguments of the representative from the National Conference of Bishops, Antônio Carlos **Biscaia**,[19] it is clear that he presents "religion" as the foundation of law, citizenship and,, secularism. Biscaia was the former Federal Prosecutor of Rio de Janeiro and Federal Deputy. He justifies the Agreement's constitutionality, understanding that the optional character of Religious Education is sufficient to ensure the principle of secularism. Speaking on behalf of the highest hierarchy of the Catholic Church and also on behalf of the State, as the CNBB was summoned by the Court to appear at the Public Hearing, it is interesting to note the naturalness with which he universalizes "religion" as an ethical-moral condition inherent to humanity:

> [. . .] the crisis of humanity is a crisis of ethical and moral principles and values, which is why I find it strange that they intend to attack Religious Education; it's very strange to me. It's the crisis of ethical principles and values that lead to criminal violence in our country [. . .]

Based on the self-evident premise that humanity is in crisis, Biscaia proposes a solution regarding values. The transition from humanitarian crisis to violence and criminality in the Brazilian context causes the same remedy: to reestablish moral values. In his speech, he confers this responsibility on the State via public schools. However, the State is not conceived here as capable of providing ethical values by itself: it is implicit in this speech that it is up to the Catholic Church, as an auxiliary institution of the State, to teach the values necessary for the foundation of the State itself.

This abstract and universal identification between religion and moral allows, in an apparently contradictory way, Biscaia's support of the confessionality of Religious Education, the transfer of the power of its regulation to ecclesiastical authorities and,

[19] In 1997, he joined the *Partido dos Trabalhadore*s (PT) (Workers' Party). Two years later he took over as an alternate seat in the Chamber of Deputies. In 2002 he was elected federal deputy for RJ. He headed the National Secretariat for Public Security in 2007.

at the same time, to assert Religious Education as a guarantee of civil rights defined as "the principle of religious freedom, cultural diversity and confessional plurality [...] and, (as a result) of the integral formation of the person" (ADIN – 4439). In this fundamentally Catholic model, religious doctrine takes the place of foundation in the ethical moral support of the constitutional legal order. It is not very clear, however, in this speech, how the transfer of regulation of this education to the hands of the Church would leave room for "confessional plurality". Nevertheless, it can be seen in this excerpt that religion, confession (doctrine) and moral values are thought of as equivalent and universal dimensions of humans. Religious pluralism would only represent variations of a morphological nature that can be easily brought together in this more abstract genre that is "religion". The particularities pertaining to the species would not affect the presumed equivalence as the genus "religion" and values that determine it are conceived as abstract and universal.

Now if we turn to the other end of the spectrum, we will see that the position of **Tereza Cristina Soares de Carvalho**, representing the Non-Governmental Organization (NGO), Brahma Kumaris does not fit well into this architecture. Although she was invited to take the floor as a representative of a variety, or "sort" of "religious genre", what she proposes—teaching meditation in schools—is itself a form of knowledge, a technique that makes "life an uplifting experience leading to well-being". More than favoring the "transmission of rites or beliefs", what should be encouraged, in her view, is the "practice of virtues". Rather than proposing to transmit a doctrine, its action is "a project that offers a variety of experimental activities and practical methodologies for teachers and facilitators to enable children and young people to explore and develop virtues" (ADIN – 4439). According to her, teaching these virtuous practices, such as developing collaborative personal and social skills, would be more important than the "transmitting information about religions and philosophies of life". In this position, the use of the term "religion" was entirely devoid of doctrinal content and separated from the idea of "confession". The decision on the best model—"confessional", "interfaith" or "non-confessional"—loses, in this perspective, all meaning because, in terms of transversality, her program "is compatible with any model" and "can be conducted by the teachers, as it is the case of environmental education".

Another position that also breaks with the equivalence between "religion" and "confessionality" is that of the representative of the National Federation of Afro-Brazilian Cults (FENACAB), **Antonio Gomes da Costa Neto**. In his view, Religious Education should focus not on the transmission of a doctrine, but on the "implementation of education in ethnic-racial relations". Neto holds the *Conselho Nacional de Educação*—CNE (National Council of Education) accountable for defining the curriculum guidelines for this school subject and training qualified teachers. To do this, he proposes to create "a bachelor's degree course in Religious Education in which all religious denominations and religious beliefs will be part of the curriculum". It is interesting to note here that the problem of Religious Education is formulated quite differently from the previous cases.

On the one hand, for the CNBB representative, the problem to be faced by Religious Education would be the "crisis of ethical and moral principles", and on the other hand, for the Brahma Kumaris NGO it is about achieving "personal well-being" and for FENAC to fight racism and intolerance that are expressed, according to him, in three different ways: institutionally "[. . .] due to inequality", culturally "[. . .] due to the devaluation of cultures of African origin", individually "[. . .] due to individual racism". If, as Gunsfield (1981) suggests, the way to define the public problem and understand its causes is related to the way to determine who should be held responsible for implementing the solution to the problem, we see in this case that church, civil society and the state alternate here as authorized entities to regulate this school subject. Contrary to Biscaia's proposal to leave teacher training and the content of this school subject to the ecclesiastical authorities and Tereza Cristina, whose NGO would be responsible for developing the project, Costa Neto believes that the National Council of Education should assume this responsibility including all "religious denominations". This way of formulating the solution to the problem of racism via Religious Education is expressed in his manifestation: this subject should not have a confessional content, but rather transmit "[. . .] their racial history to black children" by teaching "[. . .] Afro-Brazilian and indigenous history and culture [. . .]". "Religion" and "confession" appear again here as dissociated, but in a different way: in the evangelical case described above, "religion in general" to be offered at school would differ from the "faith" taught at home; in the Buddhist case, "religion" would be indifferent to "confession"; in the case of Afro-Brazilians, religion would be a "cultural legacy". Speaking on behalf of the The Brazilian Israelite Confederation, Roseli Fischmann reiterates this distinction, noting that "not all religious groups consider themselves confessional." Disagreeing with the idea that Religious Education is "the father of citizenship", she considers that Religious Education should be offered only within the religious communities themselves.

The position of the representative from the Brazilian Spiritist Federation, **Álvaro Chrispino**, who also "is not in favor of Religious Education in public schools", argues that "this education should be given to family and religious institutions, leaving the State to protect this right". He also provides a precise understanding of what he means by "religion". Quoting the work of Allan Kardec, he distinguishes "[. . .] the words which served to the foundation of the dogmas of the church[. . .]" and the "moral teaching". The first ones concern the doctrine, "[. . .] men's interpretation of religious things[. . .]" which includes the debate on "[..] which would be the best religion[. . .]". On the other hand, "moral education" would constitute the "[..] study of universal values that guide human and social relations based on goodness and peace [. . .]". Thus, contrary to the Catholic position, Chrispino defends the distinction between doctrine and morals. But he goes even further in deconstructing the Christian notion of religion as a universal gender. In addition to presenting himself as a "movement" and not a religion, he explains that people "[. . .] are not obliged to attend Spiritist centers", but they do it voluntarily; those who "are in the Spiritist Centers [. . .] are not required to join [. . .]"; those that associate "[. . .] are not require to believe [. . .]", [. . .] there is no control, there is no policing[. . .]. The Spiritist movement proposes to "offer its ideas in an organized way to those who want to know [...] we don't go out in search, we don't trap interested parties [...] at no time do we take over public spaces, public advantages for the diffusion [...]".

In this specification of the Spiritist movement by contrast with Christianity, the inadequacy of the rules of the game implicit in the debate for the game that Spiritists would like to play is clear. In fact, here, as in the cases of Buddhists and Afro-Brazilians mentioned above, we can see a certain tension between the rules that organize the arena of debate—to support the choice between two models of Religious Education, "confessional" or "non-confessional" such as less onerous for laicity—and non-Christian positions whose diversity in understanding the religious phenomenon itself offer reasons that go far beyond the narrow alternative proposed in the terms of the debate.

Analyzing religious representatives´ presentations, it is worth noting that from the five Protestants present, four were against Religious Education in public schools, in clear opposition to the Catholic manifestation. Apart from **Douglas Batista**, President of the Council of Education and Culture of the Assemblies of God, the evangelical representatives consider that Religious Education understood as dogmas, doctrines, biblical teaching, rites and liturgies should not be taught in schools, but, in the family, in religious organizations or even in private confessional schools. The President of the National Juridical Committee of the Assembly of God, Abiezer Apolinário da Silva defends that this school subject should be optional, according to the parents' choice and that its content be geared towards the "sciences of religion". The President of the Baptist Convention Wanderley Marins, on the other hand, considers that the "unification of the religious discourse" that is intended with this school subject would falsify the dogmas. The Universal Church of the Kingdom of God, represented by its lawyer **Renato Herani** and Bishop Domingos Siqueira, presented a surprisingly secularized position. According to Herani, schools do not support this school subject, regardless of the model: "this position is the only one that actually leads to fulfilling secularism [...]". However, as long as the first paragraph of Article 210 of the Constitution is not repealed, Herani observes quite sharply, it will "have to be interpreted".

> If the original constituent thought of confessional Religious Education, the normative force of the facts must today lead to adapting the text to reality, a reality marked by the need to create a constitutional formula that accommodates religious and non-religious diversification. What formula is this? [...] if Brazil was born Christian, matured multi-religious and open to non-religious ideologies, this maxim must be included in the current conception of Religious Education.

Herani, a Doctor of Law from PUC-SP, was the only representative of religious organizations who referred to the need to contemplate non-religious concepts in Religious Education. Furthermore, he also points to the paradoxical implications of the legal recognition of religious pluralism expressed in the Constitution on the decision of the "original constituency" to maintain Religious Education. According to him, "The Universal Church sees the provision of Religious Education in public schools with concern, as the State is not properly prepared to ensure its realization with equality for all religions and beliefs." The guarantee of legal protection of equality in providing religious literacy would make the proposal to maintain its

Table 5 Positioning of civil society representatives

	Manifestation of the representatives	
Institutional representation	Non confessional	Against religious education
ANAJUBI	1	
IAB	1	
Clinica DH e Gênero/UERJ	1	
Amicus DH/USP	1	
ANIS	1	
Conectas DH	1	
OLE	1	
ANPTECRE	1	
ASSINTEC	1	
FONAPER	1	
CNTE	1	
LHIS		1
Ação Educativa		1
Total	11	2

Source: the authors

confessional format unfeasible. Herani's suggestion on behalf of the Universal Church is that Religious Education curricula be *about religion* and not *on religion*.. This "religiosity at the service of public education" would have as content "[. . .] the common philosophical foundation [. . .] (of all religions) [. . .] regarding the aspirations of ethics and humanity [. . .]" and would be regulated by the State: the teaching staff would not be able to have institutional links with churches and the admission criteria would be public. The argument of equality in supply forces a denaturalization of the synonymy between "religion" and "confession". Although he sees religions as a universal gender inherent to the human condition (just as the Catholic jurist Biscaia), their common foundation would be philosophical and not doctrinal in nature.

In an paradoxical way, the set of religious positions does not defend, therefore, "confessional" Religious Education in schools, as many are even against the existence of this school subject. This diversity highlights the predominance of the Catholic Church in circulating this political agenda and the urgency of its interests in formulating, and defining this issue.

Now let us see how other civil society entities, activists, specialists, jurists, and unionists dealt with this way of formulating the problem.

3.8 Demonstration by Representatives of Non-Religious Organizations

As seen from Table 5, the thirteen representatives of non-religiouscivil society put forward numerous recommendations for non-confessional Religious Education, stating outright that it would be better not to offer Religious Education in public schools.

However, if the various previous religious positions indicate agreement with the non-confessional model to preserve the integrity of religious doctrines, the secular positions analyzed in this section argued in favor of supporting "the unshakeable principle of the State's laicity" (C. Schlesinger, Brazilian Association of Jewish Lawyers and Jurists (ANAJUBI),).[20] Therefore, let us begin our analysis with the lawyers who, in our view, set the tone for what is at stake in the debate.

Legal experts argue that the Action of Unconstitutionality against the Agreement between the Brazilian State and the Vatican is well-founded. Carlos Schlesinger considers that article 11, paragraph 1 of the Agreement, which concerns Religious Education, conflicts with article 19,[21] paragraph 1 of the Constitution, which refers to State secularism. Daniel Sarmiento,[22] proponent of the *Ação Direta de Inconstitucionalidade*—ADI (Direct Unconstitutionality of Action) sets a similar tone, also considering the same article of the Agreement as unconstitutional. Virgilio Afonso da Silva,[23] from the Culture and Extension Group at the USP Law School, states that articles 19 and 210 of the Fundamental Standard contradict each other. This contradiction causes, in his view, great perplexity, as Religious Education and State secularism cannot be harmonized. Moreover, according to Salomão Barros Ximenes[24] from *Ação Educativa* (Educational Assistance), these articles would be

[20] He graduated in Law at Candido Mendes University (1977). He was President of the Commission on Human Rights and Vice President of the Special Commission on Law and Religious Freedom at the *Instituto dos Advogados do Brasil* (IAB) from 2015 to 2017.

[21] **Art. 19 of the Constitution**—The Union, States, Federal District and Municipalities are prohibited from: I—establishing religious cults or churches, subsidizing them, hindering their functioning or maintaining relationships of dependence or alliance with them or their representatives, except, in accordance with the law, for collaboration in the public interest.

[22] Daniel Sarmiento is a professor, coordinates the Laicity Laboratory, and the *Fundamental Rights Clinic* of the State University of Rio de Janeiro (UERJ) *Law* School, both at UERJ. In addition, he was a student and is a friend of the STF judge Roberto Barroso rapporteur of the ADI in the STF.

[23] Graduated in Constitutional Law from the Faculty of Law at the University of São Paulo (1995). It is dedicated to the study of fundamental rights, especially from the perspective of the theory of principles, especially focusing on the analysis of proportionality, as well as deliberative processes in the Supreme Court.

[24] Doctor in State Law from the University of São Paulo (2014), who holds a Master's in Education from the Federal University of Ceará (2006). He was a researcher at the Center for Applied Legal Research at the São Paulo School of Law, *Fundação Getúlio Vargas* (FGV Direito SP) and coordinator of the *Ação na Justiça* program at *Ação Educativa Assessoria, Pesquisa e Informação* (from 2006 to 2014).

facing a "practical impossibility, that of reconciling what by definition is irreconcilable".

Therefore, the legal scene organized around Barroso in this Public Hearing, revolves around this oxymoron. As a constitutional change is not at stake, how can the protection of laicity be reconciled with the provision of Religious Education? The suggestion offered by legal experts was, in the words of Schlesinger, to "modulate the principle of secularity with the precept of article 210", or more clearly, "to make a lemonade out of a sour lemon," as proposed by Sarmiento. Therefore, this entire argumentative exercise staged at the Public Hearing aims, from a Constitutional point of view, to find a way to reinterpret the rule relating to Religious Education so that it "fits the commandment to carry out the greatest measure of laicity possible" in the formulation of Virgílio da Silva. The options laid out on the table—"confessionality" or "non-confessionality"—were considered too narrow because, as Silva observes, they do not clarify who would be responsible for the syllabus of this school subject, how teachers would be selected and with what criteria. It can be inferred from the positions presented that the gordian knot in the matter is the dispute between secular and Catholic Church leaders to define and control this school subject's governance.

Débora Diniz,[25] an activist at the Institute of Bioethics, Human Rights and Gender (ANIS) NGO, clearly formulates the terms of this dispute. According to her, Religious Education is the only school subject that does not have any State regulation regarding both the teaching material offered and teachers´ qualifications. In her reading, there is a public policy that refrains from regulating its teaching. As a result, it "moves as if protected by a State' safe conduct". Everything happens as if "the religious fact had precedence concerning the political [...], and as if religion [...] should not be subject to the political agreement of what should promote citizenship".

Diniz is right when she suggests that this controversy only reached the Supreme Court because large sectors of Brazilian society, including jurists, conceive the religious fact as "natural", that is, prior to the political and, therefore, as we have seen, universal. The set of forces that shaped the 1998 Constitution placed, side by side, the premises of religion "as a foundation of citizenship" and as a guarantee of "equality in diversity". Currently, at the moment when the practical implementation of these premises in schools was starting to take place, the Agreement with the Vatican made explicit the silent pact that sustained the Catholic monopoly on religious school education. The debate around the unconstitutionality of this Agreement and the paradoxical notion of "non-confessional religious teaching" concerns precisely the attempt to redefine this pact: it is about deciding in which new terms Religious Education would be acceptable to citizenship and laicity.

[25] Graduated in Anthropology at the University of Brasília (1992) where she also completed her Doctorate (1999). Professor of Law at the University of Brasília, she studied issues of bioethics, feminism, human rights and health. In 1999, she became co-founder of ANIS.

The responses offered by the actors were varied but converged on one point: "religion" and "confessional" religious teaching could no longer coincide. It must be purged of dogmas, beliefs, teaching gestures and rites, in short, everything that could define it as "catechetical" and "proselytist". According to Oscar Vilhena Vieira, an activist at *Conectas* Human Rights NGO, the Constitutional article 210 should be understood as a subordinate norm, an exception to article 19, which expressly prohibits any form of subsidy to religious action. As this norm is binding, Religious Education could not be "confessional", that is, proselytizing, nor could it be given by people accredited by the churches.

The state cannot "allot the educational system to cults and religions", he asserts, nor should it be "a supplier of souls to churches". In the view of Salomão Ximenes,[26] it would be necessary to formulate "a more contemporary interpretation" of this constitutional article 210, since this "terminology would have become anachronistic". For him, considering Religious Education as "part of common basic education and respect for cultural and artistic, national and regional values" as stated in article 210 or as "an integral part of basic citizen education" as required by article 33 of the National Education *Guidelines* and Framework *Law*, is unconstitutional: "with the advent of Human Rights, it would not be necessary to resort to religious ethics in schools to teach universal secular values". The representative of the Permanent National Forum of Religious Education (FONAPER), Leonel Piovesana,[27] speaking on behalf of all Religious Education teachers in Brazil, says that this school subject aims to "developing the learning of religious diversity". According to him, "if we decide for religious teaching of a confessional nature, we will be authorizing indoctrination in schools."

Therefore, for him, Religious Education would be a space in which the students would be prepared for the democratic challenge "of coexistence between different cultural matrices in a multicultural context". Thus, Piovesana proposes a shift in perspective in which the focus of this school subject would no longer be "religion", but diversity itself. The knowledge of diversity in their religious or cultural expression would favor the "development of training based on mutual respect, reciprocity and democratic coexistence between people and groups who assume different religious convictions". In this formulation, it is no longer "religion" that offers moral values of collective coexistence, but, on the contrary, it is the ethical and democratic principles of civility and tolerance that underlie the peaceful coexistence between religions.

---

[26]Doctor in Law from the University of São Paulo (2014) and professor in the Public Policy Program at the Federal University of ABC. He is a member of the Latin American Campaign for the Right to Education (CLADE/Brazil).

[27]Doctor in Regional Development from UNISC (2010). Professor at the Community University of the Chapecó region of the Master's Program in Education at Unochapecó. .Consultant for updating the 2014 Santa Catarina Curriculum Proposal on Indigenous Education. He was Coordinator of the Bachelor in Education Degree in Sciences of Religion from 2014 to 2018 and Coordinator of the Graduate Program *Stricto Sensu* Master's in Education at Unochapecó 2016 to 2018. Specialist in the National Common Curriculum Base 2014–2016.

If there were a consensus among civil society actors that the "non-confessional" model of Religious Education would be the least costly for the laicity, its syllabus content remained in abeyance. Despite its inopportune presence in public schools, on behalf of science of religion professors, Piovesana proposed that Religious Education could benefit citizenship by teaching the value of religious diversity.

Willem Wachholz, from the *National Association of Graduate* Studies and *Research* in *Theology* and *Science* of *Religion* (ANPTECRE), considers that Sciences of Religions should provide this approach; Roberto Leão of the National Confederation of Education Workers (CNTE) is inclined towards the sociology or philosophy of religion; Eloi Santos from Interfaith Association of Education and Culture (ASSINTEC) prefers phenomenology. Whatever the approach to be adopted, for the non-religious actors present there—academics, activists or teacher representatives—religion should be taught as an object of reflection, not as a doctrine to be followed.

4 Final Considerations

Although it may seem a marginal issue, at first glance, Catholic Religious Education in public schools has been a long-term public problem. This is because its consequences affected not only those interested in the Catholic religion but also those who had no interest in it and, above all, those who were, and still are, against its influence. Disputes against Religious Education began to be organized, as we have seen, in the nineteenth century. However, the enormous collective effort channeled by the Judiciary in this 2015 Public Hearing indicates that this problem has not yet been properly addressed. Pluralism as a political principle started to demand that all religious and non-religious representations could be heard. If until the 1960s the dispute revolved around the question of defining whether the teaching of religion should or should not be a function of the State, the 1988 Constitution, by defining citizenship as the regulated and peaceful coexistence of differences, introduced something new in the debate: it is now a matter of determining how the State should regulate diversity in Religious Education. The 1996 National Education *Guidelines* and Framework *Laws* aimed to formulate a first response to this problem by proposing "interfaith" or "non-confessional" teaching. However, its implementation and the resistance of the Catholic Church gave rise to new controversies that shifted to the control of the content of this school subject and teacher education management.

Considering the complexity of the views on the subject, in order to define his position on the unconstitutionality of item 11 of the Agreement with the Vatican, the rapporteur preferred to "listen to society" beforehand, as Carlos Schlesinger put it.

This long and intricate staging of society and its voices in this legal arena explains the diversity of perspectives on the problem. It also indicates that the formulas for regulating the past -preponderantly occupied with defining and controlling the limits of the Catholic Church's action in public life—are not enough to regulate religious freedom in this new legal, and political framework, which requires respect for diversity. In this context, what should be the object of regulation and what would be the best possible regulation are still not entirely pacified issues. Observed as a whole, on the one hand, the scene reveals the surprising minority position of the Catholic Church in the field of religions regarding the benefits of the existence of this school subject in public schools; on the other hand, it shows the consistency and the political weight of the secularist positions that question the moral laws of Christianity as a legal basis for citizenship and supports opening up this school subject to other religious, non-religious and anti-religious perspectives.

The way in which we grouped the institutions present in the debate—executive bodies, representatives of parliament and civil society—enabled us to identify narrative patterns in relation to the topic of laicity. Perhaps because this Public Hearing was motivated, organized and represented basically by lawyers, the representatives linked to the jurists' organizations mobilized categories and developed a way of arguing closer to that proposed by the rapporteur. At the center of the debate was the unconstitutionality of article 11, paragraph 1 of the Agreement with the Vatican, which would threaten the secular character of the State. They also dealt with the contradictions inherent in the Constitution concerning the protection of the secular state defined by a strict separation between State and religion, "one of the greatest achievements of the civilizational advance" in the words of the representative from ANAJUBI.

According to Schlesinger, by introducing Religious Education in schools and making it available to all religions, the Constitution posed a new problem of identifying "which religions would be accepted as good or worthy of this approval". In general, this segment contrasts Religious Education with teaching human rights in public schools, as the solution for training Brazilian citizens. On the other hand, representatives of the government's executive bodies, all with extensive experience in planning educational policies, preferred to direct the debate towards the strengthening of national guidelines that should guide the contents of this school subject. The most important thing for them would be to curb catechetical teaching. Important sectors of civil organizations allied with the positions of the executive argue in favor of a non-doctrinal understanding of religion.

The associations that bring together the interests of teaching professionals in this field guided the debate to determine what would be the most appropriate contents and formats to prevent the teaching *about* religion from being oriented towards the teaching *on* religion. Despite the differences and nuances observed between the actors in the way of mobilizing categories and articulating propositions, it is interesting to note that, in terms of positions, non-confessional Religious Education was chosen by most members of non-religious organizations (eleven of thirteen) and executive and legislative branches (four out of six). On the other hand, the issue divided the thirteen representatives of religious organizations that mainly focused against Religious Education in public schools.

This paradox in which the interest of most religious advisors and activists converged indicates that the controversy described here was not restricted to a polarity that places religious actors and non-religious or anti-religious actors in opposing camps. Compared with the 1960s debate around the National Education *Guidelines* and Framework *Law,* which divided the positions around only two possibilities—for or against Religious Education in public schools—it can be seen that the diversification of participants in the audience, expanded considerably the range of actors qualified to speak publicly and introduced a third term into the debate, the "confessional" category.

The meaning of this category was disputed over the following decades and its avatars emerged in different editions of the National Education *Guidelines* and Framework *Law*. The term "religious confession" first appeared in the 1961 National Education *Guidelines* and Framework *Law* to indicate students' beliefs. The post-constitution National Education *Guidelines* and Framework *Law*, edited in 1996, split, as we have seen, this term into two: "confessional" Religious Education, which corresponds to the personal conviction of the student or guardian, and "interfaith" Religious Education, one resulting from an agreement between the various religious entities, who would be responsible for planning the respective program. As there was no consensus on the best format, the 1997 National Education *Guidelines* and Framework *Law* version suppressed all reference to this term. Even so, in the same year, due to the demands of the CNBB, Congress voted on law 9.475 proposed by Padre Roque (PT/PR), reiterating the "confessional nature of education" (Cunha 2005). More than a decade later, Brazil's Agreement with the Holy See rekindled the debate by reintroducing the term to qualify the format of Religious Education.

In the context of this controversy, the Public Hearing, organized to debate the constitutionality of the Agreement, scheduled the vote around this opposition: "confessional" or "non-confessional" education. The displacement of the dispute from the presence/absence binomial of Religious Education at schools to the model of confessionality produced, at the same time, a broadening of the concept of secularity and a shift in the meaning of the category of "religion". In the previous debate, which did not mention confessionality, Religious Education defenders ensured that the principle of secularism was guaranteed by the fact that "religion" was a private and autonomous choice of families and that the churches were responsible for the cost of its teaching; in the following debate, the legislator, pressed by the need to safeguard laicity and diversity at the same time, proposed this new term, the "interfaith religion." This new configuration would be able to add to the existing protection of secularism, granting State control of the guardianship of religious diversity through management, financing and teacher training.

In this movement, new academic and union associations were created, such as those of Religious Education teachers (ASSINTEC, 1973; FONAPER, 1995), which started to promote meetings, events, and research aimed at subsidizing the pedagogical practices of this education. The professionalization of this education, anchored in an expanding academic formation in this field, gradually distanced it from the sacristy and re-signified it as a tool to produce public morality, regardless of any religion, but capable of making respect for diversity the foundation of citizenship. This new form of knowledge is based, no longer on brotherhood and the truth of beliefs, but on philosophical knowledge, cultural heritage and political equality.

We should bear in mind that, despite the majority position of these actors for non-denominational education at the Public Hearing (56%), the final vote on the matter by the Supreme Court in 2017 dismissed the ADI arguments and by a narrow margin of votes (six to five) the justices defeated the rapporteur, understanding that Religious Education in public schools may have a "confessional nature" and be taught by representatives of a religion. The understanding that Religious Education is an integral part of basic citizen training was also maintained and reinforced in the Supreme Court's vote.

Regardless of this result and the division of forces in the Supreme Court, it seems to us that the performance of the Public Hearing reveals the different ways in which the categories of "religion" and "laicity" are operated in the current context. As we said, the controversy described here has not only placed religious and non-religious positions in opposing camps, but also Catholic and non-Catholic positions. Non-Christian churches were either indifferent or preferred the "non-confessional" model. On the other hand, Evangelical leaders were mostly against Religious Education in public schools, under any modality. According to Cunha (2005), these denominations were not interested in Religious Education in public schools for fear of the advantage of Catholic organizations, which have more resources, experience and capacity to prepare teachers.

However, the enactment also reveals the ideological and political overdetermination of the game, whose rules do not concern all the participants, given their need to be stronger in order to change the terms of the debate. In any case, the very requirement of the game, which forces the actors to make the protection of laicity compatible with the plural religious literacy, end up modulating the principle of secularity and the very hegemonic definition of "the religious". The great loser was the catechetical model of Religious Education. The peculiar emergence of the term "non-confessional" Religious Education and its wide circulation indicates that in contemporary pluralism, there is no longer any way to make the public school a supplier of souls to churches. However, it is significant that Religious Education, when modulated by the principle of diversity, can be considered capable of offering souls to the Republic.

References

Asad T (2003) Formations of the secular modern: Christianity, Islam, modernity. Stanford University Press

Baubérot J. El origem del estado laico (2016). Available at: <http://www.jornada.unam.mx>. Accessed 1 abr 2020

Braga LG (2008) Na lei e nas escolas. Debates do NER 14:89–110

Calhoun C (2012) Time, world and secularism. In: Kim DK, Torpey J, VanAntwerpen J, Gorski PS (eds) The post-secular in question: religion in contemporary society. New York University Press, New York

Casanova J (2011) Public religions in the modern world. University of Chicago Press

Cefai D (2017) Públicos, Problemas Públicos, Arenas Públicas. Novos Estudos do Cebrap 36:187–213
Connolly WE (1999) Why I am not a secularist. University of Minnesota Press, Minnesota
Connolly WE (2011) Some theses on secularism. Cult Anthropol 26(4):648–656
Cunha LA (2005) Autonomização do campo educacional: efeitos do e no Ensino Religioso. Colóquio AFEC, Sèvres, França, pp 139–154
Cunha LA (2006) Ensino Religioso nas Escolas Públicas: a propósito de um seminário internacional. Educação e Sociedade 27(97):1235–1256
Cunha LA, Gondra AM, Magaldi JG, (org.) (2003) A Reconstrução do Campo Educacional: manifestações, manifesto e manifestantes. Rio de Janeiro: 7Letras
Cury CRJ (1984) Ideologia e Educação Brasileira: Católicos e liberais, 2a. edn. Cortez Editora/ Autores Associados, São Paulo/SP
Esquivel JC (2008) Laicidades Relativas: avatares de la relación Estado-Iglesia en Brasil. In: Roberto J. Blancarte (Coord.). Retos de la Laicidad y la Secularización en el Mundo Contemporáneo. El Colegio de Mexico, Mexico
Giumbelli E, Carneiro SS (2006) Religião das Escolas Públicas; questões nacionais e a situação no Rio de Janeiro. Revista Contemporânea de Educação. 2
Giumbelli E, Carneiro SS (2007) O ensino religioso na sala de aula. ANPOCS
Giumbelli E, Carneiro SS (2010) A religião nos limites da simples educação: notas sobre livros didáticos e orientação curricular de Ensino Religioso. Revista de Antropologia 53(1):39–78
Gunsfield JR (1981) The culture pf public problems. Drinking, driving and the symbolic order. The University of Chicago Press
Lima D (1978) Educação, Igreja e ideologia: uma análise sociológica da elaboração da Lei de Diretrizes e Bases. Livraria Francisco Alves, Rio de Janeiro/RJ
Lui JÁ (2006). Em nome de Deus. A implementação do Ensino religioso nas escolas públicas de São Paulo. Tese de Mestrado, UFSC
Luiz AA (2009) A educação na Concordata Brasil-Vaticano. Educação e Sociedade 30(106): 263–280
Mainwaring S (1989) A Igreja Católica e a Política no Brasil: 1916–1985. Brasiliense, São Paulo/ SP
Modood T (2009) Muslim, religious equality and secularism. In: Brahm G, Modood T (eds) Secularism, religion and multicultural citizenship. Cambridge University Press, Cambridge
Montalvão SS (2010) A LDB de 1961: apontamentos para uma história política da educação. Mosaico 2(3):21–39
Oliveira GG (2014) Educação, Laicidade e Pluralismo: elementos para uma genealogia dos debates sobre o ensino religioso no Brasil. Revistas Teias 14(36):43–60
Portier P, Lagrée J (2010) La Modernité Contre la Religion? Pour une Nouvelle Approche de la Laïcité. Presse Universitaire de Rennes, Rennes
Santos MS (2016) Religião e demanda: o fenômeno religioso em escolas públicas. Unicamp
Taylor C (2007) A secular age. Belknap Press of Harvard University, Cambridge

Evangelical Jurists and Human Rights in Brazil: A Case Study of the National Association of Evangelical Jurists (ANAJURE)

Cleto Junior Pinto de Abreu

Abstract Over the last decade, evangelical jurist groups have emerged in Brazilian courts. Intervening in public controversies about the meaning of human rights, they confronted the agendas of the feminist and LGBTQI+ movements. This phenomenon did not occur as a denial of the importance of advancing the issue of human rights, but, on the contrary, in accordance with the normative public sphere and the procedures for demanding rights in modern democratic societies. From a genealogical approach, this chapter addresses the collective mobilization process of jurists on behalf of evangelicals' interests in Brazil, focusing on the relationship these groups maintain with LGBTQI+ movements in contentious processes involving rights claims. From the public controversy surrounding criminalizing violence against homosexuals to the judgment of this issue by the Supreme Federal Court, the mobilization of evangelical groups in the legal world is analyzed. The material comprises documents, interviews and statements on the themes of homophobia and homosexuality made by members of the National Association of Evangelical Jurists (ANAJURE). They redefine human rights claims made in the courts by LGBTQI+ subjects, contesting the legitimacy of the acceptance of these demands by these institutions of power. Although they emerged at the intersection of law and religion, these groups use their legal identity to gain public recognition and intervene in controlling the borders between the worlds of law and politics.

1 Introduction

In recent years, evangelical jurist associations have emerged in Brazilian courts, intervening in the name of the values and rights of their religious confession and confronting demands for rights from the feminist and LGBTQI+ movements. Christian groups are very active in Supreme Courts of countries such as the United States and Canada. Courts are bodies for accepting and resolving their demands for

C. J. P. de Abreu (✉)
Center for Historical Research, HSE University, Saint-Petersburg, Russia
e-mail: cletojunior@alumni.usp.br

P. Montero et al. (eds.), *Religious Pluralism and Law in Contemporary Brazil*, Law and Religion in a Global Context 4, https://doi.org/10.1007/978-3-031-41981-2_3

religious freedom, particularly concerning their grievances against secular state policies (Hoover and den Dulk 2004). In addition, Supreme Courts also serve these groups as instances to impede or delay the implementation of sexual and reproductive rights made by feminist and LGBTQI+ movements, which they consider to be moral opponents. Entry of conservative or religious groups into the courts against these demands is a global phenomenon and the cases of Colombia and Brazil are examples in the Latin American context (Sales 2015; Lehoucq 2021). In this context, the legal education of its members is a key point for activism of the Christian right in its confrontation with secular law, politics and culture (Wilson and Hollis-Brusky 2018).

For many Christian lawyers, the practice of law entails a divine calling or vocation, which can also involve a perspective of cultural and spiritual warfare against the forces of evil. In this case, legal training is used to restore Christian values to the public sphere (Wilson and Hollis-Brusky 2014). This phenomenon refers to Christian lawyers' views about the functions and uses of law. This dimension can also be observed among members of Brazilian Evangelical jurist associations. However, this study addresses the collective mobilization process of these actors in the name of their evangelical identity, focusing on the relationship they establish with LGBTQI+ movements within contentious processes involving human rights claims. Evangelical jurist associations in Brazil have emerged within a mobilization process of legal practitioners in different evangelical churches, where the characterization of religious freedom as a right threatened by demands of LGBTQI+ groups to higher courts gains centrality. The phenomenon reveals that disputes involving religious groups and feminist and LGBTQI+ movements extend beyond the parliamentary scenes, also moving to the legal arenas, where new actors emerge and increase in importance.

The chapter begins by presenting the public controversy surrounding criminalizing violence against homosexuals in Brazil and the way in which religious actors and members of the LGBTQI+ community acted in this process. Then, I try to demonstrate how the mobilization of evangelical jurists occurred in articulation with this phenomenon. Afterwards, I describe how these disputes were expressed in the Supreme Court and how the association of evangelical jurists acted in the judgment of criminalizing violence against homosexuals. Finally, I try to demonstrate that disputes involving religious groups and LGBTQI+ are not limited to the legal world, as they seek ways of resolution in global institutions of power.

2 Methods

The time frame covers the period between 2011 and 2019. In this period of time, the legal world began to suffer more and more from the effects of public controversy between Evangelical groups and LGBTQI+ concerning Bill 122/2006 (PL 122/2006), which deals with criminalizing homophobia. ANAJURE's trajectory proved to be an analytically important phenomenon, as it emerged at the time immediately after the controversy arose in 2012, and it has been constituted as a relevant actor throughout this period, playing the role of *amicus curiae* in the Supreme Federal Court (STF) in 2019, concerning the consequences of this controversy in the legal world. The time frame allows us to analyze more accurately the phenomenon of displacement of disputes between evangelical groups and LGBTQI+ movements from the political arena to the legal arena.

The materials collected were documents published by ANAJURE on its website and in other media on the themes of homophobia and homosexuality; reports and news in the media about PL 122/2006, street demonstrations of Christian activists in 2011, and the trial of criminalizing homophobia in the Supreme Federal Court in 2019; and, finally, the Supreme Court's ruling on the matter. Most of the material corresponds to ANAJURE's public presentation and the image that the association seeks to convey to public opinion. It reveals the association's public positions over time around the theme of homophobia and homosexuality and its performance in the worlds of law, politics and religion, highlighting the way in which evangelical groups organize and question the agendas of the LGBTQI+ movements in the legal arena.

The analysis of the material involved mapping the way ANAJURE acted in relation to the themes of homophobia and homosexuality. Concerning this, I identified these categories from the first documents published by the association until they were judged by the Supreme Federal Court. This analysis enabled us to pinpoint ANAJURE's role in the political, religious and legal worlds and the way in which it sought to make itself visible from these categories. Finally, the analysis identified themes related to these categories, networks of interested actors and the association's relations with the Supreme Federal Court.

3 The Political Context of the Emergence of ANAJURE

In 2007, Dilma Rousseff's statements on the topic of abortion and women's reproductive rights were the subject of public controversy. Rousseff was head of the Office of the Chief of Staff and a pre-candidate for the Workers' Party (PT) for the presidential succession of Lula da Silva. Her statements echoed the rights claims of the feminist movements. Controversies heightened in the 2010 presidential elections when Rousseff's speeches were remembered and criticized by Evangelical and Catholic groups (G1 2010).

Disputes between religious groups, LGBTQI+ and feminists started having more visibility and the issue of human rights was a key element in 2009 when the 3rd National Human Rights Plan (PNDH-3 in Portuguese) was drafted in Lula da Silva's second presidential term (2006–2010). Among other objectives, the PNDH-3 sought to increase the participation of civil society groups in the development of public policies. It represented the third stage (after the PNDH-1, in 1996, and the PNDH-2, in 2002) of a long process of articulating the Brazilian legal and political order with the international agenda for the protection of human rights, leading to consequences to develop public policies. Proposals such as the decriminalizing abortion, civil unions between people of the same sex and the right of adoption by same-sex couples were foreseen in the PNDH-3 and sought to fulfill demands of the feminist and LGBTQI+ movements (Adorno 2010).

In 2011, in the first year of Dilma Rousseff's presidency, there was a mobilization of the *Frente Parlamentar Evangélica*—FPE (Evangelical Parliamentary Front) and street demonstrations by Christian groups (Evangelical and Catholic) in opposition to pushing through Bill 122/2006, in the Federal Chamber. The author of the project was a PT parliamentarian and the text provided for criminalizing homophobia in the country. Evangelical leaders from different denominations, including Pastor Silas Malafaia, one of the most controversial and most visible people, organized a rally in front of the National Congress, in Brasília, the hub of the country's political power, bringing together about 25,000 people. Using banners, posters, sound trucks and slogans, the protesters sought to pressure parliamentarians to shelve the bill. Malafaia stated that the law would result in the privilege of a minority, referring to LGBTQI+ people, and the persecution of pastors against homosexuality (Castro 2011). The posters and banners at the demonstrations evoked biblical verses, showed phrases against abortion, homo-affective civil unions and decriminalizing marijuana, and many of those present carried Brazilian and Israeli flags. The defense of religious freedom appeared as one of the demands and on many posters there were phrases, such as: "In favor of family and freedom of speech and religion", "Is the Bible homophobic? What are they going to do now, tear up the bible?", "They'll soon be saying that the bible is homophobic" (Cavallera 2011).

This was a period in which mobilization episodes of evangelical and Catholic groups on the theme of human rights became increasingly frequent, especially in opposition to the demands of the feminist and LGBTQI+ movements, and most often involving deputies linked to the Evangelical Parliamentary Front. Examples are disputes surrounding the School without Homophobia project (G1 2011), the appointment of federal deputy Pastor Marco Feliciano to the Chamber's Human Rights and Minorities Commission (CDHM) in 2013 (Freitas 2013), and the presence of religious advisors in the public hearings at the Supreme Federal Court about religious teaching in public schools in 2015 (Montero and Girardi 2019).

4 The Process of Mobilizing Jurists on Behalf of Evangelicals

The relationship between evangelicals and the legal world is not new in Brazil. When drawing up the New Civil Code in 2003, evangelical groups mobilized their legal frameworks in order to measure the consequences of the new law on their churches and on the right to religious freedom (Mariano 2007). They feared an increase in state regulation of their denominations. Lawyers, judges, appellate judges and practitioners of the right to evangelical confession mobilized at that time, but they did not constitute an association or movement of jurists in the name of their religious identity.

In 2012, a group of evangelical jurists created the National Association of Evangelical Jurists (ANAJURE). It joined other associations of religious jurists, such as the *Associação Nacional de Magistrados Evangélicos*—Anamel (National Association of Evangelical Magistrates) and the *União de Juristas Católicos de São Paulo*—Ujucasp (Union of Catholic Jurists of São Paulo) and Rio de Janeiro (Ujucarj). and the (Ujucasp) and Rio de Janeiro (Ujucarj). ANAJURE was created simultaneously using political processes involving evangelicals around demands for rights by feminist and LGBTQI+ movements. It started to bring together people who live, work and circulate between the religious world and the world of law and who are linked to international networks of actors with the same characteristics. In clashes with those who they consider their political opponents, they make extensive use of the idea of religious freedom, which is relatively pacified and recognized in Brazil, but they understand that it is a constantly threatened right, especially in the case of evangelicals, due to the advancement of gender and sexual diversity policies. From cases they perceive as violations of this right, they issue opinions and notes, which they publish on their media and digital social networks, and prepare official letters, which they address to government authorities.

ANAJURE expressed a form of public religious activism that did not emerge in a vacuum, but had correspondents in a public culture before creating it and which began with the polemicization and confrontation of demands for sexual and reproductive rights by the Catholic Church, since the 1990s (Steil and Toniol 2012). It is in line with Catholic actions on the topic, whose representatives make frequent use of the Supreme Federal Court's public hearings to express their positions[1] (Sales 2015). Catholics sought to politically confront demands for rights based on gender policies, such as abortion, demands made in the name of fetuses and embryos and traditional family rights, using the category "gender ideology" and echoing positions on the topic externalized by the Vatican (Junqueira 2018). ANAJURE incorporated the Catholic political agenda, adding to these rights the demand for protection of religious freedom, as well as freedom of worship and speech.

Despite this historical background, there is no precedent for an entity such as ANAJURE in Brazil. Although evangelical denominations have claimed the right to religious freedom on numerous occasions in the country's history and, in these cases, have called their own jurists for this purpose, there is no record that legal practitioners have mobilized around an evangelical identity. Due to this, ANAJURE's activities follow the example of Christian jurists in other countries, especially in the United States. For example, the Religious Liberty Partnership (RLP), a network created in 2006 with links in 20 countries. It provides training, research and assistance services to Christian organizations focusing on religious freedom

[1] For an analysis of public hearings related to the "beginning of human life", referring to embryonic stem cell research and the possibility of anticipating the delivery of anencephalic fetuses, see the chapter written by Sales in this volume.

(O'Connell 2020) and the Alliance Defending Freedom (ADF), created in 1994 whose actions are focused on litigation in the United States Supreme Court (Freedom 2021). ANAJURE acts similarly to the ADF, as it has been increasingly claiming and occupying the role of *amicus curiae* in public hearings promoted by the Brazilian Supreme Court (ANAJURE 2020a). In the Latin American context, the association maintains links with the *Federación Interamericana de Juristas Cristianos*—FIAJC (Inter-American Federation of Christian Jurists), founded in 2001, whose headquarters are in Montevideo, Uruguay. One of the FIAJC presidents is Uziel Santana, founder and president of ANAJURE. In 2012, the association published Gerardo Amarilla's speech on its website, a Uruguayan parliamentarian and at the time president of the FIAJC, against what he saw as criminalizing opinion through homophobia (ANAJURE 2012a).

ANAJURE's administrative structure reflects the issues of interest to the association. Thus, its departments include legal and academic affairs, refugees, humanitarian aid and development, mission agencies, denominational affairs, denominational educational institutions, and the Third Sector. Guidance is given by two councils, the Referential Consultative Council and the National Directive Council. The members of the first council are not legal practitioners, but people who have a background in theology, theological education organization leaders and members of evangelical ecclesiastical elites. Some of the members of this council are not Brazilian and include presidents and directors of religious organizations from other countries, especially from the English-speaking Protestant world, who share the theme of defending religious freedom and are interested in the debate around human rights. Thus, through these actors, ANAJURE is part of an international network of Christian organizations that address religious freedom and human rights. The second board is ANAJURE's decision-making and administrative body. Its members belong to traditional Protestant churches and differ from the members of the first council in their professional identity, as they are all legal practitioners.

ANAJURE consists of an evangelical public that comprises mostly Presbyterian and Baptist Protestants. The board members are Mackenzie Presbyterian University graduates, and many are lecturers at that educational institution. The presence of other segments of Protestantism, such as Anglicans, Methodists, Pentecostals, Neo-Pentecostals, etc. is the minority, at least as far as the association's management positions are concerned. Thus, ANAJURE represents evangelical jurists from a specific segment of the Brazilian Protestant world.

The association works on several fronts and, by and large, its work is characterized by constructing figures of victims, in line with constitutional guidelines, paying special attention to cases involving religious advisors, but not only them. This work is done in reaction to the demands of groups considered by it to be adversaries. In the evangelical world, ANAJURE's work is based on raising awareness and training members of the ecclesiastical body of denominations regarding the legal instruments they can use in case they perceive that their right to religious freedom is being threatened, as well as their freedom of worship and speech. This work is interdenominational, that is, it takes place in historic Pentecostal and Protestant churches, which expands the network of actors mobilized by the association.

In 2013, leaders from the Evangelical Lutheran Church of Brazil, Evangelical Church of the Lutheran Confession in Brazil, Presbyterian Church of Brazil, Independent Presbyterian Church, United Presbyterian Church, Methodist Church, Wesleyan Methodist Church, and Evangelical Holiness Church supported ANAJURE's activities and suggested their respective denominations to jurists to affiliate to the association. The episode demonstrated an advance in mobilizing evangelical jurists around the agenda proposed by ANAJURE (ANAJURE 2013a). The association sought to articulate a network of jurists from their respective denominations, making use of the religious leaders of each church. This process gradually resulted in an interdenominational network of legal practitioners in different segments of the evangelical world and committed to defending their religion.

The universe of evangelical denominations in Brazil is fundamentally diverse in theological, social and political terms. However, ANAJURE in the national arena and the way in which it brings together actors of theological and denominational reference in the Protestant world strengthens and publicly projects it as an entity representing evangelicals in the field of law. Its "Denominational Support Plan" offers courses to pastors and evangelical leaders on administrative and legal issues related to religious work. This resource allows ANAJURE to be included, for example, in the world of Pentecostal denominations, such as the Assembly of God (ANAJURE 2013b).

Mobilizing jurists does not only involve organizing events, congresses, meetings and consultancies, but also the offer of legal training courses. The "ANAJURE Academy" was created to "create the identity of evangelical jurists of the institution from the beginning", according to the president of the association (ANAJURE 2019a). The course is aimed only at students and people trained in the field of law (it is not open to students from other academic disciplines), and its main objective is "to train in a Christian worldview applied to Legal Sciences" (ANAJURE 2021a). Participation in the "ANAJURE Academy" entails a two-step selection process. First, candidates must present a motivation letter, a letter of recommendation from a teacher and the pastor of the church that they attend, as well as a review on the following topic: "The relationship between the Christian worldview, the Law and the defense of Religious Freedom." In the second stage, those who were selected are interviewed by ANAJURE members.

Since its foundation, ANAJURE's staff is composed by members of the judicial system. This feature remains and is constantly expanding. The association's members have been playing the role of evaluators of candidates for judiciary positions (Mazza 2020). The evaluation method involves criteria among which the candidates' (Christian) religious belonging and their defense of moral guidelines. Although some members may be dissatisfied with these institutions whereby the association interferes in the selection process, ANAJURE evaluates candidates and imposes new strategies on those who attempt to be successful in their evaluation, among which is the interest in defended agendas by the association. In the legislative branch, the association maintains a Directorate of Parliamentary Affairs. The first occupant of this department was Damares Alves, an evangelical pastor and current head of the Ministry of Women, Family and Human Rights.

As the dispute for the meaning of human rights also passes through non-legislative channels and refers to international agreements and treaties, in 2017, ANAJURE started the accreditation process in the United Nations Committee on Non-Governmental Organizations (NGOs). Through this body, NGOs can give their opinion in UN forums and have access to events held by other bodies of the entity. However, China and Cuba objected to the association's request, delaying its accreditation process (Frazão 2020).

On another occasion, ANAJURE took a stand against the actions of the Inter-American Commission on Human Rights (IACHR) regarding violence against homosexuals. The IACHR is an organ linked to the Organization of American States (OAS) and part of the inter-American system for the protection and promotion of human rights. The president of ANAJURE declared that the IACHR's decision revealed "ideologization, partisanship and appropriation by a specific group in the society of public human rights policies that should really address those who are vulnerable in society, in this case, children themselves who are victims of the mistaken choices of those who insist that homosexuality is a normal and natural pattern of human beings" (ANAJURE 2013c). The association noticed the influence of entities from the international system for the promotion of human rights on public opinion and political life in different countries, as it began to demonstrate an indisposition towards the actions of these entities regarding the agendas of interest of the LGBTQI+ movements. Due to this fact, ANAJURE aims to qualify for spaces of influence in UN commissions.

Although it aims to keep up an image as an actor in the world of law, the association does not set aside the world of politics. In 2019, at an event on religious freedom, one of the main guests was former judge Sergio Moro. Minister of Justice and Public Security at that time, Moro was nominated to the position by former President Bolsonaro because of his visibility as a kind of anti-corruption hero. At the ANAJURE event, the former judge sought to give greater publicity to his proposals in public safety and get closer to evangelical congregations (ANAJURE 2019b). Since then, the association has become Moro's main institutional support among evangelicals, especially after former President Bolsonaro's statement regarding his intention to nominate a "terribly evangelical" minister to the Supreme Federal Court and the possibility of Moro's candidacy for presidential succession to Bolsonaro. In addition to Moro, ANAJURE's "International Congress on Fundamental Civil Liberties" also brought together Minister Damares Alves, the Presbyterian pastor and head of the Attorney General of the Union, André Mendonça, as well as Evangelical parliamentarians such as Roberto de Lucena (PODE-SP), ambassadors, religious missionaries, theologians and social workers.

5 The Supreme Federal Court's Criminalization of Violence Against Homosexuals

In an interview with the president of ANAJURE, it can be observed that the initial group of evangelical jurists was small and their agenda did not represent a broad demand from sectors of this confession. Furthermore, it was not initially born in the world of law, but in the world of politics, and its main interest was in the defense of evangelical churches, in the figure of their pastors and leaders. ANAJURE mobilized the right to religious freedom to that end. An important point concerns the relationship of jurists with the context in which the association was created. They define this period negatively, as they see it as a time of regression for the right to religious freedom, as the federal government's policies on sexual diversity and gender identity have advanced.

> When we started ANAJURE as a movement from 2008 to 2009, we had no idea of what the future of our work at ANAJURE would be or what the national association would be like. We saw the demands and concerns, it was a time of many uncertainties, the various actions that we were aware of were taking place against the church, the famous PL 122, which deals with homophobia. And you see, ten years later, the Supreme Federal Court comes and decides on this. And, at that time, our concern was to safeguard some of the historic freedoms, not some, but all the historic freedoms that a modern democracy must have and, therefore, our right to religious freedom. In this context, I remember well, in the first meetings with Dr. Ênio Araújo and Dr. Valter Valnício, both from Paraíba, we thought that we should run the country so that new members, new legal persons, we did not know exactly what this movement would be so that they could understand the dangers that our country was beginning to have in that context. And from 2008 to 2012, we prepared the foundation of exactly what the National Association of Evangelical Jurists would be. It was launched in November 2012, there at the National Congress, in a solemn act, with the participation of many parliamentarians from the Evangelical Parliamentary Front and also from other segments and our initial group there had, I believe, about 10 jurists who were part of the first National Board of Directors" [Speech taken from the ANAJURE Cast episode from November 30, 2019 (ANAJURE 2019a)].

The group of lawyers who created ANAJURE saw in PL 122/2006 the beginning of a persecution of Christians in Brazil. In their view, it was not about safeguarding the physical and psychological integrity of LGBTQI+ subjects, but rather a strategy of social movements in defense of these subjects to reduce the influence of Christianity on Brazilian society. Thus, the group saw in PL 122/2006 a regression and an attack on the rights of religious. In 2012, the president of ANAJURE expressed his point of view on the context. He gave the following interview to an evangelical publisher, *Edições Vida Nova*.

> In 2007, in the midst of serious discussions and concerns regarding PL 122/2006 (...) Evangelical jurists, first of all, from the Northeast, began to discuss creating an entity that would be willing to defend fundamental civil liberties, particularly, in the Christian case, our freedom of religion and speech. This is because, definitely, the possibility of approving legislative projects such as PL 122/2006 - among others - was taking our country to a typical scenario of Islam and the West: a scenario of persecution of Christianity and its values (...), developing public policies of the deconstruction of the Christian ethos and the persecution of institutions and people from the Christian segment. Thus, in the last 5 years, this group of

> jurists started to meet, with members from all over the country and to form what is today ANAJURE. On August 18 of this year, in Campina Grande, Paraiba State, where it all started during one of the *Visão Nacional para a Consciência Cristã* - VINACC (National Vision for Christian Consciousness) meetings, we founded our association. (ANAJURE 2012b).

According to its members, the association originated from a group of evangelical lawyers who recognized the insufficiency of the public polemic instrument concerning the rights claims of the feminist and LGBTQI+ movements. As we have seen, this instrument was extensively used by the Evangelical Parliamentary Front parliamentarians in the 2011 demonstrations. "They summed up that the evangelical parliamentarians made more noise giving their spectacular speeches than producing practical results." (Mazza 2020). They considered opening a new front of confrontation, complementary to the world of politics, and the defense of religious freedom served as a flag for mobilizing jurists in the evangelical world.

From that moment on, ANAJURE members began to map what they called "state PL 122", which were state legislations that sought to criminalize homophobia in some federative units, despite PL 122/2006 that was processed in the Senate. This phenomenon occurred in the states of São Paulo, Minas Gerais, the Federal District, Bahia, Sergipe, Mato Grosso do Sul and Rio Grande do Sul. In its view, approving these laws was the result of pressure from the LGBTQI+ movements, the press and sectors from the political left in the state legislative chambers (ANAJURE 2013d). In the same year, the association promoted the online course "PL 122 in the States: the new strategy of the LGBT movement", aiming to "demonstrate how to defend against the dangers of the new LGBT movement strategy". The event announcement featured an illustration of a heterosexual couple and a child (ANAJURE 2013e). The association not only acted as an observatory of the state legislative chambers in relation to the demands of LGBTQI+ subjects, but also offered courses to sensitize evangelical congregations concerning their political agenda. Although it presented itself as an entity in the legal world, ANAJURE's actions focused mainly on the world of politics and mobilizing actors around its agendas.

Prior to filing the PL 122/2006 in the Senate, ANAJURE also began mapping a broad spectrum of government initiatives around the issue of LGBTQI+ people's rights. For its members, advancement of these guidelines did not only imply criminalizing pastors and religious leaders against homosexuality, but also the encouragement of "homosexual behavior". In 2013, it became concerned about what it considered to be a promotion of homosexuality in public schools. The federal government decided to include topics on the rights of LGBTQI+ subjects in the National Education Plan, which ANAJURE members saw as an "exaggerated ideologization and partisanship" of educational policy, as well as "early eroticization" of children and the "promotion of homosexual behavior". The association became increasingly interested in and acting in the educational arena, denouncing what it called "the theory of gender" in schools and legally disputing the parameters of confessional education (ANAJURE 2013f).

Evangelical jurists' reactions also occurred as a countermovement to the process of expanding the citizenship of LGBTQI+ subjects through infra-legal normative acts. Integrating the norms of international treaties on human rights into the Brazilian legal system allows governments to develop infra-legal normative acts (Gonçalves 2019), that is, not within the legislative scene and outside the Evangelical Parliamentary Front's scope of action. The groups in defense of the expansion of citizenship of LGBTQI+ subjects started to rely on this resource, as the evangelical benches in the legislative chambers impeded their claims (Luna and Owsiany 2019). The effects of using this resource were opposed by evangelical groups organized on other fronts besides the Evangelical Parliamentary Front, for example, in the field of psychology (Gonçalves 2019).

It was because of the issue of criminalizing homophobia, the object of PL 122/2006, that ANAJURE participated for the first time in a public hearing of the Supreme Federal Court as an *amicus curiae* in 2019. The Supreme Federal Court promotes public hearings before making its decisions because they serve, at the same time, to clarify ministers' votes and as a device to legitimize their decisions (Marona and da Rocha 2017). From the civil society participants' perspective who play roles in these audiences, they also serve as a stage for the audiences they are interested in representing. In playing the role of *amicus curiae*, ANAJURE members not only seek to convince ministers of their positions on the matter, but also aim to represent what they think is in the interest of evangelicals.

In 2015, the *Partido Popular Socialista* - PPS (Popular Socialist Party) entered the Supreme Federal Court with an *Unconstitutionality Direct Action* by *Omission* due to the omission of the legislative power in relation to the criminalization of homophobia. Considering the beginning of the new legislature in the same year, the Senate had filed PL 122/2006, which dealt with the issue, and which had been the subject of controversy. The *Unconstitutionality Direct Action* by *Omission* aims to implement a rule that is provided for in the Federal Constitution, but which has not yet been the object of action by the competent authorities (Mendes 2008). In the judgment, the parties against the *Unconstitutionality Direct Action* by *Omission* were civil, religious organizations and pro-traditional parliamentary groups: in addition to ANAJURE, the "Mixed" Parliamentary Front for Family and Life Support and the *Convenção Brasileira das Igrejas Evangélicas Irmãos Menonitas*—COBIM (*Brazilian Convention of Evangelical Mennonite* Brethren *Churches*). On the side in favor of the *Unconstitutionality Direct Action* by *Omission* are political parties, professional councils, members of the Judiciary and groups defending the rights of minorities and LGBTQI+ agendas: *Grupo Dignidade Pela Cidadania de Gays, Lésbicas e Transgêneros* (Dignity Group for the Citizenship of Gays, Lesbians and Transgenders), *Partido Socialista dos Trabalhadores Unificados*—PSTU (Unified Socialist Workers' Party), *Conselho Federal de Psicologia, Associação Nacional de Travestis e Transsexuais*—ANTRA (Federal Council of Psychology, National Association of Travestis and Transsexuals), *Defensoria Pública do Distrito Federal* (Federal Public Defender), *Grupo Gay da Bahia*—GGB (Gay Group of Bahia) *Associação de Lésbicas, Gays, Bissexuais, Travestis e Transexuais*—ABGLT (Brazilian *Gay*, *Lesbian*, *Bisexual*, Travesti, *Transsexual* and Intersex *Association*) e *Grupo de Advogados pela Diversidade Sexual*—GADVS (Group of Lawyers for Sexual Diversity) (Supreme Federal Court 2019).

ANAJURE disclosed on its website that it sought to communicate to the Supreme Federal Court that the judiciary did not have "the competence to set legal parameters" and to assume "typical functions of Legislative Power" (ANAJURE 2019c). However, the ten minutes of intervention by Luigi Braga, a member of ANAJURE, was mainly guided by the issue of the right to people's freedom of speech who, due to their religious convictions, manifest positions contrary to homosexuality (Poder360 2019).

In fact, there were not any evangelical organizations specialized in human rights in the Judiciary Power, particularly in using the *amicus curiae*; the Catholic participation, via the *Conferência Nacional dos Bispos do Brasil*—CNBB (National Conference of Bishops), was minimal. Since its foundation, ANAJURE has been accepted at least fifteen times as *an amicus curiae* in Supreme Federal Court actions and is awaiting admission in other actions (Mazza 2020).

6 ANAJURE's Ambiguous Relationship with the Supreme Federal Court

ANAJURE aims to create a public image of a moderate and impartial actor and uses this representation to counteract actors who, in its view, do not comply with the etiquette of the legal world. In this case, it has in mind not only the demands of the LGBTQI+ movements that, in its opinion, should be made in the parliaments, but also the Supreme Federal Court decisions in favor of these demands.

The association regularly publishes notes on debates and topics of its interest in the legal world. In 2019, the association issued a "Press Release" in which it used a speech by former President Bolsonaro to the legal world. In an event at the Church Assembly of God Ministry Madureira, the president said that the Supreme Federal Court would be legislating by making the crime of homophobia equivalent to the crime of racism. In May of that year, the Supreme Federal Court decided that forms of violence against LGBTQI+ people would be classified as crimes of social racism. Bolsonaro asked to an eminently evangelical audience: "Isn't it time we had a minister in the evangelical Supreme Federal Court?" (Santana 2019). The speech was widely seen in the media and had repercussions. ANAJURE was thus challenged by a speech from the world of politics to the world of law and could not help giving an opinion on the matter as it was an entity comprising jurists and evangelicals.

> Likewise, ANAJURE understands, in line with President Bolsonaro, that there has been growing and worrying judicial activism on the part of the Supreme Federal Court in recent years, particularly, on moral issues that have social impact, as is the current case of the judgment of the ADO 26 (*Unconstitutionality Direct Action* by *Omission)* on the so-called "homophobia", where the country's supreme court is about to innovate in the Brazilian legal system, creating a penal type, as if the legislator were it, in a clear violation of classic penal-constitutional principles, such as that of the legal reserve, that of the precedence of the criminal law (...). But that, precisely because we are against the exacerbated judicial

> activism of the Supreme Court, ANAJURE clarifies that we, evangelical jurists, do not necessarily intend that a Protestant will become one of the members of the apex body of our judicial system to influence him/her by his/her condition as a religious advisor. What we strive for and aspire to, in the Supreme Federal Court and other high bodies of the Judiciary Power, is that we have judges who respect and adhere to the Federal Constitution of our country, whether they profess a religion or not, refraining from joining, without due reflection, to this undemocratic wave of judicial activism (ANAJURE 2019d).

ANAJURE made two movements on the release. On the one hand, it disagreed with the presidential speech, contradicting expectations regarding its possible position in favor of the declaration, as an entity representing evangelicals in the legal world. It used the speech to position itself as a defender of the legal world against illegitimate demands from the political world and as a maintainer of the secular separation between the spheres of law, religion and politics. On the other hand, the presidential speech served for ANAJURE to accuse the Supreme Federal Court of judicial activism, in which it agreed with Bolsonaro's accusation to the Supreme Federal Court.

Gender inequality litigations do not usually reach the Supreme Federal Court, which shows that the feminist political issues, such as abortion, advance slowly both in the legislature and in the judiciary. In the latter, they are met with resistance by religious advisors through the National Conference of Bishops and ANAJURE. Despite slow progress, they tend to benefit from the "lens of feminist constitutionalism" present in some Supreme Federal Court decisions, through the function of counter-majoritarian power (de Barboza and Demetrio 2019).

The process of expanding citizenship to LGBTQI+ subjects involved the judicialization of politics, given that constitutional grammar has increasingly become the preferred language of social movements for the construction of LGBTQI+ agendas in Brazil. A negative reaction policy also accompanied the court decisions favorable to this audience (Cardinali 2017). This type of reaction, known as backlash, has a negative connotation in the legal world, as it represents a political movement that seeks to contradict a court decision (Eskridge 2013). Thus, ANAJURE aims to present its challenges to the decisions of the courts through a performance in accordance with the world of law, avoiding backlash. Although it seeks to establish a critical relationship with the Supreme Federal Court, especially when the court decides in favor of the rights of LGBTQI+ subjects, it seeks to publicly demonstrate respect and proximity to the court, as what occurred, for example, at an event promoted by ANAJURE and the Evangelical Parliamentary Front with the president of the Supreme Federal Court, Dias Toffoli, in 2020 (ANAJURE 2020b). This relationship is key for the association to request the Supreme Federal court to participate as an *amicus curiae* in litigation regarding matters of interest to it.

The association played a minority role in influencing Supreme Federal Court decisions and in the broader arena of disputes for human rights meanings, given the historical hegemony of lay and Catholic groups in this field. The NGO called *Conectas*, the *Ordem dos Advogados do Brasil*—OAB (Brazilian Bar Association) and the National Conference of Bishops are the organizations that most managed to position themselves in public hearings at the Supreme Federal Court, at least between 1990 and 2017 (Nery and Ferreira 2018). However, ANAJURE has been gaining more space in this dispute. After Bolsonaro's accession to the presidency in 2018, ANAJURE started playing the role of balance sheet in executive branch decisions on issues involving the judiciary. Thus, it often takes a position in nominating Supreme Court ministers, even backing specific names (ANAJURE 2021b).

7 Conclusion

ANAJURE's case study can serve as an analytical framework for understanding the reach of these institutions. Social movements never operate in isolation. They must constantly respond to the demands of opposition movements. In the United States, for example, the emergence of Christian Anti-Gay Activism changed the landscape of political action for the Lesbian and Gay Movement, altering their way of formulating claims and developing strategies for framing certain issues and expressing their viewpoint (Fetner 2001; Dugan 2004; Stone 2016; Williams 2018). In Canada and France, the limits of multiculturalism and state secularism are challenged by disputes between groups seeking to extend human rights through the legalization of same-sex marriage and those seeking to prevent it on cultural and religious grounds (Reidel 2009; Carnac 2020). Finally, in Australia, Christian activist groups organize campaigns in the name of religious freedom and against the expansion of human rights (Ball 2012).

The contentious process of forming evangelical jurist associations in Brazil reveals that disputes involving religious groups and feminist and LGBTQI+ movements extend beyond the parliamentary scenes, also moving to the legal arenas. Throughout this collective experience, new actors emerge and gain importance. In this case, the idea of religious freedom appears as the key code by which the political strategies of religious groups can be translated into legal language. The defense of religious freedom works as an instrument capable of, at the same time, confronting demands for sexual and reproductive rights and producing new demands for rights by religious advisors.

ANAJURE works as a channel through which groups that speak on behalf of evangelicals can act politically in the legal world as actors belonging to the legal arena. In fact, although the association seeks to act according to a legal performance, making use of traditional reverences from this universe and giving opinions on litigation involving topics of its interest, the evangelical identity remains a key element for its performance, and it is in its name that it manages its members in the evangelical world. The association acts on behalf of a specific religious group and what it considers its real issues. Its actions do not concern the defense of the professional class of evangelical law practitioners, but the defense of a specific evangelical identity. Its members interpret PL 122/2006 in a specific way, as evidence of a strategy that takes place in a broader dispute over the meanings of morality. This perception also derives from evangelical leaders 'reflections in the congresses they hold. The dispute over morality is seen as the exercise of a cultural mandate ordained by God to men in Genesis 1.26-29 and whose objective is to rescue the original marks of Creation in a decaying culture (Van Til 2001).

Thus, ANAJURE's actions express the same phenomenon that its members say they are fighting: the indeterminacy of the borders that separate the world of law, politics and religion. It is in the name of a specific evangelical identity, whose defenders see it constantly threatened by demands from LGBTQI+ subjects, that ANAJURE seeks to assume the role of whistleblower of this problem and show itself as a defender of the legal world, establishing guidelines for the performance of actors who can intervene in it.

ANAJURE's trajectory expresses a collective work of inquiry by political groups that speak and act in the name of evangelical identity in the arenas where different actors claim rights. In this case, this study addresses an inconvenience concerning the phenomenon of displacing disputes around the demands of LGBTQI+ movements from the legislative scene to the legal scene. In parliaments, these demands are more difficult to advance due to evangelical and conservative politicians' actions. Evangelical groups experience the phenomenon of redirecting LGBTQI+ demands from parliaments to the courts as a problematic situation. It is a creative experience, as new organizations, actors, discourses and practices result from it (Cefaï 2016). Throughout this experience, jurists from different Protestant denominations reconfigure their professional skills and transform them into defense instruments of a religious identity that they consider threatened. ANAJURE is part of this collective work of inquiry, as it works as a platform to organize a field of intervention for these actors, redefining their perspectives and the meanings of religious freedom, as well as freedom of worship and speech. These themes are no longer relatively pacified issues and start to appear as controversial issues of interest to evangelicals.

Using the role of the *amicus curiae* in the Supreme Federal Court's public hearings works as a visibility and mobilization instrument for the group and is part of the inquiry work. Evangelical jurists, in addition to seeking to persuade Supreme Court justices of the validity of their positions on the issues in question, also aim to speak to evangelical congregations who are interested in publicly representing, defining for them their problems, causes and responsible people. In the case discussed here, there is also an attempt to create a negative public image of the Supreme Federal Court, in cases where it decides favorably on LGBTQI+ demands. In these cases, by characterizing the Supreme Federal Court as an element that generates legal instability and not consensus, the association intensifies pressure of evangelical hearings on the Court's ministers.

The production of rights presupposes a process in which groups involved in situations of suffering demand and conquer the status of subjects of rights. The relationship between the world of law and the world of politics is unavoidable. On the border between these two worlds, groups define the nature of their experiences of suffering, identify and name those responsible for degrading situations, and make complaints in terms of justice and according to norms and laws (Felstiner et al.

1980). Under a normative public sphere, litigants cannot delegitimize rivals' demands without jeopardizing the legitimacy of their own demands. A possible combat strategy is to define the political and legal reality as an agonistic clash between different demands for rights, demonstrating to the public opinion how the advancement of the agendas of one group puts the rights conquered by another at risk. Another strategy is to define rivals' demands as inappropriate in the instances where they seek resolution. In these terms, these demands are no longer legitimate complaints, according to the constitutional grammar and consistent with the language of human rights and are now qualified as illegitimate demands and inconsistent with the instances of power where they seek resolution.

ANAJURE tries to create an image of natural belonging to the legal world. Based on this image, its members aim to legitimize it as a defender of the borders of the legal world against the invectives of the political world. As an actor in the legal world, it is possible, then, to define, from this place, the nature of disputes over human rights policies. This feature is important, because whoever defines the nature of disputes also defines the rules of the dispute and the legitimacy of its actors and scenes. Using this political tool, ANAJURE is able to politicize the demands of minorities in the legal world and denounce them, given that it speaks and presents itself in the name of the law.

Disputes between evangelical groups and LGBTQI+ movements do not seem to have just followed the path from the legislative power to the judiciary. When analyzing ANAJURE's trajectory, we can see that the confrontations occur in different arenas of disputes and disciplinary fields, such as psychology, education and religious education. What articulates the different scenes is the growing mobilization of rights by actors in clashes. Legal language increasingly becomes the parameter of disputes and movements between groups occur based on signs from the legal world, especially from the Supreme Federal Court. We also saw that disputes shift to global arenas of confrontation, causing associations to articulate themselves in networks with similar purposes in an attempt to intervene in international systems to promote and defend human rights. Intervention in UN commissions and in developing international agreements and treaties is not dissociated from intervention projects in local contexts.

References

Adorno S (2010) História e desventura: o 3° Programa Nacional de Direitos Humanos. Novos Estud CEBRAP:5–20. https://doi.org/10.1590/S0101-33002010000100001

ANAJURE (2012a) Discurso do Presidente da FIJC no Parlamento Uruguaio: "Desnaturalizando el matrimonio y la familia". ANAJURE. https://ANAJURE.org.br/discurso-do-presidente-da-fijc-no-parlamento-uruguaio-desnaturalizando-el-matrimonio-y-la-familia/. Accessed 23 June 2021

ANAJURE (2012b) Edições Vida Nova entrevista o Presidente da ANAJURE, Dr. Uziel Santana. In: ANAJURE. https://ANAJURE.org.br/edicoes-vida-nova-entrevista-o-presidente-da-ANAJURE-dr-uziel-santana/. Accessed 24 June 2021

ANAJURE (2013a) Novas associações: Líderes de denominações históricas fecham parceria com a ANAJURE e incentivam seus juristas a participarem da mesma. ANAJURE. https://ANAJURE.org.br/novas-associacoes-lideres-de-denominacoes-historicas-fecham-parceria-com-a-ANAJURE/. Accessed 24 June 2021

ANAJURE (2013b) Liderança da Assembleia de Deus de Alagoas apoia PAD da ANAJURE. ANAJURE. https://ANAJURE.org.br/lideranca-da-assembleia-de-deus-de-alagoas-apoia-pad-da-ANAJURE/. Accessed 29 June 2021

ANAJURE (2013c) Comissão Interamericana de Direitos Humanos da OEA decide instituir relatoria especial para tratar dos Direitos de Lésbicas, Gays, Bissexuais, Trans e Intersexuais (LGBTI). ANAJURE. https://ANAJURE.org.br/comissao-interamericana-de-direitos-humanos-da-oea-decide-instituir-relatoria-especial-para-tratar-dos-direitos-de-lesbicas-gays-bissexuais-trans-e-intersexuais-lgbti/. Accessed 24 June 2021

ANAJURE (2013d) Parecer Jurídico da ANAJURE revela que movimento LGBT tenta aprovar PL 122 em todo o País. ANAJURE. https://ANAJURE.org.br/parecer-juridico-da-ANAJURE-revela-que-movimento-lgbt-tenta-aprovar-pl-122-em-todo-o-pais/. Accessed 24 June 2021

ANAJURE (2013e) Novo curso online da ANAJURE abordará a estratégia do movimento LGBT para aprovação do PL 122 nos Estados brasileiros. ANAJURE. https://ANAJURE.org.br/novo-curso-online-da-ANAJURE-vai-abordar-a-estrategia-do-movimento-lgbt-para-aprovacao-do-pl-122-nos-estados/. Accessed 24 June 2021

ANAJURE (2013f) ANAJURE e entidades representativas de universidades e escolas cristãs do Brasil emitem Nota conjunta sobre Plano Nacional da Educação que está em discussão no Senado Federal. ANAJURE. https://ANAJURE.org.br/ANAJURE-e-entidades-representativas-de-universidades-e-escolas-cristas-do-brasil-emitem-nota-conjunta-sobre-plano-nacional-da-educacao-que-esta-em-discussao-no-senado-federal/. Accessed 29 June 2021

ANAJURE (2019a) ANAJURECAST#4 está no ar, com participação do Pr. Igor Miguel, Dr. Luigi Braga e Dr. Uziel Santana. In: ANAJURE. https://ANAJURE.org.br/ANAJUREcast4-esta-no-ar-com-participacao-do-pr-igor-miguel-dr-luigi-braga-e-dr-uziel-santana/. Accessed 17 June 2021

ANAJURE (2019b) Ministros Sérgio Moro e Damares Alves participarão do 6º Congresso Internacional sobre Liberdades Civis Fundamentais. ANAJURE. https://ANAJURE.org.br/ministros-sergio-moro-e-damares-alves-participarao-do-6o-congresso-internacional-sobre-liberdades-civis-fundamentais/. Accessed 30 June 2021

ANAJURE (2019c) ANAJURE faz sustentação oral no julgamento conjunto da ADO 26 e MI 4733 no Supremo Tribunal Federal. ANAJURE. https://ANAJURE.org.br/ANAJURE-sustentacao-oral-julgamento-ado-26-e-mi-4733-supremo-tribunal-federal/. Accessed 29 June 2021

ANAJURE (2019d) ANAJURE emite NOTA DE IMPRENSA sobre as declarações do Presidente da República a respeito da indicação de um evangélico ao STF. ANAJURE. https://ANAJURE.org.br/ANAJURE-emite-nota-de-imprensa-sobre-as-declaracoes-do-presidente-da-republica-a-respeito-da-indicacao-de-um-evangelico-ao-stf/. Accessed 17 June 2021

ANAJURE (2020a) ANAJURE é admitida como *Amicus Curiae* pelo STF na quinta ADPF que trata da ideologia de gênero na educação municipal. Desta feita, é sobre Tubarão/SC. ANAJURE. https://ANAJURE.org.br/ANAJURE-e-admitida-como-amicus-curiae-pelo-stf-na-quinta-adpf-que-trata-da-ideologia-de-genero-na-educacao-municipal-desta-feita-e-sobre-tubarao-sc/. Accessed 17 June 2021

ANAJURE (2020b) Fortalecimento das liberdades civis fundamentais é tema de debate em webinar promovido pela ANAJURE e FPE com o presidente do STF. ANAJURE. https://ANAJURE.org.br/webinar-organizada-pela-ANAJURE-com-stf-e-fpe-assista-na-integra/. Accessed 28 June 2021

ANAJURE (2021a) Academia ANAJURE. In: Acad. ANAJURE. https://espinoladev.com.br/academia. Accessed 28 June 2021

ANAJURE (2021b) Recomendação da ANAJURE para a nova vaga de ministro do STF. ANAJURE. https://ANAJURE.org.br/recomendacao-da-ANAJURE-para-a-nova-vaga-de-ministro-do-stf/. Accessed 24 June 2021

Ball R (2012) Human Rights and Religion in Australia: false battle lines and missed opportunities. https://doi.org/10.1080/1323-238x.2013.11882124

Cardinali DC (2017) A judicialização dos direitos LGBT no STF: limites, possibilidades e consequências. Universidade do Estado do Rio de Janeiro

Carnac R (2020) Imaginary enemy, real wounds: counter-movements, 'gender theory', and the French Catholic church. Soc Mov Stud 19(1):63–81. https://doi.org/10.1080/14742837.2019.1708307

Castro G (2011) Religiosos entregam 1 milhão de assinaturas contra projeto que criminaliza homofobia. VEJA. https://veja.abril.com.br/brasil/religiosos-entregam-1-milhao-de-assinaturas-contra-projeto-que-criminaliza-homofobia/. Accessed 17 June 2021

Cavallera R (2011) Protesto e manifestação contra PLC 122 do Pr Silas Malafaia - Brasília. Notícias Gospel. https://noticias.gospelmais.com.br/protesto-manifestacao-contra-plc-122-silas-malafaia-brasilia-20417.html. Accessed 17 June 2021

Cefaï D (2016) Publics, problèmes publics, arènes publiques.... Que nous apprend le pragmatisme ? Quest Commun 30:25–64. https://doi.org/10.4000/questionsdecommunication.10704

de Barboza EMQ, Demetrio A (2019) Quando o gênero bate à porta do STF: a busca por um constitucionalismo feminista. Rev Direito GV 15. https://doi.org/10.1590/2317-6172201930

Dugan KB (2004) Strategy and "Spin": opposing movement frames in an anti-gay voter initiative. Sociol Focus 37(3):213–233. https://doi.org/10.1080/00380237.2004.10571243

Eskridge W (2013) Backlash politics: how constitutional litigation has advanced marriage equality in the United States. Fac Scholarsh Ser

Felstiner WLF, Abel RL, Sarat A (1980) The emergence and transformation of disputes: naming, blaming, claiming . . . Law Soc Rev 15(3/4):631–654. https://doi.org/10.2307/3053505

Fetner T (2001) Working Anita Bryant: the impact of Christian Anti-Gay activism on Lesbian and gay movement claims. Soc Probl 48(3):411–428. https://doi.org/10.1525/sp.2001.48.3.411

Frazão F (2020) Após China, Cuba retarda adesão de associação de juristas evangélicos na ONU - Internacional. Estadão. https://internacional.estadao.com.br/noticias/geral,apos-china-cubaretarda-adesao-de-associacao-de-juristas-evangelicos-na-onu,70003169724. Accessed 18 June 2021

Freedom AD (2021) History. Alliance Defending Freedom. https://adflegal.org/about-us/who-we-are/history. Accessed 17 June 2021

Freitas S (2013) Comissão de Direitos Humanos da Câmara terá pastor como presidente. https://noticias.uol.com.br/politica/ultimas-noticias/2013/03/05/psc-confirma-pastor-feliciano-para-presidir-comissao-de-direitos-humanos-da-camara.htm. Accessed 17 June 2021

G1 (2010) Saiba o que Dilma, Serra e Marina já disseram sobre o aborto. In: Eleições 2010. http://g1.globo.com/especiais/eleicoes-2010/noticia/2010/10/saiba-o-que-dilma-serra-e-marina-ja-disseram-sobre-o-aborto.html. Accessed 17 June 2021

G1 (2011) Projeto de distribuir nas escolas kits contra a homofobia provoca debate. Educação. http://g1.globo.com/educacao/noticia/2011/05/projeto-de-distribuir-nas-escolas-kits-contra-homofobia-provoca-debate.html. Accessed 18 June 2021

Gonçalves AO (2019) Religião, política e direitos sexuais: controvérsias públicas em torno da "cura gay.". Religião Soc 39:175–199. https://doi.org/10.1590/0100-85872019v39n2cap07

Hoover DR, den Dulk KR (2004) Christian conservatives go to court: religion and legal mobilization in the United States and Canada. Int Polit Sci Rev 25(1):9–34. https://doi.org/10.1177/0192512104038165

Junqueira RD (2018) A invenção da "ideologia de gênero": a emergência de um cenário político-discursivo e a elaboração de uma retórica reacionária antigênero. Rev Psicol Política 18(43):449–502

Lehoucq E (2021) Legal threats and the emergence of legal mobilization: conservative mobilization in Colombia. Law Soc Inq 46(2):299–330. https://doi.org/10.1017/lsi.2020.28

Luna N, Owsiany L (2019) Aborto e luta por direitos humanos na ALERJ: religiosos e feministas em disputa. Religião Soc 39:49–77. https://doi.org/10.1590/0100-85872019v39n2cap02

Mariano R (2007) A reação dos evangélicos ao novo Código Civil. Civ - Rev Ciênc Sociais 6(2):77. https://doi.org/10.15448/1984-7289.2006.2.57
Marona MC, da Rocha MM (2017) Democratizar a jurisdição constitucional? O caso das audiências públicas no Supremo Tribunal Federal. Rev Sociol E Política 25:131–156. https://doi.org/10.1590/1678-987317256206
Mazza L (2020) No reino do poder: o lobby discreto – e cada vez mais eficaz – dos juristas evangélicos. Rev. Piauí. https://piaui.folha.uol.com.br/materia/no-reino-do-poder/. Accessed 17 June 2021
Mendes GF (2008) Jurisdição Constitucional no Brasil: o problema da omissão legislativa inconstitucional. Congresso da Conferência das Cortes Constitucionais Europeias
Montero P, Girardi D (2019) Religião e laicidade no STF: as figurações do secular no debate brasileiro sobre o ensino religioso público. REVER - Rev Estud Religião 19(3):349–366. https://doi.org/10.23925/1677-1222.2019vol19i3a21
Nery PF, Ferreira D (2018) Como se relacionam os influenciadores do Supremo. https://www1.folha.uol.com.br/poder/2018/03/como-se-relacionam-os-influenciadores-do-supremo.shtml. Accessed 17 June 2021
O'Connell B (2020) History - Religious Liberty Partnership. https://rlpartnership.org/. https://rlpartnership.org/about/history/. Accessed 17 June 2021
Poder360 (2019) Julgamento do STF sobre a criminalização da homofobia - parte 2/3 - 13.fev.2019
Reidel L (2009) Religious opposition to same-sex marriage in Canada: limits to multiculturalism. Hum Rights Rev 10(2):261–281. https://doi.org/10.1007/s12142-008-0079-x
Sales L (2015) "Em defesa da vida humana": Moralidades em disputa em duas audiências públicas no STF. Religião Soc 35:143–164. https://doi.org/10.1590/0100-85872015v35n2cap06
Santana V (2019) "Será que não está na hora de termos um ministro no Supremo Tribunal Federal evangélico?", diz Bolsonaro em evento religioso. G1. https://g1.globo.com/go/goias/noticia/2019/05/31/sera-que-nao-esta-na-hora-de-termos-um-ministro-no-supremo-tribunal-federal-evangelico-diz-bolsonaro-em-evento-religioso.ghtml. Accessed 28 June 2021
Steil CA, Toniol R (2012) A trajetória dos direitos humanos na Igreja Católica no Brasil: do discurso político ao discurso moral. In: Mobilidade religiosa: linguagem, juventude, política. Paulinas, São Paulo.
Stone AL (2016) The impact of anti-gay politics on the LGBTQ movement. Sociol Compass 10(6): 459–467. https://doi.org/10.1111/soc4.12373
Supremo Tribunal Federal (2019) ADO n° 26 DF. http://portal.stf.jus.br/processos/downloadPeca.asp?id=15344606459&ext=.pdf. Accessed 23 June 2021
Van Til HR (2001) The Calvinistic concept of culture. Baker Academic, Grand Rapids, Mich
Williams HH (2018) From family values to religious freedom: conservative discourse and the politics of gay rights. New Polit Sci 40(2):246–263. https://doi.org/10.1080/07393148.2018.1449064
Wilson JC, Hollis-Brusky A (2014) Lawyers for god and neighbor: the emergence of "Law as a Calling" as a mobilizing frame for Christian Lawyers. Law Soc Inq 39(2):416–448. https://doi.org/10.1111/lsi.12061
Wilson JC, Hollis-Brusky A (2018) Higher law: can Christian conservatives transform law through legal education? Law Soc Rev 52(4):835–870. https://doi.org/10.1111/lasr.12364

Formalizing Religious Intolerance in Police Records: A Picture of a (De)Construction Problem

Camila Nicácio

Abstract Against the backdrop of growing conflicts due to religious reasons in Brazil, this chapter investigates how public security agencies deal with complaints based on religious discrimination or prejudice, particularly in the state of Minas Gerais. Having this objective in mind, I asked about the formalization process or *mise en forme* of a complaint, understood as the transposition of the social language, in which conflicts are expressed, to the language of the law, in which they are processed. My analysis focused on empirical material formed by a set of data extracted from police reports registered from 2016 to 2018. The main results point to the insufficiency of relevant data for the continuation of cases, as well as to the invisibility of the category "religious intolerance" in the record of occurrences. In conclusion, I affirm that the standard of filling in the data in the initial phase of the aforementioned *mise en forme* seems to interfere both in the process of (de)-construction of the victim's figure and in the demand itself, impacting, as a consequence, on highlighting religious intolerance as a problem that needs state intervention.

1 Introduction

Official and unofficial data show an increase in violence related to religious discrimination or prejudice in Brazil.[1] The issue of intolerance or, preferably, the contrary, tolerance, is fundamental for democracies and forms part of the broader

The present work is the result of research financed by the São Paulo Research Foundation (FAPESP), process: 2018/18140-7.

[1]Please find some sources: *Disque 100* (Dial 100) (Brazil/MDH); *Relatório sobre Violência e intolerância religiosa no Brasil* (RIVIR) (Report on Violence and Religious Intolerance in Brazil),

C. Nicácio (✉)
Law School, Federal University of Minas Gerais (UFMG), Belo Horizonte, Brazil
e-mail: cnicacio@ufmg.br

P. Montero et al. (eds.), *Religious Pluralism and Law in Contemporary Brazil*, Law and Religion in a Global Context 4, https://doi.org/10.1007/978-3-031-41981-2_4

context of dealing with differences, whether from official institutions or not. I point out the officiality of how it is dealt with in parallel with the non-official one because, in a pluralism framework, both legal and social, there is a diversity of arenas, actors and ways of approaching the same problem,[2] which can complement each other, alternate, compete with each other, depending on a series of factors, for example, the intensity and context in which violence occurs. In this work, I only deal with approaches of the first type.

At the level of official institutions, public security and justice systems make up this mosaic, in their dual claim to control and regulate. This claim increased significantly considering the expansion of guarantees and fundamental rights stipulated by the 1988 Constitution, a normative framework for the proliferation not only of new rights, but also of new subjects and new legal tools available, in what was called by some the "normative short circuit" (Santos 2009).

Once the scope of rights has been expanded, the ways to mobilize them and the subjects who are their recipients, the transposition of demands made on the social plane to the legal-judicial field, however, remains a complex process. Based on its own code, often seen as dry and with little social capillarity, the law is the object of translation: in order to understand it, forms, brochures and technical expressions are decoded in a language accessible to citizens in environments such as the offices of public defenders, law firms or popular legal advice bureaux. For some, a strong conception of access to justice must necessarily consider access to what the legal technique does not reveal (Cappelletti 1984). The opposite must necessarily take place, the decoding also taking place in the opposite direction: from street language, collectives and associations or individuals to the language of the law.

It turns out that, as in any translation, the process is laborious and potentially problematic, especially if we take into account that two different fields meet—the social and the legal-judicial—not only with their own languages, but with their own "cultures", to appeal to an expression broad enough to cover practices, discourses, commonplaces, *topoi*, etc. Considering this, translation is not just the "fixing equivalences between different repertoires" (Montero 2013, p. 844), as linguists want, but the encounter—interested and situational—of alterities in presence. Its nature is necessarily negotiation.

The critique of translation has already been made in different contexts and it proves itself to be useful for my purpose in this chapter. In the work referred to above and elsewhere (2006a, 2009a), when examining the Salesian missionary textuality, Montero tried to restore the way in which religious advisors represented native life, based on their descriptions and narrations of Indigenous Peoples. Her finding is that there is no empirical "other" that existed before the arrival of the religious

carried out by the then Ministry of State for Women, Racial Equality, Youth and Human Rights (SDH-PR 2016); Santos et al. (2016); and Latest Trends in Religious Restrictions and Hostilities (Pew Research Center 2015).

[2] Discussions about deep equality in the Canadian context are instigating in the sense of pointing out alternatives for managing religious diversity within the scope of everyday relationships, beyond institutions. Cf. Beaman Lori (2017).

missionary, either to resist, appropriate or submit to their speech. Hence the author preferentially speaks of "mediation", and no longer of translation, when of a cultural "encounter", referring to the discursive construction of bridges between one universe and another. In this construction, the codes are agreed upon by the actors in the negotiation itself, that is, in the "encounter" [3] itself.

This perspective is directly related to what I would like to develop in this chapter, even though the empiricisms in question differ in everything: just as the missionary textuality "produces" the "native in their difference" (Montero 2013, p. 846), the formalization process or *mise en forme* (suggested by Acosta 1987, and according to which I will work below) of the complaints based on religious violence produce the complainant as the victim or non-victim, as well as the object of complaint in aggression or non-aggression. In other words, there is no *a priori* "victim" or "crime", but, on the one hand, the letter of the law, on the other, a claim, and between them the counter and the state bureaucracy inscribing in official documents "an agreement circumstantial on the order of the world whose format cannot be anticipated in advance" (Montero 2013, p. 23).

In the passage from the social code to the law code, questions arise: how do demands arise in the legal-judicial field? How do the complainants refer to the alleged violence suffered? How is it described? How detailed are they? How are such descriptions or narratives understood by the interlocutors across the counter? How are they transposed into official documents? Are they pre-identified to a specific type of violence? Among others, I concentrated on such questions when I pored over information extracted from the Minas Gerais Civil Police databases, from which I intend to address the problem of translation or mediation, in the terms explained, and its possible dialogue or equivalence with the idea of "formalization" raised by Acosta (1987) in the context of Critical Criminology. This parallel can be productive in the sense that both approaches to social reality are based on the denial of the aprioristic existence of subjects and processes.

I organize the itinerary of this investigation in three moments. In the first, I locate the conceptual problem about religious intolerance and the course of dispute over the meaning that it has been and is an object to this day (2). Then, I will analyze, in light of the concept of "*mise en forme*", the formalization of social demands related to discrimination on religious grounds in legal language in police records, in dialogue with the idea of "cultural mediation" proposed by Montero (2006a, 2009a, 2013) (3), as well as the apparent consequences of such formalization for the publicity and visibility of religious intolerance as a public problem (4).

[3] In the author's words: "The missionary wants to understand and describe native culture in order to better conquer it; the native calculates what would meet the missionary's expectations and how to do it, so that he/she also appropriates this type of knowledge of him/herself and of the Other in order to better control it. This game is expressed in Salesian missionary textuality in a very paradoxical fashion: description very frequently slides from the missionary's writing quill to the immediate indigenous voice. In these juxtapositions of narratives, the discrepancy between their different 'programs of truth' can be seen clearly (Veyne 1984)". (Montero 2009b, p. 15).

2 Religious Intolerance or Racism?

Attentive readers will have noticed that I have used at least three different expressions so far to refer to conflicts related to the diversity of religions: religious discrimination or prejudice, violence against religions and, finally, religious intolerance. Purposely inserted in the text, this apparent hesitation reveals the curvy paths of defining a phenomenon that still struggles to find its place in both the social and legal fields.

The first terms, discrimination and prejudice, are those found in the law that covers the subject in the Brazilian legal system. Known as the "racism law" or "Caó act", Law No. 7716 was emblematically enacted in 1989, as one of the fruits of the campaign for the Constituent Assembly, and established racism as an unbailable and imprescriptible crime at the constitutional level. Initially aimed at repressing prejudice based on race or color, the aforementioned law expanded its scope to reach discrimination based on ethnicity, religion or national origin in 1997, according to the Law No. 9459.[4]

The expression "religious intolerance" is another story. I will concentrate on this next.

In Brazil, the issue of "religious intolerance" has already been the target of few, but very fruitful academic approaches.[5] For the purpose of this topic, I especially highlight the studies conducted by Silva (2007a, b), Miranda (2010, 2012, 2014, 2015, 2016); Miranda et al. (2017a, b), Bortoleto (2014, 2015), Fernandes and Adad (2017) and Hoshino Thiago and Bueno (2019).

Initially, I mention the works produced and organized by Silva (2007), which bring together numerous occurrences in São Paulo, which he calls "attacks", such as

---

[4]In a recent discussion, it was intended that the interpretation of Law No. 7716 should also include homophobia, equated with the crime of racism, on grounds of discrimination and prejudice based on sexual orientation and/or gender identity. Decision of the Federal Supreme Court (STF), under the Direct Action of Unconstitutionality by Omission (ADO) 26, established, in January 2019, the unconstitutional omission of the National Congress for not enacting a law that criminalizes acts of homophobia and transphobia. The understanding was that the congressional moratorium implies direct aggression to the fundamental rights of the LGBT community and that such acts must be classified as a crime defined in Law 7716/1989 until the National Congress enacts a specific law on the matter (for a look at the opposition of parliamentarians and evangelical leaders to Bill 122/2006, which intended to criminalize prejudice and discrimination based on sexual orientation, see Bortolin's chapter in this volume). To expand the scope of the Racism Law, the STF understood that the configuration of this type of crime does not depend solely on biological and/or physiological aspects, and that damage to the dignity of vulnerable groups must be taken into account, regardless of such aspects. An essential point in the decision was, equally, the reaffirmation of the exercise of religious freedom, as long as it does not encompass hate speech against that public. See http://www.stf.jus.br/portal/cms/verNoticiaDetalhe.asp?idConteudo=414010, consulted on August 19, 2020.

[5]These studies focus on religious violence against Afro-religious people. This concentration cannot be discussed in this chapter, although it does not seem anodyne to me, especially considering the little availability of data on religious intolerance in Brazil in general and the data found by this research in particular.

aggression during services at neo-Pentecostal churches, as well as in their means of dissemination (radio stations, publishers, television networks) to Afro cults, physical aggression against members and objects of worship in *terreiros* (place where rituals take place), and, equally, offenses to Afro-Brazilian religious ceremonies in different public spaces. The author classifies these events as religious intolerance against the public image of Afro-Brazilian religions. In this work, there is restitution of only one properly legal analysis, carried out by Silva Júnior, in which the author, in addition to presenting the historical passage, from repression to protection, from the legal repertoire in relation to the Afro-descendant public, places religious intolerance as a discrimination crime, unbailable and imprescriptible.

Regarding Miranda's investigations, in 10 years of work, it seems that her research agenda can be divided into at least two moments. The first works focused on understanding the dynamics by which Afro-religious people presented themselves as victims of religious intolerance, as well as the means used to give visibility to their demands, such as complaints in the media, records in police stations and, residually, lawsuits arising from them. At this moment, there are ethnographies dedicated to investigating the institutional treatment and conflict management about religious intolerance on the part of State agents, especially police officers, prosecutors, judges, conciliators and mediators (2010, 2012). In the second block of investigation, one can place the attempt to identify and analyze the ways in which Afro-Brazilian religious organize themselves in a public space to claim their citizenship rights. Based on ethnographic studies, Miranda examines the different practices, discursive operations and vocabulary of motivations used by those agents to legitimize themselves in the public space and situate religious intolerance as a public problem, demanding adequate treatment by public authorities and social institutions (2014, 2015, 2016), Miranda et al. (2017a, b).

Bortoleto will, in turn, demonstrate how a case that occurred in 2008 in the city of Rio de Janeiro contributed to defining religious intolerance as a "crime". In addition to analyzing the specific case, this author was responsible for an in-depth reconstruction of the category "religious intolerance". Based on a vast bibliography, Bortoleto reviewed more than two decades of reflection on what is called "the conflict between adherents of neo-Pentecostal churches and those of Afro-Brazilian religions" (2014; 2015). The author systematizes this scientific production in three phases, describing them as a movement from the notion of "holy war" to that of "religious intolerance", in which the very nature of the conflict is transformed. The first, of an essayistic nature, dates back to the 1980s and is based on journalistic material that, at the time, accounted for the exponential increase in Pentecostal churches whose practices encouraged attacks on the manifestations of Afro-Brazilian religion faith, hence the expression, coined at that time, "holy war". This first approach laid the foundations for developing a research agenda that is still ongoing today. A second phase was based on making a more in-depth analysis of this new Pentecostalism, called by some, since then, neo-Pentecostalism, which has its strongest expression in the Universal Church of the Kingdom of God (IURD), and whose practices, based on the rituals of Liberation from Evil and the Theology of Spiritual Warfare, signify greater opposition to Afro-Brazilian religions. Thirdly, studies converged on the understanding of how Afro-Brazilians behaved, via organization or not, considering the so-called "attacks" imposed by their antagonists. It is in this third phase that the term "religious intolerance" gains strength as a discursive category, not only because of the action of militant groups and associations, but also because of the involvement of sectors of the justice system, as demonstrated by the concrete case analyzed by Bortoleto (2014, 2015).

In turn, Fernandes and Adad (2017) discuss a possible shift from the notion of "religious intolerance" to that of "religious racism", in which the color/race markers overlap with the religion marker. Based on decolonial reading and supported by data from the Report on Violence and Religious Intolerance in Brazil (RIVIR in Portuguese) (SDH-PR 2016), the authors relate the notion of religious intolerance to the colonial enterprise in Latin America, which, from naturalization onwards and from the hierarchy of differences, it could dominate and control. By citing RIVIR, the authors will situate racism as a religious "double intolerance", given the difficulty in complaining and prosecuting cases of violence and intolerance suffered by the Afro-Brazilian religious community, which are justified "both due to the lack of structure of the bodies, as well as recognition and acceptance by employees who receive these complaints" (SDH-PR 2016, p. 14).

Finally, in an article in which they comment on the result of the vote, by the Supreme Federal Court, of Extraordinary Appeal (RE) 494601, Hoshino Thiago and Bueno (2019) inquire about the possible recognition, by that Supreme Federal Court, of religious racism as an element of structural racism in Brazil.[6] In the words of the authors:

> For years, the concept has been claiming that, instead of its liberal counterpart – "religious intolerance" – demarcating "the seriousness and, above all, the specificity of the experience of violence perpetrated against African-based religions, which has in racism its mainstay of legitimation and destructive action", since the aggressions suffered by them are not limited to a purely religious character, but to a civilizing dynamic full of values, knowledge, philosophies, cosmogonies, in short, amalgamated Black Africans' ways of living and existing in the *terreiro* communities.

Along these lines, it is the same Miranda who, in a recent article published in the media, inquires about the correlation between religious intolerance and the "genocide of black people" (2019). The author points to the growing violence against adherents of African-based religions in Rio de Janeiro, according to an evolution that migrates from religious intolerance to racism and, later, to their genocide. Such a gradation has already been institutionally recognized, given the technical note from the Federal Public Ministry, in 2018, in which it classifies cases of violence either as "hate crimes" and "religious racism", or as "terrorist acts" or "genocide". Instigated by supporters of neo-Pentecostal churches or by the militia and drug trafficking

[6]The insufficiency of the notion of religious "intolerance" in relation to religious racism and structural racism was developed in another study that critically analyzed RE 494601, in which it pointed to the partiality ("whiteness", the authors would say) of the liberal notion of "tolerance", as well as for the explanation of the racialization and white normative devices that the case involved (Hoshino Thiago de Azevedo and Karam de Chueiri Vera 2019).

organizations, such attacks constitute a strategy for dominating territories long abandoned by the State. According to the author, the advance of disputes that use religious confrontations tends to create a "smoke screen" for the domination of territories. By indicating the expression "narco-Pentecostalism" and the arrest of a group called "*Bonde de Jesus*", Miranda points out the relationship of such events with the penetration of neo-Pentecostal evangelicals in the prison system. These incidences also have repercussions in states such as Pará, Amazonas, Alagoas, Bahia, Pernambuco, São Paulo, Sergipe and Rio Grande do Sul. Viewed by specialists not only as a problem in the field of religious disputes, but as a matter of public safety, such a trend requires new tools and intervention strategies to prevent the cultural and physical attack on Afro-religiosity in Brazil.

These debates allow us to have a glimpse of a dispute about the expression and the predominance—we can even speak of a synonymy—of the correlation between violence against religions and the racial issue in Brazil. Different arguments seem, however, to organize themselves to claim a specific content of the phenomenon. Thus, while it matters for some actors to highlight the amalgamation between religious prejudice and racism, others aim at the generality of an expression that encompasses prejudice against any and all religions, indiscriminately. The institutional choice of RIVIR (SDH-PR 2016), the main report dealing with the issue at the national level, by the term "religious intolerance" points in this sense.[7] These disputes leave open the question of the difficulty in locating religious intolerance in Brazilian law in general, and in criminal law in particular, as I analyzed in Nicácio (2020) and I return, only incidentally, below.

3 Religious Intolerance in Police Records: From the Act to the Infraction

In this section, based on some primary data, it is important to analyze the beginning of the process of formalizing demands based on religious discrimination or prejudice in police records, as well as pointing out gaps found in this process. As indicated initially, I assume that this formalization converges to what Montero designated, in another context, as cultural mediation, that is, the "negotiation of the meanings of cultural repertoires in a situation of interaction" (Montero 2006b). As mentioned above, the language of law needs to be mediated, even if the parties—claimants and State agents—are part of the same cultural context, after all, as already stated in a catchphrase: "the native is us" (Kant de Lima 1997).

[7]Due to its scope, this definition has the "inconvenience of advantage", and seems to have been chosen precisely because of this: "The set of ideologies and attitudes that are offensive to different beliefs and religions, and in extreme cases can become a persecution. Religious intolerance is understood as a hate crime that harms freedom and human dignity, violence and persecution for religious reasons are extremely serious practices and are usually characterized by offense, discrimination and even acts that threaten life" (SDH-PR 2016, p. 8).

By "formalization" or "*mise en forme*", I mean the passage from the social fact to the legal and judicial fact. Such an operation cannot be considered vulgar as it is able to decide on the future of what deserves, to a greater or lesser degree, attention and care by the justice system and, at another level of intervention, by public policies. According to Acosta (1987), specifically about the *mise en forme pénale*, there are two decisive moments for the transition from the social to the judicial sphere that deserve to be highlighted: "the inquiry and the judicial proceedings. Both carry out the essential operations of reconstitution, interpretation, and legal codification of the facts. Each of these operations is accomplished by anticipating subsequent operations, to ensure the validity of the product" (Acosta 1987, p. 1).[8]

In short, by formalization or *mise en forme pénale*, the author called the study of the way in which the criminal offense is constituted from the progressive transformation of what, from the outset, is a "plot of life" into a "legal fact" (1987, p. 2). By distinguishing between two possible meanings of the expression "infringement", on the one hand as a "legal definition" and on the other as a "construct" itself, Acosta highlights the process of construction of the notion of "crime", in addition to its expression in penal codes or sparse legislations. While the infraction, as a legal definition, consists of a "formal frame of reference for judicial intervention", such intervention constitutes a "set of operations aimed at cutting reality and reconstructing it in function, among others, of a given definition frame" (1987, p. 2), the infraction as a construct being the result of these operations or process, named by the author of formalization or *mise en forme pénale*.

The interest in Acosta's perspective comes from the fact that he, once critical of the classic separation between primary criminalization (making of norms) and secondary (application of norms),[9] shifts the tone from the functioning of the judicial system to the movement of transforming "primary matter" into matters likely to be appropriated and subjected to a criminal-law examination. Considering this way of proceeding, the author offers a comprehensive analytical tool to investigate not only the functioning of police and justice institutions, but the relationship between them and their surroundings, in the transition from the social plane to that of public security and the justice.

This perspective matches my approach since, when working with what precedes and grounds investigations and lawsuits, I assume that the formalization of an event in the legal context, and the consequences that flow from it, represent a special contribution to force and the breadth that a given fact takes on in a public debate. This formalization thus participates in the "translation processes that transform the meaning of ordinary language into a social problem" (Montero 2012, p. 178), giving it visibility and legitimizing it.

[8] All translations from the original texts are my authorship.

[9] Based on this separation, many works "[...] implicitly postulate the anteriority of the infraction as a construct in relation to judicial intervention; in other words, the infraction is considered as constituted at the level of the social fabric ('life fabric'), even before the incidence of the judicial approach" (Acosta 1987, p. 3).

In light of these conceptions, I will analyze some data according to the hypothesis that the quality of the referred formalization or *mise en forme* tends, on the one hand, to lead to differentiated institutional treatment of issues brought to the public authorities as social demands, and on the other hand, to contribute for the recognition of more or less legitimacy to them and their actors, by placing them in the public debate as central or marginal discussions. In other words, the beginning of the process of formalizing social demands at the level of State institutions, in my case, public security institutions, is fundamental for the unfolding of those demands not only in the legal and judicial sphere but also in the political and administrative sphere. The, let's say, "success" of a demand in an eventual criminal process, and its visibility, depends on this beginning, as well as on it (but not only) depends on the approach of this demand as a public problem that deserves organized state intervention.

My presupposition is, then, that the record of occurrences actively composes such formalization or *mise en forme pénale*, as one of its first steps or steps toward the reconstruction—in fact a construction—of the fact in terms of law, constituting at a crucial moment for the "fate" of the case in the criminal domain, since such fate is "closely linked to that authorized narrative" (Lévy 1985, p. 409), that is, to the administrative record. In other words, the referred operation of "reconstruction" is inseparable from the "writing" of occurrences (Lévy 1985, p. 421), in the transposition between the "plot of life" and the "legal world" (Acosta 1987). In this transposition, the attempt at description finally creates its own object.[10] Such a transposition does not take place, however, in an environment in which the equality of the parties involved can be assumed (Montero 2006b). On the contrary, it is inequality that is present as a presupposition, since State agents, when describing and naming it, make a cut – always selective – of the reality that is reported to them, which does not precede the record (Montero 2009a).[11]

In the action of occurrence records, as I will point out, at least two moments can be highlighted for the referred "reconstruction", the first concerns the framing of the fact according to a previous criminal or administrative classification, identifying it and naming it as a criminal fact. The second moment refers to "telling the story" of the fact (Miranda et al. 2010, p. 129), that is, collecting and describing, in a space reserved for this, called "history of the occurrence" or "dynamics of the fact", the characteristics of the fact that may eventually serve for further investigation.

[10] According to Montero, in relation to her own research context: "By trying to describe native experience realistically, Salesian narrative actually builds its object". (2009a, p. 8).

[11] A retrospective reading of literature already based on social sciences reinforces the need to pay attention to the issue of inequality: historically in Brazil there has been unequal recognition of what can be recognized as religion and the protection of freedom that comes with it. Although Brazilian constitutions have not (except for the first, in 1824) constituted Catholicism as an official religion or discriminated against citizenship on the basis of religion, the country was slow to recognize non-Catholic practices as religious, relegating them to the field of criminality. In this sense, see Schritzmeyer Ana Lúcia (2004); Giumbelli (2008); Montero (2009b); Oro (2011); Machado (2012).

A brief parenthesis is pertinent at this point to show that the Brazilian social sciences have so far been prodigal in investigations in the area of public policies and human rights in general and with regard to public security in particular. Specifically, in the area of public security and criminal justice, and using records or police reports as a source of research, numerous works can be found (Kant de Lima 1995; Misse 1997; Beato Filho 1999; Battitucci Eduardo 2007; Miranda et al. 2007, 2010). In this domain, the studies converge on some points: the direct connection between the success of the investigation and the quantity and quality of information collected in its scope; the precariousness or insufficiency of filling in these administrative documents; its bureaucratic, "notary" and subjective character, since "registration is an interpretive act of the State through the police" (Miranda et al. 2010, p. 125). In another context, in a work on the French *procès-verbal*, equivalent to Brazilian records of occurrences, Lévy pointed out years ago that these were "often considered by those in charge of it as the most tedious, where it is necessary to "produce bureaucracy", in other words, to sacrifice the need to produce information which, linking (or not) a criminal act to the person in question, will lead to implementing the repressive process to continue (or will interrupt it)" (Lévy 1985, p. 408, my italics).

In my approach, supported by this literature, it is less important to demonstrate the weaknesses of institutions at the time of transposing the "plot of life" to the "matter of law", to return to Acosta's expressions, but relating such transposition or formalization to the sequence, which it comes from it and with it, it is necessarily connected, referring to the visibility of the infraction in question and the impact of such visibility to the constitution of a public problem. Furthermore, I am interested in investigating its gaps more than the formalization itself, that is, I focus on what, theoretically presupposed as essential to an investigation process, is obscured or even excluded from the result of the *mise en forme*.

Before moving on to the data, I present a brief methodological note. Inspired by the methodological strategy of field research, especially the ethnography of documents (Lowenkron and Ferreira 2014; Ferreira and Lowenkron, org., 2020), my work was based on the investigation of police reports in Minas Gerais called Records of Social Defense Events (REDS in Portuguese), dealing with the theme of religious intolerance, carried out by the State's public security agencies and made available by the Public Security Observatory.[12]

Data for the period from January 2016 to May 2018 were used, which I had access to through two complementary forms of filtering occurrences. The first, more automated, consisted of extracting all crimes in which the option "Religious Intolerance" and "Religious Discrimination/Prejudice" were used in the "Cause or Presumed Motivation" field. As I pointed out security agents filling this space is the first step in formalizing the "plot of life" for the legal sphere. The second, more manual, was based on the reading and analysis of the "History" field, with its textual

[12] Access to such data was granted via the Technical Cooperation Agreement signed between the Federal University of Minas Gerais and the State Secretariat for Public Security (SEJUSP), on May 31, 2019, published in Minas Gerais on June 4, 2019.

account of the facts, to compare them to the options used in the parameterized fields. Because it was not found, in absolute numbers, a very high total of occurrences, the analyses could be made by the universe found, and not by sampling. The low number of occurrences does not seem anodyne to me, and I will address this again later. If the statistical numbers are timid, the fundamental, qualitative question is likely to arouse attention.

Among the existing fields in the researched database, the following can be mentioned: the main nature and up to three secondary natures of the fact; date and time of the event; type of place where the event happened; target, means used, and presumed cause or motivation; history of the occurrence, among others. All occurrences were analyzed in order to verify: (a) the existence (or not) of a crime or conflict motivated by religious intolerance; (b) the nature(s) of the crime or conflict motivated by religious intolerance (with the possibility of more than one nature per occurrence); (c) the existence (or not) of another type of intolerance as a motivator for the actions of those involved; (d) the religion of the person involved who was the victim of the action motivated by religious intolerance and, finally, (e) the relationship between the victim and the author of the action motivated by religious intolerance.

The data set was already analyzed in Nicácio (2020), which is why I will focus, in this work, specifically on the problematization of formalization. Thus, from the totality of data, I will highlight the sequences that allowed me to advance in the correlation between formalization/visibility/public problem, namely, the inconsistency of some reports and the absence of relevant data.

First, I call attention to the absolute number of occurrences found according to the pre-established search. Of the 168 incidents allegedly originating from conflict or crime motivated by religious intolerance, 101 (60.1%) were identified as typical[13] and 35 (20.8%) as atypical. From 32 occurrences (19%), it was not possible to extract information about the typicality or not of the behaviors, due to the inconsistency of the reports. Representing 1/5 of the universe found, such reports are not without impact on the analysis as a whole, and are presented, as an example, as follows:

(a) The VICTIM,[14] who is staying at the Evangelical Hotel, goes to this police station to inform an officer that he is being threatened with death by a black, thin individual, of medium height, who is staying at the same hotel.
(b) At the site in contact with the parties, both had called the Military Police, and according to the VICTIM today's conflict arose with his neighbor, the person INVOLVED 1 and that this person have shown him a gun, and that this conflict is happening constantly because of religion. According to the victim, these conflicts have been happening because of the construction of INVOLVED

[13]Technical term used to indicate that the fact described corresponds to the conduct abstractly provided for in the law.

[14]Personal names changed in compliance with the confidentiality clauses contained in the Technical Cooperation Agreement that provided access to the data.

1, which was supposedly invading his/her lot, and that today INVOLVED 1, on the second floor of his residence, have shown a genital organ to the applicant and his/her family members. In view of the facts, the parties were instructed to appear before a Civil Police Station for the appropriate measures. The alleged gun has not been found. Hence, this is a record for future measures.

(c) According to the report of the VICTIM, her neighbor, a woman named INVOLVED 1, is telling relatives that she, the victim, is having an affair with INVOLVED 2, the Pastor of an Evangelical Church, which is located at the VICTIM's residence, as well as with INVOLVED 3, a churchgoer of the aforementioned Evangelical Church. Also, according to the VICTIM, relatives of INVOLVED 1 told her that she, INVOLVED 1, spoke the following words: "I'm going to catch her (the victim) and beat her up". Besides that, according to the report, INVOLVED 1 is telling people that the Evangelical Church that the VICTIM has in her home in fact is a "cabaret."

(d) The police officer, in contact with the VICTIM, narrated that he was at the aforementioned address and the INVOLVED 1 was there; For futile reasons there was a conflict between those involved and a heated discussion began, even shoving each other; they were advised about the other measures. Registered for future purposes.

(e) We received a call from a person who preferred not to be identified, realizing that a woman already known in the city for committing various crimes "INVOLVED" was in the Church at the Central Square, causing a scandal and speaking profanity.

Found under the heading "conflicts motivated by religious intolerance", the brief reports of the different events above leave the reader in suspense about the conditions under which the registration took place and how much was communicated between the whistleblowers and State agents. Can it be supposed, in a puerile way, that the relationship between complaints and religious intolerance is due only to the fact that those involved stay in a hotel called "*Evangelical*" or due to an involvement between the victim and pastor "*of an evangelical church*"? The conflict that "*has been going on constantly because of religion*" refers to exactly what kind of conduct? What are the religions causing the clash between those involved? What is at stake? A material legal asset? Or the honor or religious feeling of the alleged victim? Which articulation did the complainant intend to expose by associating "*evangelical church*" and "*cabaret*" and which apparently remained unrelated in the historical text? How are offense and discrimination on religious grounds articulated here? Why does the fact that a woman—"*already known in the city for committing various crimes*"—in a church who was supposedly disturbing a religious cult deserve a report of three brief lines, without knowing anything more about what happened? What religious connotation is behind the "*futile reasons*" that gave rise to the conflict between those involved? Were they really so futile? What was said and that in the record was silent? And how? Or does the essay express exactly what the complainants were able to communicate within the limits of the emotion of the lived scene?

What constitutes reason for speculation for the unsuspecting reader, takes the shape of a greater problem when we pay attention to the fact that, as I mentioned above, the formalization or *mise en forme* implies steps or procedures of which the sequence of an eventual legal action is dependent. The inconsistency of the reports observed in my work points to a persistent problem in the filling pattern of a document that is theoretically founding the formalization: the record of occurrences.

Joined together, reports containing atypical behavior (35) and inconsistent reports (32) form a significant number when compared to the total found (168), and are prejudiced for the purpose of further analysis by public security agencies. Atypicality and inconsistency are not confused, and the police officer cannot simply invent a crime, even if he/she participates in its reconstruction. Nevertheless, it is interesting to ask to what extent the lack of the quality of filling does not produce, somehow, its own atypicality: when there is no crime or infraction, there is no victim, there are no aggressors who deserve to be called such. This question takes on an ironic contour if associated with the fact that police officers are convinced that the "criminal fate" of a case definitely depends on the work they perform (Lévy 1985, p. 421), hence, according to Ferreira (2013, p. 41), "documents function (...) as spaces for taking positions" by police officers. Between a claim of right and a legal provision, the claimants and State agents, police officers in the case, have reciprocal interests, according to which mediation/formalization is carried out. In general, such interests vary between asserting the claim, on the one hand, and making the claim intelligible to the law, on the other hand. This variation may, however, contain surprises, since, without being possible to assume the existence of an "authentic victim", "prior to the discourse of knowledge that (Montero 2009, p. 851), the role of the victim and the outline of the eventual infraction is drawn or blurred as elements are brought or omitted from the "paperwork" during interactions at the counters of the state bureaucracy. While I assume that this is the *modus operandi* of the construction of any and all infractions, I also assume that, for crimes and infractions based on religious discrimination, the formalization of the complaints points not only to the mere "disregard" of the data, but also due to a certain difficulty for complainants and, above all, for State agents to imagine that type of violence.[15] I will return to this relationship at the end of this work.

I also mention the absence of relevant information. I am referring here, for example, to data such as the relationship between the victims, or their religion, or the central characteristics of the allegedly offensive situation reported. Thus, in 18 (17.6%) occurrences, the victim's religion was not informed. Approaching a 1/5 of the universe of typical behaviors, such data arouse interest when we think not only about the formalization (with investigations and subsequent court proceedings), but also about the formatting of public policies to face the problem of religious intolerance. This absence is particularly noteworthy if we consider what I pointed

[15] Some works have already explored the relationship between the possibility of recognizing violence, considering it unacceptable and demanding its punishment, and the ability to imagine that violence is possible. Thus, see Sliwinski (2006, 2009) and Hunt (2007).

out at the outset: the concentration of the discussion on religious intolerance in the racial key. Examples of what I mean can be found below:

(f) The victim appears at this Police Station claiming that she is constantly being threatened and verbally abused by the residents of apartment 03, a student house. The victim reports that at the end of last year, she had to cut a clothesline that had been placed in the window of her residence, by the residents of the apartment. The victim alleges that in addition to the threats uttered, against his physical integrity, the residents acted with religious intolerance. The victim informs that she is afraid, and she fears the residents of the aforementioned property and that, for this reason, she requests protective measures. The victim emphasizes that she was on the phone, talking to a client, and she made a joke saying that the apartment's residents were offended and called the military police for her. Therefore, register for future purposes.
(g) The victim, who told us the following, went to these Military Police Station and informed the authorities: that due to a religious meeting that would be held at her residence from 10/27/2017 to 10/29/2017, she is suffering threats on the telephone, in which it was said that they would end the event. The author of the threats is a person known religiously as "God's light"—a preacher of the Christian faith.
(h) We traveled to the district of São João da Chapada, where, according to the victim, when he was in the company of his son, he made a personal comment on the religion of his brother-in-law, INVOLVED 1. Due to this, INVOLVED 1 created a verbal conflict with the victim. However, with the spirits calmed, both were guided and the occurrence was resolved there.
(i) The victim appeared at the Police Station together with her legal representative, reporting that she has been frequently suffering from bullying at the school environment, and that this situation is the result of her religious belief and physical appearance. Moreover, according to the victim's mother, this has been happening for a long time, however she thought it would stop, and this is the reason why she did not report the situation before. Yet this situation is hindering her young daughter's school progress and also affecting the psychological state of the student. In view of the narrated facts, we advised the mother to carry out a representation.

In this part, there is a notable lack of essential information for a follow-up investigation, if one takes into account the fact that investigations need the minimum information to determine a line of investigation and that "the more detailed the circumstance of the crime at first, the police work will be better developed in the elucidation process" (Miranda et al. 2010, p. 125). Although a little more consistent than the previous block, the reports fail to indicate more clearly the relationship between the offense and religious prejudice. In the case of example "f", for instance, it cannot simply be assumed that the fact that the complainant is being "*threatened and verbally abused*" by neighbors addresses religious prejudice only, although the expression "religious intolerance" appeared in the record—which, incidentally, was rare in the research group. This is repeated in occurrence "h", in which it is plausible to ask what is behind the expression "*verbal conflict*" and to what extent this conflict refers to specific religious prejudice. Current in police jargon, this expression is useful to cover a wide range of possibilities, without, however, revealing the nature of the aggression or insult. For the rest, the lack of indication of the religion of those involved seems regrettable not only because it compromises possible future actions in terms of public policy intervention, but because it reveals "*two weights and two measures*" of a State whose classification and inspection fury has been known since the remote year of 1872, when the first National Demographic Census was carried out.

In light of these considerations, I wonder if the fate of most of the records of social defense events (REDS) would not be destruction. How many of them could support inquiries, in turn, prematurely archived due to a lack of minimum elements? Without an inquiry, there is no action, there is no lawsuit, there is no victim constituted before the State and individuals. On the other hand, if the possible crime in question is prejudice or discrimination for religious reasons, what place should be reserved for the victim's religion in the data set, especially in view of the complementarity of the State's actions to face a specific problem?[16] I will deal with some of these issues in the next section.

Before proceeding, I insert something that seems important to me in the correlation between *mise en forme* and public problems: the visibility of the category "religious intolerance" in the records. The expression appears in only 14 out of a total of 168 hits. No fewer than 20 types of crime or conflict motivated by religious intolerance were found. Among this "normative tangle", there are various types of violence. In these types of violence, both physical integrity and patrimony, as well as honor and freedom, can appear as violated goods, to which religious sentiment seems to be amalgamated not as the main actor, but as a supporting actor. I note that the racism law, No. 7716/89, was not mobilized even once. This is not, as in the previous hypotheses, a problem of formalization, but something that formalization captures: a possible relationship between the low (albeit growing) incidence of violence linked to religious intolerance and a relative lack of knowledge or confusion about what it encompasses. The dispute over the expression "religious intolerance", indicated above, may be at the origin of this relationship and brings us back to the difficulty in imagining such intolerance as a crime (or offense that deserves state attention), despite a national past marked by the attempt of erasure or overlapping between religions and of a present in which the amalgamation of racism and religious intolerance is still claimed by some religious groups.

[16] I emphasize that the data set pointed to the preponderance of Evangelicals in the pole of alleged victims of religious violence, in a total of 35 (34.3%) occurrences, while the African-based religions, added together, account for 31 (29.4) %) occurrences. These data should, however, be read with caution, since, in proportional terms, and in relation to data from the last Census (IBGE 2010), the preferential target of manifestations of violence is, unquestionably, Afro-Brazilian religions as they are numerically inferior than (0.31% of the population) evangelical Christianity (22.16% of the population). (Nicácio 2020). For the Census, see: https://biblioteca.ibge.gov.br/visualizacao/periodicos/94/cd_2010_religiao_deficiencia.pdf, consulted on August 13, 2020.

4 Connection Between Formalization and Public Problems

In this topic, I intend to analyze how the formalization process described and exemplified above connects with the issue of making religious intolerance visible as a public problem, as posed by some authors affiliated with the French sociology of public problems.

As I stated earlier, one of the possible approaches to the issue of confronting religious intolerance is the official one, that is, through the State and its institutions. It is the State itself and its right that claim the task of confrontation, which may be necessary, although not exclusive in relation to other interventions. For this to happen, the demand that takes place in the social environment must be properly transposed to institutions, such as those of public security, and from them to legal institutions. The answers given in the scope of such institutions are presented as complementary in that, in the scope of public administration, social issues are approached from other perspectives, notably prevention, by implementing coping and care public policies.

As a feedback loop, what happens in one field serves as an indication for possible changes, adjustments or alterations in the other field, according to a framework of integrated management of public affairs (Müller 1990). The increase in crime in relation to a given legal asset tends to draw the attention not only of the public security and justice system to the search for a more efficient and effective approach to the problem, but also subsidizes, if necessary, a change of course in public policies aimed at that specific problem, if they already exist or, otherwise, in the production of new policies, having the problem as their object.[17]

It just so happens that, for there to be public policy, there must be a problem within society that has been constructed, voiced and subsequently absorbed by the State in its agenda, as a problem that deserves attention as such. A "public problem" is included in these cases. According to authors influenced by North American pragmatism, and here I make use of the work of Daniel Cefaï, largely inspired by John Dewey, by "public problem" one must understand what emerges when the consequences of an action are perceived as extending to those who are not directly engaged in it (Cefaï 1996; Cefaï and Terzi 2012).

Many elements can block the constitution or emergence of a problem as public, among which the unwillingness of decision makers to the situation can be pointed out, disguising it or making it invisible or even contesting its "public" character (Cefaï 1996; Cefaï and Terzi 2012). There can also be a tension between represented and representatives, within the framework of representative democracies, in which

[17] According to Padioleau (1982), the notion of public policy removes the State from its place as a "teleological machine", destined simply to govern social life according to an organicist and obsolete institutional vision, and relocates it as a set of actors who hold interest and force—even if not convergent—of which society is an operating and active part. Public policy thus reinforces the State's place as an actor "of the concrete," as well as its and the social actors' role in achieving the legitimacy of decisions.

the publicizing of a problem is impaired, hence the importance of asking to what extent assuming a problematic situation provides a dynamic of mobilization or, on the contrary, of paralysis and withdrawal.

On the other hand, several elements and dynamics participate in the construction of a problematic situation in a public problem, such as the mobilization of rights by actors or the intensity and capillarity of the media in reverberating, as a social resonance chamber, such issues, especially those of great media reach, seen as emblematic, such as the case involving Mãe Gilda[18] or the 11-year-old child who was hit by a stone when leaving a *Candomblé* ceremony.[19]

The question of naming the problem is equally important. As I pointed out in section I of this work, the category "religious intolerance" does not seem to enjoy unanimity, whether in the academic, associative or institutional milieu. On the contrary, it has been, in recent years, the target of constructions and deconstructions, given the need on the part of some groups to add content to the expression that connotes not only intolerance toward minority religions, but the racism embedded in some behaviors, as an epiphenomenon of intolerance itself. Thus, the terms "religious racism" or even "genocide" directly compete with "religious intolerance". The almost absence of expression in the researched data, as I have already mentioned, does not seem to me to be anodyne. Considering, in the context of a sociology of public problems, that the search and mobilization of actors to name a problematic situation is part of the construction of the issue as a public problem, makes the hypothesis that, in the case of religious intolerance, this process is still ongoing and without any horizon of consensus.[20]

Media, social actors, appointments, flows, and dynamics count. These were not, however, my focus of analysis. In fact, my interest was based on examining the role of the State, via its agents, especially those who are at its "gateway" in relation to civil society, such as police stations, in making visible or (de)constructing religious intolerance as a public problem, subject to state intervention through public policies. To demonstrate this, I resorted to the argument that the formalization or *mise en forme pénale*, or even mediation, carried out even in the occurrence recording phase contributes—I would even say: it is decisive—to scale to size and importance of the problem, and, consequently, the visibility it will have in the public arena.

If compared to the actors and dynamics that give visibility and consolidate religious intolerance in an agenda that is understood as legitimate and of interest to a broad public, the formalization that is made of demands about religious

[18] *Yalorixá* Mãe Gilda filed a lawsuit against Folha Universal, a newspaper of the Universal Church of the Kingdom of God, on account of crimes against honor related to religious intolerance. She died a short time later from a massive heart attack and her death marked the establishment of the National Day to Combat Religious Intolerance (January 21st). For an analysis of this and related episodes, see: Silva (Silva 2007b).

[19] See https://m.folha.uol.com.br/cotidiano/2015/06/1642819-apos-sair-de-culto-de-candomble-menina-de-11-anos-leva-pedrada-no-rio.shtml, accessed on August 14, 2020.

[20] For an analysis of the claim of religious intolerance as a public problem in Rio de Janeiro from the perspective of religious actors, see Miranda et al. (2017a).

intolerance by the State can be considered, on the contrary, more as a form of "erasure" or invisibility. In other words, they do not contribute to broadening the conditions for greater publicity around the problematic situation, thus expanding the public experience of the problem. Now, a problem needs to be experienced or felt by the public as a disturbance, to be enunciated and become a public problem, gaining public dimension or publicity (Cefaï 2017 p. 137).

It should be considered that the initiation of a police inquiry is mandatory in the presence of minimal elements of information or evidence that lead to developing an investigation. Given the notorious absence and insufficiency of data in the records, as I have indicated, what about the visibility of religious intolerance as a public problem, in the Cephaean sense, that deserves state intervention? Moreover, what can be said about the impact of that formalization in the context of elaborating public policies to confront the issue?[21]

What I observe from these questions is that public security institutions, through their actors, as agents of "hegemony in the criminal process" (Lévy 1985, p. 422), contribute to modulating the issue of religious intolerance as a public problem, at first, reducing its importance and, at the limit, making it invisible, given the lack of data and the consequent scarcity in the investigations that depend on them.

This finding is supported by data that, in the past, have already demonstrated the difficulty of the security and justice system to deal with some issues, when the necessary transposition from the social to the institutional environment, or by "euphemizing" the terms of the problem (Kant de Lima 2013), either for not recognizing them in their specific demand (Cardoso de Oliveira 2002), or even, in the present case, for simply neglecting the quality when producing data on a given situation.

Some works had already pointed in the same direction, namely, the difficulty of the justice system in translating an event as a crime that deserves punishment by the State. This is the argument we found in Fullin Carmen (1999, 2015), when considering that the gradual upsurge of laws on racism in Brazil has not resulted in more criminal actions and convictions so far, either because of its poor wording or the difficulty of proving in the context evidence or even a biased reading of legal professionals, tending to disqualify the actions as crimes. According to the author, recalling DaMatta (1990), "[. . .] the agent's intention to discriminate can hardly be found in 'Brazilian racism'" (1999, p. 117), which is associated with the difficulty of encouraging a public that, although discriminated against, has a negative view of the judicial system to report (Fullin Carmen 1999, p. 118). The authors Machado et al. (2016) reach similar conclusions, in a study on racial insults, as well as Miranda

[21] These "absences" and "insufficiencies" bring us back to a central question, that arose in a crystal-clear way by Ferreira about the production of truth, authority and authentication in modern States: "Documents play a fundamental role in the chain of acts, authorities and authorizations that structure the bureaucratic field (Bourdieu 1996) and, in this sense, they are key pieces in the *production of both categories and procedures* from which agents, *departments and sectors of the state public administration intervene in the social world, as well as the very need for intervention*". (2013, p. 41, emphasis added).

(Miranda 2010, Miranda 2012, Miranda 2014) on religious intolerance itself, in the context of Rio de Janeiro.

Based on these works and on the results found in my own research, I suppose that what precedes the difficulties of an eventual affirmation of religious intolerance as a public problem is, among other factors, the difficulty of recognizing this type of intolerance as a crime itself.

5 Final Considerations

Based on what has been developed, it seems plausible to affirm that conflicts involving religious intolerance are ranked as minor problems, especially if one takes into account a context in which the rate of elucidation of crimes considered extremely serious, for example homicide, is very low.[22] These conflicts related to religious intolerance can be found in a scenario of institutional saturation, in which institutions tend to selectively protect rights. In this regard, I return to Lévy, in a blunt statement:

> [...] for a case to be effectively taken forward by the penal apparatus, it must necessarily go through the police 'format' (Robert, 1985). This does not mean that all cases brought to the attention of the police or found by the police will have a criminal fate. *On the contrary, it can be said that one of the essential functions of the police in criminal matters, from a sociological point of view, consists of operating a selection among such cases, and that it has multiple means for this, among which are mentioned simply the fact of discouraging or dissuading the claimants from filing a complaint, or the fact of not continuing a demand based on in-depth investigations, which ends up condemning the case to shelving by the Public Ministry* (1985, p. 421, my emphasis added).

As I said, in this work I did not aim at a comprehensive analysis of the factors and elements that account for the emergence or construction of a controversy or problematic situation in a public problem, nor am I claiming that religious intolerance already presents itself or should present itself as a public problem. I was only interested in the place of the security system, via its agents, as a specific element in this (de)construction process, beyond the semantic dispute around expression; the growing number of incidents (which can be described as an increase in the mobilization of the police and justice system); news in the media reporting episodes of violence, or even creating specialized police stations (such as in São Paulo, Rio de Janeiro and Minas Gerais) to specifically address demands based on prejudice or discrimination for religious reasons.

The issue of the invisibility of some offenses, here religious intolerance, there racism or racial injury interests me particularly because it seems to relocate, updating

[22] The data is difficult to trace. However, estimates show that for every 100 (one hundred) homicides in Brazil, only 8 (eight) are duly investigated, encompassing the authorship and circumstances of the crime. See https://oglobo.globo.com/politica/sol-quatro-mil-dos-cerca-de-50-mil-homicidios-cometidos-por-ano-no-pais-sao-resolvidos-2773316, consulted on April 3, 2020.

it, the discussion on the protection of legal assets at a time of strong legalization and judicialization[23] of social relations, in which the state machine is requested by social actors authorized to participate in the public debate—and in it to assert their rights—within the framework of pluralism inaugurated by the 1988 Constitution.

A question underlying the invisibility of religious intolerance as a possible public problem is, therefore, the tension between the permanent construction/creation of new rights and new subjects of rights, by the normalizing and regulatory ambition of the State, and the (de)construction—or at least the restraint—of such ambition in view of the capacity and interest of the competent institutions to deal with demands anchored in social pluralism in the day-to-day of official bureaucracies with equality.

References

Acosta F (1987) De l'événement à l'infraction: le processus de mise en forme pénale. Déviance et société. 11(1):1–40

Arnaud, André-Jean et al. (1988) Dictionnaire encyclopédique de théorie et de sociologie du droit. Paris: L.G.D.J, Bruxelles, Story-Scientia

Battitucci Eduardo C (2007). As limitações da contabilidade oficial de crimes no Brasil: o papel das instituições de pesquisa e estatística. São Paulo em Perspectiva, São Paulo, 21(1):7–18

Beaman Lori G (2017) Deep equality in an era of religious diversity. University Press, Oxford

Beato Filho CC (1999) Políticas Públicas de Segurança e a Questão Policial. São Paulo em Perspectiva 13(4):13–27

Bortoleto M (2014) *Não viemos para fazer aliança.* Faces do conflito entre adeptos das religiões pentecostais e afro-brasileiras. Dissertação (Mestrado em Antropologia Social). Faculdade de Filosofia, Letras e Ciências Humanas da Universidade de São Paulo, São Paulo

Bortoleto M (2015) Não cultuais imagens de escultura": alguns aspectos do debate público acerca da tipificação jurídica da "intolerância religiosa" e da "liberdade religiosa. In: Montero P (Org) *Religiões e Controvérsias Públicas:* Experiências, Práticas Sociais e Discursos. Campinas. Editora Unicamp, pp 127–162

Cappelletti M (dir) (1984) Accès à la justice et État-Providence. Economica, Paris

Cardoso de Oliveira LR (2002) Direito legal e insulto moral: dilemas da cidadania no Brasil, Quebec e EUA. Relume Dumará, Rio de Janeiro

Cefaï D (1996) La construction des problèmes publics. Définitions de situations dans des arènes publiques. Réseaux, volume 14, n°75. Le temps de l'événement I. pp 43–66

Cefaï D (2017) Públicos, Problemas Públicos, Arenas Públicas: O Que Nos Ensina o Pragmatismo (Parte 2). Novos Estudos - CEBRAP 36(02):128–143. https://doi.org/10.25091/s0101-330020170002000

Cefaï D, Terzi C (dir.) (2012) L'expérience des problèmes publics. École des hautes études en sciences sociales, Paris

[23]The term "legalization" refers to the "extension of law and its legal processes to a growing number of domains of economic and social life [...]", see Arnaud et al. (1988, p. 319). In turn, "judicialization" means "the extension of the role of Justice as an institution in the treatment of 'problems of society', some of which involve the political field, and for which Justice was not requested in the past or for which it did not intend to intervene", see Commaille Jacques (2002), p. 1.

Commaille Jacques (2002). *La judiciarisation*. Une nouvelle économie de la légalité face au social et au politique? Note de bilan d'étape du groupe « Judiciarisation de la société et du politique », CERAT, 17 février
Fernandes NVE, Adad CJC (2017) Intolerância ou racismo religioso: discriminação e violência contra religiões de matriz africana. Intolerância Religiosa 2(1):2–17
Ferreira L, Lowenkron L (Org.) (2020) Etnografia de documentos: pesquisas antropológicas entre papéis, carimbos e burocracias. FAPERJ, Rio de Janeiro
Ferreira Letícia Carvalho de Mesquita (2013) "Apenas preencher papel": reflexões sobre registros policiais de desaparecimento de pessoa e outros documentos. Mana 19(1):39–68. https://doi.org/10.1590/S0104-93132013000100002
Fullin Carmen S (1999) A criminalização do racismo: dilemas e perspectivas. Dissertação de Mestrado. Universidade de São Paulo, São Paulo
Fullin Carmen S (2015) Direito e racismo: observações sobre o alcance da legislação penal antidiscriminatória no Brasil. Revista Da Faculdade De Direito De São Bernardo Do Campo 6(2)
Giumbelli E (2008) A Presença do Religioso no Espaço Público: Modalidades no Brasil. Religião & Sociedade 28(2):80–101
Hoshino Thiago AP, Bueno W (2019) RE 494601: reconhecimento do racismo religioso? Disponível em http://www.jusdh.org.br/2019/04/04/re-494601-o-reconhecimento-do-racismo-religioso/, consultado dia 13 de agosto de 2020
Hoshino Thiago de Azevedo P., Karam de Chueiri Vera P (2019) As cores das/os cortes: uma leitura do RE 494601 a partir do racismo religioso. Rev. Direito e Práxis. Rio de Janeiro, 10(03): 2212–2238
Hunt L (2007) Inventing human rights. New York et Londres, W.W. Norton et Cie
Kant de Lima R (1995) A Polícia da Cidade do Rio de Janeiro: Seus Dilemas e Paradoxos. 2ª edição. Forense, Rio de Janeiro
Kant de Lima R (1997) A Antropologia da Academia: quando os índios somos nós. EdUFF, Niterói
Kant de Lima R (2013) Sensibilidades Jurídicas, moralidades e processo penal: tradições judiciárias e democracia no Brasil contemporâneo. Revista de Estudos Criminais 48:7–34
Lévy R (1985) Scripta manent: la rédaction des procès-verbaux de police. Sociologie du travail, 27ᵉ année n°4, Octobre/décembre. Spécial Police. pp 408–423
Lowenkron L, Ferreira L (2014) Anthropological perspectives on documents: Ethnographic dialogues on the trail of police papers. Vibrant – Virtual Braz Anthropol 11(2) July to December. Brasília, ABA. Available at http://www.vibrant.org.br/issues/v11n2/laura-lowenkron-leticia-ferreira-anthropologicalperspectives-on-documents-ethnographic-dialogues-on-the-trail-of-police-papers/
Machado MR, Lima M, Néris N (2016) Racismo e insulto racial na sociedade brasileira, dinâmicas de reconhecimento e de invisibilização a partir do direito. Novos estudos. Cebrap. São Paulo. v35.03. 11–28
Machado Maria das Dores Campos (2012) Religião, cultura e política. Religião e Sociedade, Rio de Janeiro, 32(2):29–56
Miranda APMd (2009) Entre o privado e o público: considerações sobre a (in) criminação da intolerância religiosa no Rio de Janeiro. Anuário Antropológico 2:125–152, 2010
Miranda APMd (2010) MOTA, Fabio Reis; PINTO, Paulo Gabriel Hilu da Rocha. Relatório sobre a Comissão de Combate a Intolerância Religiosa. UFF, Rio de Janeiro
Miranda APMd (2012) A força de uma expressão: intolerância religiosa, conflitos e demandas por reconhecimento de direitos no Rio de Janeiro. *Comunicações do ISER*, Rio de Janeiro, n. 66, Ano 31:60–73
Miranda APM (2014) Como se discute Religião e Política? Controvérsias em torno da luta contra a intolerância religiosa no Rio de Janeiro. Rio de Janeiro, Comunicações do ISER 69:10–23
Miranda APM (2015) The Rebirth of religious intolerance: controversies regarding state secularisation in Rio de Janeiro. In: Resende JM, Martins AC (eds) The making of the common in social relations. Cambridge Scholars Publishing, pp 115–128

Miranda APM, Beraldo OM d, Ferreira PV (2010) A reinvenção da "Cartorialização": análise do trabalho policial em registros de ocorrência e inquéritos policiais em "Delegacias Legais" referentes a homicídios dolosos na cidade do Rio de Janeiro. Segurança, Justiça e Cidadania: Pesquisas Aplicadas em Segurança Pública 4:119–152

Miranda APM, de Mello CR, Rodrigues AR (2017a) Intolerância Religiosa: A Construção de um Problema Público. Revista Intolerância Religiosa, Rio de Janeiro 2:1–19

Miranda APM, de Mello CR, Pinto Vinicius C (2017b) Conciliação No Papel: O Tratamento Dado aos Casos de Intolerância Religiosa em Juizados Especiais Criminais no Rio de Janeiro. Confluências - Revista Interdisciplinar de Sociologia e Direito 18:21–43

Miranda APM, Oliveira MB, Paes VF (2007) Antropologia e políticas públicas: notas sobre a avaliação do trabalho policial. Cuadernos de Antropología Social, Buenos Aires, 25:51–70

Misse M (1997) Cidadania e Criminalização: o problema da contabilidade oficial do crime. In: Misse M (org.) *O Crime Violento no Rio:* um exame preliminar das fontes. Rio de Janeiro, laboratório de Pesquisa Social (IFCS – UFRJ), Rio de Janeiro, Série Iniciação Científica, n° 8

Montero P (2006a) Introdução. In: Deus na aldeia: missionários, índios e mediação cultural. Globo, São Paulo

Montero P (2006b) Religião, pluralismo e esfera pública no Brasil, *Novos Estudos*, Cebrap, 74, março

Montero P (2009a) Salesian ethnographies in Brazil and the work of cultural mediation. Soc Sci Missions (Print) 22(1):9–27

Montero P (2009b) Secularização e espaço público: a reinvenção do pluralismo religioso no Brasil. Revista Etnográfica 13(1):7–16

Montero P (2012) Controvérsias religiosas e esfera pública: repensando as religiões como discurso. Religião e Sociedade, Rio de Janeiro 32(1):167–183

Montero P (2013) Saberes missionários: da autoria à tradução. Revista De Antropologia 55(2)

Müller P (1990) Les Politiques Publiques. PUF, Paris

Nicácio C S (2020) Intolerância religiosa no Estado de Minas Gerais: considerações a partir de uma pesquisa empírica. (Aguarda publicação – Revista Direito GV /Fundação Getúlio Vargas)

Oro AP (2011) A laicidade no Brasil e no Ocidente: algumas considerações. Civitas 11(2):221–237

Padioleau J-G (1982) L'Etat au concret. PUF, Paris

Pew Research Center (Feb. 26, 2015) Latest Trends in Religious Restrictions and Hostilities

Santos Babalawô Ivanir dos *et ali.* (org.) (2016) *Intolerância religiosa no Brasil:* relatório e balanço. Klíne: CEAP, Rio de Janeiro

Santos BS (2009) Sociología Jurídica Crítica, para un nuevo sentido comun en el derecho. Editorial Trotta/Ilsa, Madrid

Schritzmeyer Ana Lúcia P (2004) *Sortilégios de saberes:* curandeiros e juízes nos tribunais brasileiros. Instituto Brasileiro de Ciências Criminais, São Paulo

SDH-PR – Secretaria Especial de direitos humanos (2016) *Relatório sobre intolerância e violência religiosa no Brasil* (2011–2015): resultados preliminares/Ministério das Mulheres, da Igualdade Racial, da Juventude e dos Direitos Humanos

Silva JH (2007c) Notas sobre o Sistema Jurídico e Intolerância. In: Silva V (org.). Intolerância Religiosa: impactos do neopentecostalismo no campo-religioso brasileiro. EDUSP, São Paulo, pp 303–331

Silva V (org.) (2007a) *Intolerância Religiosa:* impactos do neopentecostalismo no campo-religioso brasileiro. São Paulo: EDUSP

Silva VG (2007b) Neopentecostalismo e religiões afro-brasileiras: Significados do ataque aos símbolos da herança religiosa africana no Brasil contemporâneo. Mana, Rio de Janeiro 13(1): 207–236

Sliwinski S (2006) The childhood of human rights: the Kodak on the Congo. J Visual Cult 5(3): 333–363

Sliwinski S (2009) The aesthetics of human rights, culture. Theory Critiq 50(1):23–39

Evangelicals Against the Criminalization of Homophobia: The "Christian Majority" and the Dispute Over Public Morality

Paula Bortolin

Abstract This chapter examines evangelical parliamentarians' speeches and arguments against Bill 122/20061 that intended to criminalize prejudice and discrimination based on sexual orientation. We will demonstrate how these actors formulated their speeches from a repertoire supported by legal norms. We observe that the justifications, developed in conformity with the democratic field, often resorted to the right to freedom of speech and religious freedom to defend the unconstitutionality of the criminalization of homophobia in Brazil. Therefore, we will analyze how evangelical actors utilize the grammar of rights in order to influence public opinion. The idea of the "Christian majority" was also used recurrently in speeches to justify that the Bill in question restricts most of the population's rights of belief and opinion. In contrast to the anti-majority currents that guided the 1988 Constitution, these actors interpret democracy as a regime that must preserve the majority's morality, thus opposing legal proposals aimed at protecting minorities or differences. Thus, we will analyze the construction of a narrative that aims to legitimize a hegemonic majority, in the sense of regulating public morality in Brazil.

1 Introduction

Over the last two decades in Brazil, we have observed, albeit gradually, sociocultural, legal and political changes that converged toward the recognition of LGBTQIA+ individuals and homoaffective families, stimulated by the governments led by Luiz Inácio Lula da Silva (Lula) (2003 to 2011) and Dilma Roussef (2012 to 2016). These processes were influenced by the expansion of government agencies, programs and public policies aimed at promoting sexual and gender diversity (Lacerda 2019). Based on this scenario, the literature highlights that there was a growing engagement of evangelical leaders and parliamentarians in public disputes about themes involving sexuality, gender and family, despite the differences in the evangelical milieu (Machado 2017; Machado and Burity 2014; Facchini and Sívori

P. Bortolin (✉)
State University of Campinas – UNICAMP, Campinas, Brazil

P. Montero et al. (eds.), *Religious Pluralism and Law in Contemporary Brazil*, Law and Religion in a Global Context 4, https://doi.org/10.1007/978-3-031-41981-2_5

2017). Thus, the promotion of rights for LGBTQIA+ groups was considered a threat to the Brazilian traditional family (Almeida 2019). In light of this, in the last two decades, these actors have engaged in public disputes that involve demands in favor of increasing and recognizing sexual and gender diversity, through new dynamics that trigger elements of the democratic game, such as using secular grammars in the speeches against what they believe to be a crisis of family ties, generated by new demands linked to human rights (Vaggione 2005).

In this chapter, we analyze the public stance of evangelical leaders against Bill 122/2006 (PL122), which intended to criminalize prejudice and discrimination based on sexual orientation. Our aim is to demonstrate how evangelical leaders appropriated legal discourse and the grammar of rights to refute the legality of the bill.[1] When the controversy over this bill began, most of the evangelical actors who took part in the public debate held office in the National Congress. In this arena, the group of evangelical congressmen, represented by the Evangelical Parliamentary Front,[2] lobbied to hinder the bill's approval. Due to this strong opposition, Bill 122 was filed in 2015, following the rules of the house's bylaws, which provide for the filing of all proposals that go through two legislatures without being voted.[3]

Recent studies (Bohn 2004; Natividade and Lopes 2009; Duarte 2011; Vital da Cunha and Lopes 2013; Machado 2015) have already shown that the Evangelical Parliamentary Front resorts to argumentative strategies based on democratic values in order to limit demands that promote sexual and gender diversity. This has been an important strategy to strengthen and legitimize the group's stance regarding political disputes on these issues. However, this chapter will follow a different path, as we are interested in observing this dynamic in the media.

In a previous study (Bortolin 2018), we demonstrated that evangelical actors, especially congressmen linked to the Evangelical Parliamentary Front, presented themselves in the media as opposed to the rights of the LGBTQIA+ population.

---

[1] It is important to note that evangelicals in Brazil do not form a cohesive group and their public actions are not uniform. When it comes to issues more directly linked to sexuality and reproductive rights, there is a greater propensity for moral conservatism (Souza 2013). Even so, I would emphasize that the conservative moral stance on customs and values does not correspond to a total stance of evangelical leaders and/or churches (Jesus 2013; Natividade 2010; Machado and Piccolo 2011).

[2] "This is a supra-partisan group, consisting of congressmen linked to different evangelical churches, from the historical and the Pentecostal and neo-Pentecostal branches, who would act together to approve or reject legislation of religious interest and conduct various discussions in the Brazilian parliament" (Prandi and Santos 2017, p. 1).

[3] Since then, no other project addressing this same topic has made progress in the Federal Legislature. In 2019, aiming to repair the failure of the National Congress to legislate this demand, the Judiciary Branch, through the Federal Supreme Court, instituted discrimination based on sexual orientation and gender identity as a crime.

Since then, no other project addressing this same topic has made progress in the Federal Legislature. In 2019, seeking to repair the failure of the National Congress to legislate this demand, the Judiciary Branch, through the Federal Supreme Court, instituted discrimination based on sexual orientation and gender identity as a crime.

Their standpoint was frequently based on a theological repertoire, grounded on the religious authority of the Bible as a means to question the legitimacy of homosexuality and homoaffective families. However, mapping the controversy surrounding Bill 122 showed that several speeches and interviews by these actors triggered elements inherent to secular grammars.[4] The main criticism referred to the fact that, once approved, this law would limit the freedom of speech and religious freedom of evangelical leaders and would allow legal persecution of pastors who preached their religious convictions contrary to homosexuality. In other words, instead of the expected recourse to religious discourse and grammar, these actors positioned themselves in the media criticizing the bill through legal arguments and democratic rules. In other venues and arenas, their view against the criminalization of homophobia was based on values and a morality that recriminates homosexuality. In the mapping of the media during the period of greatest dispute, however, we identified speeches of respect in which the legitimacy of homosexuality was never questioned, but the constitutionality of the proposal. Thus, their discursive strategy and arguments were based on the legal repertoire and the democratic game.

Regarding the group in favor of approving Bill 122, advocates of sexual diversity, the core argument emphasizes the right to diversity, based on the principle of pluralism, established in the Federal Constitution of 1988. The then Senator Marta Suplicy, the rapporteur of the bill, defended its constitutionality on the grounds of the respect for minority rights, claiming that the LGBTQIA+ had suffered for years the effects of violence related to homophobia. As seen in Marta Suplicy's argument, the use of a legal framework is common in actors' demands in favor of Bill 122, especially the rights to equality and full citizenship of homosexuals. Their statements are frequently based on demands for equal treatment of homosexual individuals, enabling them to fully enjoy the rights to citizenship, provided by the Constitution (Bortolin 2018, p. 125).

Thus, we identified that actors from both sides used the same strategy—addressing democratic rules and the Brazilian Constitution—to legitimize their opinions. The dispute was, therefore, established in terms of rights, each group defending the greatest legitimacy of "their" right—freedom of speech, religion and conscience, as opposed to the right to equal treatment and full citizenship.

Our analysis was inspired by Wendy Brown's notion of "expansion of the personal protected sphere" (Brown 2019, p. 144). The later presented itself as an important analytical tool to understand how evangelical parliamentarians used the notions of "religious freedom" and "freedom of speech" beyond the private sphere. This sphere defines the activities that cannot be subject to State intervention. In this domain, personal freedom is unrestricted. Its expansion into the public space seeks to increase the activities that should be classified as private, so that they are protected from legal action. In the private domain, these activities are regulated by traditional

[4] It is important to emphasize that the notion "secular grammar" refers to the set of principles, codes, guidelines and laws that oppose the religious sphere, such as science or law. The term "religious grammar" corresponds to the values and principles which make up the Christian doctrine.

moral values, especially those related to family issues. In this sense, private actions are reinforced and expanded in the public space, opposing public policies and the legal/political order that seeks to expand the claims for equality and for the maintenance of secular rules.

According to the author, religious leaders often resort to the protected personal sphere to insert private (familist) values in public life, so that these, instead of the State, organize the public sphere. As a result, the expansion of the personal protected sphere, in the name of the right to freedom, legitimize the public presence of traditional beliefs and moral values, increasingly blurring the boundaries between the public and the private spheres in modern pluralistic democracies. Although it was formulated based on the US context, the notion of "expanded personal protected sphere" is useful to analyze the Brazilian setting, in which the resort to individual freedoms has become a recurring argument in actors' speeches who are opposed to the advance of demands of the LGBTQIA+ community. We will return to this point later.

Finally, it is important to point out that Bill 122 passed through the National Congress between 2006 and 2015, but its public repercussion occurred between 2011 and 2015, mainly due to the approval of the same-sex unions in the country in 2011 by the Supreme Court. The legal recognition of same-sex unions encouraged social movements, political parties and parliamentarians active in the struggle to expand LGBTQIA+s rights, to reinforce their demands in favor of the approval of the anti-homophobia law. In response to this scenario, prominent evangelical leaders, parliamentary pastors (deputies and senators) advocates of heterosexual family, reaffirmed their positions against the criminalization of homophobia in mainstream media and in religious media. Our research focused on this period (2011 to 2015) precisely because it was the crucial moment of the controversy, in which opposition to it by evangelical leaders became more intense. Thus, we describe and analyze the means by which these actors used the repertoire of law in their speeches aimed at the media, in order to gain social adhesion to their respective positions.

We focused our analysis on articles that presented speeches and interviews given by these actors to three newspapers with large national circulation: *Folha de S. Paulo, O Estado de São Paulo* and *O Globo*. Our mapping covered the total of 196 reports. The articles were selected, respectively, in all outlets, based on identifying the following keywords: homosexualism, homosexuality, criminalization of homophobia, Bill 122, Bill 122/2006, Anti-homophobia Law, *causa gay* (defending gay rights), homophobia, *bancada evangélica* (evangelical caucus), Evangelical Parliamentary Front, Brazil without homophobia, homosexuals' right(s).[5]

In addition, we mapped the interviews given to the religious media, using the search engine google.com. The selection criteria for these interviews were based on

[5]The mapping was carried out in the online archives of each newspaper. Qualitative analysis was applied, in which the researcher read all the selected reports, classifying them, using Excel software, based on the recurrence of terms used by the actors involved.

the number of accesses. In this regard, we selected the 28 most viewed interviews up to the time we carried out this mapping. Therefore, we are interested in investigating what these actors' standpoints were in the secular and religious media, using a legal and moral repertoire to publicly justify their arguments against the criminalization of homophobia.

2 Evangelical Parliamentarians in Defense of Individual Freedoms

Our analysis revealed the recurrence of certain specific terms. First, we highlight the use of the categories "freedom of speech" and "religious freedom." At times, each of them was used in isolation, but in general we observed that the arguments used both categories to justify the opposition to Bill 122. When evangelical parliamentarians resorted to these categories, theological and moral elements were left out. Their arguments explored the legal realm, thus highlighting the unconstitutionality of the proposal. They claimed that its approval would restrict the freedom of religious leaders to preach against homosexual unions and homosexuality. Thus, we noted that the private right to religious freedom was associated with the right to publicly express one's opinion.

To justify their stance, the group often based its arguments on the defense of the Brazilian Constitution, specifically on the fifth article, which provides for the inviolability of the rights to freedom of conscience and belief.[6] The following excerpts demonstrate this dynamic.

The speech given by Federal Deputy João Campos, leader of the Evangelical Parliamentary Front in the National Congress, did not question the extension of rights to a minority. On the contrary, it points out the legitimacy of this group in pleading demands. However, its criticism defends the unconstitutionality of the proposal which, in his assessment, compromised fundamental rights. His position is articulated through arguments that comprise the legal field.

> This bill is blatantly unconstitutional. When it proposes the criminalization of homophobia, this project attacks what upholds democracy: the freedom of speech and the inviolability of belief and conscience. This project indirectly creates the crime of opinion. You can express your opinion in relation to the priest, the pastor, the politician, the executive, the employee, the boss. But if this bill becomes law and you give an opinion about the practice of homosexuality, it becomes a crime. It is impossible in a democratic State for you to criminalize opinion. When you give an opinion, you are not against A or B. You are expressing an opinion against conduct and behavior. It is the so-called freedom of speech,

[6] Art. 5 - Everyone is equal before the law, without distinction of any kind, guaranteeing Brazilians and foreigners residing in the country the inviolability of the right to life, liberty, equality, security and property under the following terms: VI- freedom of conscience and belief is inviolable, the free exercise of religious cults being ensured and the protection of places of worship and their liturgies being guaranteed, in the form of the law" (Brazil 1988).

> which is one of the pillars of the Democratic Rule of Law. For this reason, on behalf of the whole of Brazilian society, we are against this Bill. It wants to ensure a right to a minority, which we agree with, but subtracting fundamental rights from Brazilian society (Camargo 2011).

It is interesting to note that the rejection of Bill 122 is based on the association of two rights of different orders: the freedom of speech that corresponds to a public action and the inviolability of belief and conscience, associated to the private sphere. In addition to defending the right to exercise a belief contrary to homosexuality, the Pastor and Deputy claims the right to publicly manifest it. The argument produces an equivalence between these two dimensions of law that correspond to different spheres: public and private. Thus, the speech transforms a private conduct into a public demonstration. Another movement in this speech is the association of the free exercise of belief and conscience with the category of opinion, as the passage triggers the two notions as if they were the same. Furthermore, we observe the shift from the idea of opinion to the field of moral judgments of conduct, making the two actions equivalent.

Federal Deputy and Pastor Marcos Feliciano, in turn, defended freedom of speech, calling on the public to take a stand against the anti-homophobia Bill:

> The bill that criminalizes homophobia is currently in the spotlight. I'm going through what everyone will suffer when it's approved. None of you ladies or gentlemen will be able to have freedom of speech, be able to think. If we don't do something now, I don't know what will happen tomorrow (Decath and Gama 2013).

This speech introduces a new element in relation to the previous quote. Here, the criminalization of homophobia would not only restrict the freedom to publicly express an opinion, but it would also prohibit people from thinking. This approach triggers an image of a possible catastrophic future, in which not only (public) opinion but (private) thinking against homosexuality would suffer legal punishment. Such an approach clearly seeks to incite in the public opinion the fear of suffering legal consequences if they express an opposition to homosexual behavior. Thus, the way in which Feliciano formulates his argument resorts to an important discursive strategy to trigger a popular support against Bill 122.

A similar argument was observed in the speech given by Pastor Magno Malta. His opposition to the bill was sustained by the defense of the freedom to criticize homosexuality.

> I owe homosexuals my respect and I'm not homophobic. It must stress that television ridicules homosexuals all the time. But if a pastor speaks ill of homosexuals… We need freedom of speech. For example, if you find out that your child's nanny is gay and you don't want her to influence your child, as it goes against what you believe, against God's will, can't you fire her? What´s this all about? (Não atentaremos…, 2012).[7]

[7] The bibliographic reference of quotations extracted from newspaper articles without authorship will be carried out as in this case. Between parentheses will appear the first word of the title followed by an ellipsis and the date of publication of the document

Despite criticizing the Bill, Malta's speech starts by emphasizing respect for homosexual subjects. Here, freedom of speech is extended to incorporate the freedom to pursue a certain conduct. Thus, not only the legitimacy of expressing a position against homosexuality is claimed, but also of adopting certain behaviors, such as firing an employee due to their sexual orientation.

The defense of freedom of speech was also present in the speech of the then Federal Deputy, evangelical, Eduardo Cunha. However, in addition to defending the right to freedom of speech, the deputy's concern regarding the risks that the approval of the bill would pose to the ecclesial sectors is worth noting. Cunha emphasized the restrictions that pastors and priests would suffer in their preaching:

> There are items in this project that prevent pastors and priests from preaching in their churches. This Bill is against freedom of speech. We are at a crucial moment where it seems that being homosexual is revolutionary and being heterosexual is reactionary. We have to be careful with this (Eduardo..., 2015).

In this passage, the overlapping of certain rights and freedoms becomes even more evident. Despite the politician citing the restriction of freedom of speech, his criticism emphasizes the impediment that religious leaders would suffer from preaching against homosexuality. It is, thus, not simply a matter of the right to freely criticize sexual diversity, since Cunha's speech highlights the legitimacy of religious leaders to profess their faith and the truths that support their beliefs. In other words, the criticism refers to freedom of speech, but the argument is supported by the concern that the religious freedom to preaching is restricted.

In the excerpt below, pastor and politician Marcelo Crivella makes an opposite move. Here, the argument is based on the defense of religious freedom. However, this notion is associated to freedom of speech.

> I am against homophobia. What we cannot criminalize is if the pastor on your church pulpit or the priest at your church says that homosexuality is a sin. This is religious freedom. He has the right to speak, and we have to respect him. But it's not a crime. Crime is the attack, crime is closing the doors to a homosexual. The controversy surrounding Bill 122 is simple: how far we can criminalize [one's faith]? People have the right to express their faith, as long as it is in a way that does not cause violence (Motta 2014, p. 10)

One can note that religious freedom is associated with a public dimension, in which not only the right to exercise one's faith is claimed, but also the right to publicly manifest it by preaching and reaffirming values and morals. Moreover, the Pastor proposes a specific regulation on the ways of expressing one's opinion, establishing the criteria that would turn an action into a crime.

In general, we observed two important movements that comprise the speeches above. First, the category of freedom of speech takes on a particular frame, according to the context in which it is used. In the statements above, it was associated with moral values, and it was connected to the freedom of thought, and the right to follow certain conducts and to express one's faith. Thus, by claiming freedom of speech, these actors are extending the scope of this category, in order to expands individual freedoms. We identified, therefore, that the use of the notion of freedom of speech is constantly changing, as its content varies according to discursive strategies. Finally, we also note that, by using legal discourse to justify the opposition to the criminalization of homophobia, evangelical actors highlight the right to profess one's religious beliefs contrary to homosexual behavior as an act of freedom of speech.

In her analysis of the expansion of the personal protected sphere, Wendy Brown (2019, p. 159) highlights that the combination of religious freedom and freedom of speech is a strategical move to challenge certain democratic rights and to empower traditional morality against claims of equality, making personal freedom increasingly unrestricted. The author argues that, when used separately, freedom of speech and religious freedom do not have the strength to dispute public morality. However, when combined, they create a new framework and a new power for traditional morality in the public sphere. Hence, religious freedom alone does not guarantee such innovation, as it is limited to the protection of a private right, namely, the freedom to believe and the right to being protected from discrimination. Freedom of speech, in turn, is the opposite, as it allows the dissemination of beliefs and values to be freely conveyed as opinions, successfully leaving the private sphere and entering the public space safely. Therefore, it is a right to speak freely and unconditionally.

When religious freedom is inserted in the public arena of freedom of speech, it is reinforced in a unique way. The private religious conviction about sexuality, by becoming free speech, gives political power to the public opinion against homosexuality. The convergence of these two types of freedom, therefore, allows evangelical leaders to defend traditional values as a form of legitimate expression in the public domain. This combination empowers these actors to claim the right to political dissent, contesting specific practices and laws that, in their view, contradict private religious beliefs and values. In a broader perspective, however, one can note how these speeches shed light not only on positions regarding homophobia, but on the limits and scope of some of the vital rights in contemporary democracies. Consequently, the disputes over the classification of homophobia as a crime enable us to observe some of the contradictions and tensions caused by the ways in which certain rights are appropriated and disputed in public debate.

The public dispute of the constitutionality of a bill by evangelical actors highlighted a new tension in the democratic system between the principles of religious freedom, freedom of speech, and the constraints that the new constitution placed, especially adopting pluralism as a legal framework and emphasizing the right to difference and diversity. There is, therefore, a relatively recent tension between the pluralist stance adopted by the Constitution, based on policies that promote an egalitarian differentialism, and evangelical activism, which connected the right to freedom of speech to religious freedom, creating a new scenario of disputes.

We will see that these actors also adopted a different strategy at times, investing in the notion of a Christian moral majority. This time, however, they used a narrative in which they attribute themselves to the position of victims of a secular persecution that attacks traditional and religious moral values.

3 Brazilian, Therefore, Christian

Increasing evidence can be found that the appeal to moral sentiments and values has become an essential force in contemporary politics, nourishing discourses and legitimizing practices, particularly when they focus on the disadvantaged, whether on a national level, such as the poor, the immigrants, the homeless, or internationally, such as victims of famine, epidemics, or war (Fassin 2012, p. 1). Nevertheless, in addition to building a governmentality of precarious lives, as Fassin indicates, moral sentiments can also be mobilized in public debate to construct a notion of majority that embodies the moral core of a nation.

One example of this dynamic, analyzed extensively by the academic literature, refers to the triumphalist discourse of the North American Christian Right (Rocha 2018; Lacerda 2019). Through political alliances of a self-proclaimed moral majority, the religious right claims that its values, especially linked to moral issues, represent the beliefs of the majority of Americans. The idea of a moral majority strengthens the political claims in the name of "family values," in opposition to abortion and homosexual rights. With regard to Latin America, Mariano and Gerardi's (2019) analysis of the presidential elections in Costa Rica, Colombia, Venezuela, Mexico, and Brazil demonstrates that conservative evangelical political activists tried to subordinate the legal system to the moral values of the "Christian majority."

In the case analyzed here, in parallel to the arguments that defend the inviolability of the right to democratic freedoms, we identified that the statements against the criminalization of homophobia claim the authority of traditional morality in Brazilian society, under the argument that most of the population is Christian, sharing a set of religious moral values. Thus, Bill 122 is accused of subverting fundamental values of the "majority" of the nation.

In a column he wrote for the *Folha de S. Paulo* newspaper, Pastor and Deputy Marco Feliciano defended the freedom to take a stand against homosexuality, emphasizing the democratic character of the Brazilian State. The pastor stated that the majority of the population is Christian and that, therefore, it would be unacceptable for democracy to apply only to minorities.

> Within this democratic rule of law, where the majority is Christian, is democracy only valid for minorities? The fact is that gay activists and their supporters cannot tolerate the debate. One can speak ill of the president of the republic, the judiciary, Catholics, evangelicals, but if we criticize homosexual practice, we are labeled homophobic (Malafaia 2013).

Following the previous arguments, this speech is also based on rules that shape democratic life. In this excerpt, the appropriation of the notion of democracy resorts to an idea of a government focused exclusively on the majority, based on Christian religious belonging. As a democratic exercise, he claims the right to an open debate. However, in this context, the debate is reduced to the action of "speaking ill." The pastor makes an analogy between different perspectives. Presidents and judges represent institutions that regulate everyone's life. Thus, criticizing them means evaluating whether they are working according to the attributions and rules that underlie their positions. In turn, criticizing homosexuals corresponds to a disqualification of a private personal choice. One can note, thus, that the demand for a democratic debate is used as a means to support criticisms about individual behaviors of a private nature. Again, the contours between the public and private spheres are blurred.

In turn, when asked about Bill 122, Pastor and politician Magno Malta declared that "the grotesque yearning of a minority cannot impose itself on the majority of Brazilian families" (Ato…, 2011). If in the previous passages, the opposition to homosexuality is treated as a simple opinion, here it is considered a private perversion. The idea of minority is associated with a notion of marginality, as opposed to the majority of the population, portrayed as supports of the traditional Brazilian family, based on Christian religious belonging (evangelical and Catholic).

Following the idea of a Christian majority, Pastor and Deputy Anderson Ferreira stated that "a minority cannot dictate rules for a majority, nor want privileges" (Braga et al. 2015, p. 6). Again, the category of democracy is based on the idea of a government for the majorities. This standpoint does not consider the counter majoritarian principle, which works as a counterweight to the majority power, in order to prevent the excesses of any majority through democracy, distorting constitutional values and oppressing minorities (Santos and Arteiro 2011, p. 17).

Based on the field of law, these statements address a specific idea of the democratic regime, one that legislates according to the demands of most of the population. That is, the notion of democracy is used with the purpose of defending the morality of the majority, which in this case is Christian. As a result, a Christian identity is claimed, given that the Brazilian population mostly comprises Catholics and Evangelicals. Thus, they assume that the dominant morality in Brazilian society is "Christian." This indicates that the majority of the population, permeated by Christian religious values, would be penalized if the criminalization of homophobia were regulated. According to this stance, its approval would violate the notion of a democratic regime, as it would go against the morals of most Brazilians, not granting rights for minorities, but "privileges." In this context, the category of democracy is appropriated and reinterpreted to serve the purpose of defending the morality of the Brazilian Christian majority.

Contrary to this standpoint, social scientists Reginaldo Prandi and Renan William dos Santos (2017) argue that, according to surveys carried out by the Datafolha Research Institute,[8] most evangelical voters are in favor of criminalizing homophobia (around 80% of respondents). Regarding the rejection of homosexuality, less than half of the evangelical electorate believe that "homosexuality should be discouraged by society" (40.3% among non-Pentecostals and 44.9% among

[8]This article used data from two surveys by the Datafolha Institute, one carried out in October 2015, with a statistically representative sample of 340 parliamentarians, and another carried out in September 2014, a nationwide survey, with a sample of 10,054 voters. In both surveys, opinions were collected on topics such as the death penalty, poverty, age of criminal responsibility, possession of weapons, economic issues, benefits from government programs, sexual minorities rights, etc.

Pentecostals). This rate is even lower among Catholics (21.5%). According to Prandi and Santos, there is a clear discrepancy between the stance of evangelical leaders engaged in this controversy, and the data collected referring to members of this religious segment in Brazilian society.

However, our objective here is not to show evidence or question the existence of this "Christian moral majority," but to understand how this notion is used as an argumentative resource, based on a direct association between religious belonging, morality and political stance, to justify an alleged national rejection to the proposal of the Bill. We are not interested, therefore, in addressing the possible standpoints of a moral majority in relation to homosexuality, but in the way in which this notion is used as a tool to strengthen and legitimize arguments against criminalization of homophobia. As Boltanski and Thévenot (1999) remind us, actors in political disputes often resort to general principles to mobilize broad audiences, as justifications become potent when they trigger universalizing grammars and moralities. Thus, reinforcing the link between Christian moral values and Brazilian cultural identity can be understood as a strategy to reinforce the criticisms against the Bill.

4 The Privilege of the Excluded

Based on the concept of "majority"—which assumes that the Brazilian population in almost its entirety has links with the Catholic and Evangelical religions, thus sharing their moral values and, particularly, the notion of traditional family—the statements alleged that homosexuals were demanding privileges and not equality. According to these actors, it was not necessary to make homophobia a crime, since physical or verbal assault are already typified in the crimes of bodily harm, ill-treatment, injury, slander and defamation. Thus, a series of speeches defended that the criminalization of homophobia would give privileges for homosexuals, as no one could question or take a stand against homosexuality. The statements against the Bill stated that its approval would only result in the censorship of religious preaching, as the criminalization of violence against gay people was already provided for in the laws that typify bodily harm and verbal abuse.

Senator Magno Malta, for example, stated that the Bill's text contains points that make homosexuals "untouchable," while other minorities, such as blacks, the disabled and the elderly, did not have the same "privileges." In his words:

> If you don't rent your property to a homosexual, or don't accept the affectionate act of a gay couple, you get seven years in jail. If you fire or do not take on a homosexual in your company, five years in jail. I can refuse to rent my house to a black person, I can fire a person with a disability, I can oppose affectionate gestures from a heterosexual couple at my front door and ask them to go somewhere else, away from my children. But if I do this with a homosexual couple, a simple police report will put me in jail (Magno... 2011).

In this excerpt, we can also note the concept of freedom of speech associated with the freedom to conduct one's acts based on a moral and religious value. More than criticizing homosexuality, Malta claims the legality of making decisions based on its position against homosexuality. It is not just a question of not "accepting" homosexuality and thus criticizing it, but of not extending to a homosexual individual the possibility of renting a property, exclusively because of his/her sexuality. Furthermore, it is important to highlight that the Brazilian legal system does not allow discrimination against people based on their color or disability. Thus, not renting a property to a black person due to their skin color is a crime in Brazil. Regarding the disapproval of the public kiss of a homo-affective couple, there are also laws against public obscenities that must be applied to all individuals, regardless of their sexuality.

Along the same lines, then-Evangelical Federal Deputy Anthony Garotinho stressed the importance of non-discrimination principle. Nevertheless, he is skeptical towards the Bill, "since not even the disabled, the elderly and children have so many privileges in our country" (Braga 2011, p. 4). Pastor Marcos Feliciano, in turn, wrote in a column for the *Folha de S. Paulo* newspaper where he states that, as an advocate of the Constitution, it was impossible for him to support the approval of the demands from the LGBTQIA+ group that foresee constitutional changes (Feliciano 2013). In an interview, Feliciano argued that if Bill 122 were approved, we would have to do the same with other minorities, such as "one-eyed people and toothless people" (Rodrigues 2013, p. A5).

The idea that the criminalization of homophobia implies necessarily the creation of privileges is based on the argument that there is already a legal penalty for discriminatory and violent acts of any kind. According to this perspective, LGBTQIA+ individuals, when discriminated against, would already have the support of the law. In addition, the speeches claimed that the notion of diversity refers to many groups. Thus, the respect for diversity implied not only the rights of homosexual individuals, but also the rights of all those who are somehow socially excluded, since in a plural society, where different social groups do not share the characteristics of the majority of the population, groups of different orders are victims of prejudice. These evangelical actors understand the claims in favor of sexual diversity as a demand for privileges. According to them, the anti-homophobia law would allow, on the one hand, the creation of privilege for a minority, and on the other, would weaken evangelical values. In this context, once approved, LGBTQIA + people would enjoy advantages, while the traditional Brazilian family and the pre-eminence of heterosexuality would become vulnerable, in addition to opening up a legal loophole for other minorities to claim "privileges."

To strengthen their argument, some lawmakers have resorted to the idea of a "*didatura gay*" (gay dictatorship) menace, which refers to an alleged omnipotence that gays would gain if homophobia were criminalized. Thus, the term "*mordaça gay*" (gay gag) emerges, based on the idea that evangelicals would be "forbidden" to criticize the homo-affective practice. This scenario would produce, according to the speeches mapped in our work, an "*evangelicophobia*," allowing the persecution of evangelicals who criticize Bills that aim to expand the rights of homosexuals.

Some statements even highlighted the need to value heterosexuality as a way of resisting this persecution. In early 2015, Deputy Eduardo Cunha, who had been newly elected to the presidency of the Chamber of Deputies, reintroduced two Bills of his authorship, proposed in the previous legislature. One criminalizes prejudice against heterosexuals and the other foresees the creation of the heterosexual pride day. In relation to these two proposals, Cunha stated:

> When prejudices against homosexuals are discussed, they end up creating another type of discrimination against heterosexuals. In addition, encouraging gay ideology overcomes any fight against prejudice. Soon, heterosexuals will be transformed by media propaganda into reactionaries and we want to have our stance on the family being proudly paraded (Carvalho 2015, p. A17).

Senator Magno Malta identifies in the law against homophobia a step toward the creation of a "homosexual empire" (O Preconceito.., 2011). Deputy Marco Feliciano, on the other hand, pointed out that the opposition would classify all divergent groups as "homophobic" and "racist." Feliciano condemned the position of sexual right advocates in relation to evangelicals as "persecution" and "*evangelicophobia*." The pastor also implied the existence of a conspiracy to establish a "*gay dictatorship*" that, in addition to persecuting political ideologies, would also combat religious beliefs (Malafaia 2013).

Although these are not legal categories, it is interesting to note the production of a new lexicon that refers to the political vocabulary of modern democracies, such as the use of the term "dictatorship," and the neologism "*evangelicophobia*", referring to the "xenophobic" treatment supposedly aimed at evangelical sectors of the population.

The legal recognition of claims made by the group defending sexual diversity is portrayed in an alarmist and catastrophic tone that places the traditional family, heterosexuality and evangelicals as victims. The discourses revolved around the idea of an alleged attack and persecution of heterosexuality in order to incite fears and phobias in the public opinion on the dangers of sexual and family configurations that do not correspond to those portrayed by the notion of a Christian Brazilian majority. This strategy has the potential to increase popular support for the stance against the criminalization of homophobia. According to the sociologist Richard Miskolci (2007), sexual diversity develops a fear of instability in institutions such as the family, constituting a multiple threat to biological reproduction, to the traditional power relations between men and women in the family and society and, above all, to the maintenance of values and morality responsible for an entire order and worldview. This fear could trigger forms of social control to repudiate behaviors that disrupt societal values and interests, under the pretext of preserving society and its moral order.

Furthermore, the arguments presented by these evangelical actors reinforce the idea that homosexuals are claiming privileges, and that the dispute around the antihomophobia law is delegitimizing heterosexuality, portrayed as a natural condition of human beings. On this matter, we observe that evangelical actors declare, at different times, respect for homosexuals. The strategy to escape the homophobic label was based on the criticism of homosexuality and not homosexuals. The speeches were structured by secular terms and triggered important categories, values and ideas from the political vocabulary which found echoes in Brazilian society.

However, the consolidation of the paradigm of diversity, from the National Constitution (1988), makes the notion of a political majority increasingly problematic, as it provides for the recognition of minority rights as a key element for plural democracies. Hence, one can note that, despite the obstacles presented by pluralism, this has not prevented evangelical sectors from defending the primacy of a political and moral Christian majority in Brazil.

5 Final Considerations

As highlighted in the introduction, the aim of this chapter was to use the speeches and positions against the criminalization of homophobia on the media as a gateway to understand the ways in which the legal categories are interpreted and disputed by actors, and the ways in which certain values and moral feelings are used to develop an idea of a moral and political majority. Regarding the first topic, our work demonstrated that the opposition to the criminalization of homophobia, presented in the speeches of evangelical actors, utilized a repertoire of rights related to individual freedoms. Thus, we observed how the speeches in defense of religious freedom, associated with the right to freedom of speech, gave rise to the idea of individual freedom as a public right. This standpoint allowed the expression of beliefs and values in the public space as personal opinions, even if these affronted or insulted certain segments and social groups, such as the LGBTQIA+ population. According to Wendy Brown (2019), the unrestricted appeal to the right to individual freedoms is expanding the personal protected sphere and, consequently, creating barriers amidst the democratic game for the consolidation of pluralist demands.

The dispute over the criminalization of homophobia in Brazil highlights the challenges that evangelical activism poses to democracy, given that it used arguments based on the right to individual freedoms to fight the regulation of a right claimed by a social group that sought legal protection as a minority. Thus, the dispute took shape trough notions that are vital to democratic life. This scenario demonstrates that the political agenda is being disputed in the public space through legal arguments, accepted by all as inviolable rights, including by religious actors, who, as shown in this case study, resort to traditional values, politicizing them as "freedoms." Christian morality is enlarged by this standpoint, becoming a political tool to demand that religious rights are incorporated to the public sphere.

In addition to exploring the issue of how actors appropriated the legal framework, we also identified in the arguments of evangelical leaders the appeal to traditional values to claim the idea of a Christian majority. This narrative strategy showed that the evangelical actors' claims go beyond the right of religious leaders to preach against homosexuality, suggesting that most of the population would be prohibited from taking a stand against sexual diversity. Thus, the arguments against Bill 122/2006, more than protecting religious practices, try to act on the political system and guarantee that moral values are legitimately inserted in the political game, influencing the rules and the way in which the public sphere works. Finally, we emphasize that if, on the one hand, these actors employed moral values to validate the idea of a Christian majority, on the other hand, they portrayed themselves as victims of religious intolerance, placing themselves as the real group that is harmed and persecuted.

In this clash between majority and minorities, the actual numbers are not on the agenda. In fact, the Censuses of the last three decades indicate that the rate of the population that claims to be evangelical has more than doubled, jumping from 9.1% in 1991 to 22.1% in 2000, second only to Catholics, who declined from 83.8% to 64.6%. Despite this change in the balance of forces, the census data theoretically reaffirm the idea of a Christian majority, in numerical terms. However, as Prandi and Santos demonstrated, the positions of these segments in relation to a series of themes and issues can vary and, in fact, varies a lot, which pose problems for the consolidation of the idea of a supposed moral majority. Nevertheless, it is much less about numbers, but about the construction of a narrative that allows the legitimate insertion of morality in the political arena, and the consolidation of a hegemonic majority, whose desires should supersede those of multiple minorities that insist on claiming recognition of their rights in an increasingly plural Brazil.

References

Almeida R (2019) Deus acima de todos. In: Democracia em Risco? 22 ensaios sobre o Brasil Hoje. São Paulo, Companhia das Letras, pp 35–51

Bohn S (2004) Evangélicos no Brasil. Perfil socioeconômico, afinidades ideológicas e determinantes do comportamento eleitoral. Opinião Pública, Campinas X (2):288–338

Boltanski L, Thévenot L (1999) A Sociologia da Capacidade Crítica. Eur J Soc Theory 2(3): 359–377. London, Thousand Oaks, CA and New Delhi

Bortolin P (2018) A controvérsia em torno do projeto de lei 122/2006: Uma análise da oposição de parlamentares evangélicos à criminalização da homofobia. Dissertação de Mestrado em Ciências Sociais, Universidade Federal de São Paulo, Guarulhos.

Braga, I (2011) Esquenta briga no Congresso a favor dos gays. O Globo, Rio de Janeiro, 06 de março de 2011. País, p. 04

Braga I et al (2015) Cunha vê discriminação contra bancada evangélica na Câmara. O Globo. Rio de Janeiro, 14 de fevereiro de 2015. País, p 6

BRASIL. Constituição (1988) Constituição da República Federativa do Brasil. Senado, Brasília

Brown W (2019) Nas ruínas do neoliberalismo: a ascensão da antidemocrática no ocidente. Editora Filosófica Politeia

Camargo R (2011) Ser gay não é normal, diz líder evangélico. Congresso em foco, 11 de junho de 2011. Disponível em: http://congressoemfoco.uol.com.br/noticias/questao-de-foco/ser-gay-nao-e-normal-diz-lider-evangelico. Accessed 1 May, 2017

Carvalho D (2015) Cunha quer criar dia do orgulho Hétero. O Estado de S. Paulo, São Paulo, 13 de fevereiro de 2015. Metrópole, p A17

Decath E, Gama P (2013) Pastor diz que não recuará e prega combate à lei anti-homofobia. Folha de S. Paulo, São Paulo, 12 March 2013. Poder, p A-5

Duarte TS (2011) A casa dos ímpios se desfará, mas a tenda dos retos florescerá: a participação da Frente Parlamentar Evangélica no Legislativo brasileiro. Dissertação (Mestrado em Antropologia), Universidade de Brasília

Facchini R, Sívori H (2017) Conservadorismo, direitos, moralidades e violência: situando um conjunto de reflexões a partir da Antropologia. In: dossiê conservadorismo, direitos, moralidades e violência. Cadernos Pagu (50)
Fassin D (2012) On humanitarian reason: a moral history of the present. University of California Press, Los Angeles
Feliciano M (2013) Ditadura gay e Direitos Humanos. Folha de S. Paulo, São Paulo, 06 de março de 2013. Opinião
Folha de S. Paulo (2011) O Preconceito em Pauta. São Paulo, 11 de dezembro de 2011. Editorial
Gospel Prime (2011) Magno Malta afirma que estão tentando criar um império homossexual no Brasil. 02 de junho de 2011. Disponível em: https://noticias.gospelprime.com.br/magno-malta-afirma-que-estao-tentando-criar-um-imperiohomossexual-no-brasil/ Acessado em 01 de maio de 2017
Guia-me (2015) Eduardo Cunha, novo presidente da Câmara, defende cristãos no planalto. 03 de fevereiro de 2015. Disponível em: https://guiame.com.br/gospel/mundo-cristao/eduardo-cunha-novo-presidente-da-camara-defende-principioscristaos-no-planalto.html. Acessado em 01 de maio de 2017
Jesus FW (2013) Igrejas inclusivas em perspectiva comparada: da "inclusão radical" ao "mover apostólico". Seminário Internacional Fazendo Gênero 10 (Anais Eletrônicos), Florianópolis
Lacerda MB (2019) O novo conservadorismo brasileiro. Zouk, Porto Alegre
Machado MDC (2015) Religião e Política no Brasil Contemporâneo: uma análise dos pentecostais e carismáticos católicos. Religião e Sociedade 35(2):45–72
Machado MDC (2017) Pentencostais, sexualidade e família no Congresso Nacional. Horizontes Antropológicos 47:351–380
Machado MDC, Burity J (2014) A ascensão política dos pentecostais no Brasil na avaliação de líderes religiosos. Dados 57(3):601–631
Machado MDC, Piccolo FD (2011) Religiões e homossexualidades. FGV Editora, Rio de Janeiro
Malafaia S (2013) Marcos Feliciano é a bola da vez. Folha de S. Paulo, São Paulo, 05 de abril de 2013. Opinião
Miskolci R (2007) Pânicos morais e controle social: reflexões sobre o casamento gay (28):101–128
Motta P (2014) Entrevista com Marcelo Crivella. O Globo, Rio de janeiro, 19 de setembro de 2014. País, p 10
Natividade M (2010) Uma homossexualidade santificada? Etnografia de uma comunidade inclusiva pentecostal. Religião & Sociedade 30:90–120
Natividade M, Lopes PVL (2009) Os direitos GLBT e as respostas religiosas: da parceria civil à criminalização da homofobia. In: Duarte et al (Eds). Valores religiosos e Legislação no Brasil: a tramitação de projetos de lei sobre temas morais controversos. Garamond, Rio de Janeiro
O Estado de S. Paulo (2011) Ato contra o PL que criminaliza a homofobia reúne 15 mil, São Paulo. 02 de junho de 2011. Vida, A-19
Prandi R, Santos RW (2017) Quem tem medo da bancada evangélica? Posições sobre moralidade e política no eleitorado brasileiro, no Congresso Nacional e na Frente Parlamentar Evangélica. In: Tempo Social, revista de sociologia da USP 29(2)
Rocha C (2018) Menos Marx, mais Mises: uma gênese da nova direita brasileira (2006-2018). Tese (Doutorado em Ciência Política) – Programa de Pós-Graduação em Ciência Política. Universidade de São Paulo, São Paulo
Rodrigues F (2013) *Cúpula da Câmara quer me achincalhar, diz Feliciano*. Folha de S. Paulo, São Paulo, 02 de abril de 2013. Poder, p A5
Santos BI, Arteiro RL (2011) O princípio contramajoritário como mecanismo regulamentador da soberania. I Simpósio Internacional de Análise Crítica do Direito. Universidade Estadual do Norte do Paraná (UENP). Programa de Mestrado em Ciência Jurídica. 2011. Available at: <http://eventos.uenp.edu.br/sid/publicacao/artigos/8.pdf>. Accessed 23 June 2021
Souza SD (2013) Política religiosa e religião política: os evangélicos e o uso político do sexo. Estudos de Religião 27(1)

Vaggione JM (2005) Reactive politicization and religious dissidence. The political mutations of the religious in social theory and practice. Soc Theory Pract 31(2):233–255

Verdade G (2012) Não atentaremos contra a natureza de Deus, diz Magno Malta, 30/08/2012. Available at: http://www.verdadegospel.com/nao-atentaremos-contra-a-natureza-de-deus-diz-magno-malta/. Accessed 1 May 2017

Vital da Cunha C, Lopes PVL (2013) Religião e Política: uma análise da atuação de parlamentares evangélicos sobre direitos das mulheres e de LGBTs no Brasil. Fundação Heinrich Böll, Rio de Janeiro

Verdade Gospel (2012) Não atentaremos contra a natureza de Deus, diz Magno Malta, 30/08/2012. Disponível em: http://www.verdadegospel.com/nao-atentaremos-contra-a-natureza-de-deus-dizmagno-malta/. Acesso em 01 maio de 2017

"It Is Not Solved Just by Writing It Down on Paper": Patrimonialization Policies and the Religious Use of Ayahuasca as a Brazilian Intangible Cultural Heritage

Henrique Fernandes Antunes

Abstract This chapter analyzes, on the one hand, the construction of an institutional arrangement of policies on intangible heritage of Brazilian culture. On the other hand, it maps the disputes that emerge from implementing these policies from a case study on the patrimonialization of the religious use of ayahuasca in Brazil. Based on analyzing theses, dissertations, and articles on cultural heritage in Brazil, in the first part of the study, we describe the initial moment of developing public policies in the country. Then, using interviews, institutional documents from the *Instituto do Patrimônio Histórico e Artístico Nacional*—IPHAN (National Institute of Historic and Artistic Heritage) and national legislation, we made an analysis of the emerging policies aimed at intangible cultural heritage. Based on a literature review, interviews with actors involved in the process and institutional documents produced by ayahuasca groups, the following sections map the disputes surrounding the process of recognizing the religious use of ayahuasca as an intangible heritage of Brazilian culture. Thus, the present work addresses two key objectives: (1) Apprehending the construction and consolidation of a right from the convergence of various social, historical and institutional processes that occur at different levels and with different temporalities; (2) Showing evidence that the subsequent process of implementing such rights by formulating public policies can give rise to the emergence of a new set of dynamics, tensions and unforeseen claims in the law.

This chapter is the result of postdoctoral research that was funded by São Paulo Research Foundation (FAPESP), Grant Number: 2019/11202-0.

H. Fernandes Antunes (✉)
Brazilian Center of Analysis and Planning, São Paulo, Brazil
e-mail: henrique.antunes@cebrap.org.br

P. Montero et al. (eds.), *Religious Pluralism and Law in Contemporary Brazil*, Law and Religion in a Global Context 4, https://doi.org/10.1007/978-3-031-41981-2_6

1 Introduction

By the end of the eighteenth century, as Desvallées (2003) reminds us, the notion of heritage usually referred to the theme of transmitting tangible heritage related to family assets. The impacts of the French Revolution, however, marked the emergence of a new meaning associated with the category of heritage, leaving the private domain and embracing the collective heritage expressed in historical monuments, understood hitherto as public assets. Almost a century later, in 1887, the first law for the classification and preservation of historical monuments in France was created. Despite the importance of such landmarks, Desvallés states that the emergence of the modern notion of heritage, linked to the cultural domain, gained strength only in the first decades of the twentieth century through the creation of the *Secrétariat de l'Office International des Musées* (l'OIM). The OIM developed the vocabulary and specific institutional structures for the protection of historical and artistic heritage.

In the case of Brazil, there is an intrinsic relationship between heritage and religion, which refers to the very origins of the notion of cultural heritage in the country at the beginning of the twentieth century. In fact, the preservation of the historical and artistic legacy of the Catholic Church in the country was one of the main concerns of the first patrimonialization policies. From the 1980s onwards, however, this relationship expanded considerably as the legal notion of heritage was extended to include intangible cultural manifestations (Lins et al. 2017).

This novelty substantially broadened the scope of public heritage policies. As a result, many new institutions and religious and non-religious groups began to dispute this new right, claiming recognition of their practices and their legacies as assets of national value. The vast breadth of this new landscape, which goes beyond the scope of religious manifestations and practices, encompassing rituals, celebrations, and traditional knowledge of all kinds, merits a separate study. Thus, within the scope of this chapter, we will restrict our analysis to the interface between religion, law and intangible cultural heritage.

We intend, on the one hand, to describe the convergence of a particular set of processes that enabled the construction of an institutional arrangement forged to develop, within the scope of cultural policies, forms of social recognition aimed at popular manifestations and practices. On the other hand, we seek to analyze the disputes that emerge from implementing these policies, taking a case study as a reference that has gained increasing visibility: the disputes surrounding the patrimonialization policies regarding the religious use of ayahuasca[1] in Brazil.

[1] Ayahuasca, Yagé, Santo Daime, Vegetal, Hoasca, Nixi Pae, Caapi are some of the main names by which the drink produced from two plants native to the Amazon region is known, the *Banisteriopsis caapi* vine and the leaves of a bush, the *Psychothrya viridis*. Ayahuasca has gained notoriety in Brazil and internationally, mainly because it contains, among other psychoactive properties, DMT (n,n-dimethyltryptamine), a controlled substance under the 1971 United Nations Convention on Psychotropic Substances.

Considering that the disputes on the patrimonialization of ayahuasca have emerged during the restructuring of the patrimonialization field in Brazil, we intend to provide an overview of the way in which patrimonialization policies were developed in the country, more specifically regarding intangible heritage. In the first section, we rely on the academic literature to describe the initial moment of developing public policies in the country. Then, through the analysis of interviews, institutional documents from the *Instituto do Patrimônio Histórico e Artístico Nacional* - IPHAN (National Institute of Historic and Artistic Heritage) and national legislation, we describe the emergence of policies aimed at intangible cultural heritage. The following section briefly outlines the convergence between institutional contexts and the international and national debate on intangible heritage.

The final two sections specifically address the case study on the patrimonialization of ayahuasca. Based on a literature review, interviews with actors involved in the process and institutional documents produced by ayahuasca groups, among other sources, we present the main disputes surrounding the recognition process of the religious use of ayahuasca as an intangible heritage of Brazilian culture. The final section discusses the recent role of Amazonian Indigenous Peoples in the ayahuasca patrimonialization process and in drawing up a new political agenda focused on indigenous rights.

In a broader perspective, the present work addresses two key objectives. (1) Apprehending the construction and consolidation of a right from the convergence of various social, historical and institutional processes that occur at different levels and with different temporalities; (2) Demonstrating that the subsequent process of implementing such rights by formulating public policies can give rise to the emergence of a new set of dynamics, tensions, often unforeseen in the letter of the law.

2 IPHAN's Role in Creating the Cultural Heritage Field in Brazil

The creation of the *Instituto do Patrimônio Histórico e Artístico Nacional* - IPHAN (National Institute of Historic and Artistic Heritage) in 1937 can be seen as a starting point for public policies of patrimonialization in Brazil. At the time, there was a heated debate on the dilemma of Brazilian national identity and the attributes of the nation. On the one hand, intellectuals linked to the modernist movement conceived a project to "civilize" and "modernize" Brazil, not only reproducing European nations, but affirming an authentic Brazilian culture (Gonçalves 1996). On the other hand, a political regime was inaugurated that sought a strong and centralized State, and that stipulated the foundations of national identity in the Portuguese and Catholic heritage[2] (Sala 1990).

[2]IPHAN was created shortly after the *coup d'état* that started the dictatorial regime known as *Estado Novo* (New State), under the command of Getúlio Vargas. According to Sala (1990),

IPHAN was initially conceived as an institution whose main focus was scientific research and the development of systematic studies on Brazilian art and history. Its tasks were, however, limited to the issue of tangible heritage, and its role was to identify and select, as well as protect the national historical and artistic heritage. This initiative was an important milestone in affirming the role of the Brazilian State as the holder of the nation's memory and, at the same time, of the national historical and artistic heritage (Chuva 2009, p. 173). According to Gonçalves (1996, p. 43) the goal was to build a notion of heritage as an object of scientific knowledge, but at the same time, as a key component of a nationalist cause.

It is a consensus that this initial period of heritage policies in Brazil was mainly dedicated to the "stone and lime" heritage (Sala 1990; Freitas 1999; Chuva 2009; Santos 2018a). It was only in the 1970s that the expansion of the notion of heritage in Brazil began, accompanied by an increase in public actions related to cultural preservation, and a significant increase of the network of actors and state agencies, as well as non-governmental organizations working with cultural heritage.

One of the protagonists of this new moment is, undoubtedly, Aloísio Magalhães,[3] who coordinated the *Centro Nacional de Referência Cultural*—CNRC (National Cultural Reference Center) in the 1970s and was head of IPHAN from 1979 until his death in 1982. Gonçalves (1996) credits Magalhães the changing of the notion of "historical and artistic heritage" to the category of "cultural assets". In general terms, the notion of "cultural asset" emphasized the present more than the past, highlighting the importance of close contact between local populations and heritage professionals, and underlining the cultural diversity of Brazilian society. The focus shifted, therefore, to diversity as one of the traits of the country's uniqueness *vis-à-vis* other nations, building cultural heterogeneity as one of the most important attributes of Brazilian society. According to Magalhães (Brazil 1982 as cited in Freitas 1999, p. 88):

> [. . .] the approach that the CNRC has given to the concept of cultural assets reaches an area that heritage had overlooked. In other words: the movable cultural heritage, people's activities, craft activities, cultural habits of a community. Heritage worked from top-down and, in a way, with a mainly elitist conception. Churches and monumental buildings are

---

IPHAN, which was initially linked to the Ministry of Education and Health, was part of a broader political project whose ambitions were to make Catholicism and the cult of the country's political leaders the symbolic foundations of a strong and centralized national State. For a contemporary discussion on moral majority and the role of Christianism in Brazilian society, see Bortolin (in this volume).

[3] Aloísio Sérgio Barbosa Magalhães was born in Recife in 1927 and died in 1982. In 1950, he graduated in Law from the Federal University of Pernambuco and studied Museology at the Louvre Museum School in Paris. His role in heritage policies gained ground from the 1970s, when the CNRC began its work at the University of Brasília, under his coordination. The relevance of Magalhaes' trajectory is also highlighted in the institutional narrative of IPHAN, which reaffirms the central role of his work in highlighting the value of popular manifestations in the country (IPHAN 2015, available at http://portal.iphan.gov.br/noticias/detalhes/3216, accessed on 04/04/2020). For an analysis on the CNRC formation and policies, see Londres (2000).

cultural assets, but of a very high standard. They are the most refined result of culture. The CNRC aims to work from the bottom up.

Magalhães' speech shows some tensions and divergences concerning the meaning of the notion of cultural heritage. The emphasis on popular and "cultural habits of a community" is presented as a critique of the notion of heritage in force until that moment, "elitist" and imposed "from top-down". Along the same lines, Gonçalves emphasizes Magalhães' role so that different forms of "popular culture" were valued and presented as a source of an authentic national identity. According to the author, "this pluralist and, in a way, 'anthropological' view of Brazil is, then, conceived by Aloísio and his colleagues as a fundamental instrument in the process of political and sociocultural democratization of Brazilian society" (Gonçalves 1996, p. 56).

This reading is reaffirmed by Anastassakis (2017, p. 65), who points to Aloisio Magalhães' nomination as president of the IPHAN as a shift in public policies on cultural heritage in Brazil, which became increasingly oriented by the "anthropological paradigm." According to Anastassakis, as well as Gonçalves, Magalhães carried out a significant semantic expansion of the concept of cultural heritage, not only incorporating cultural productions of an intangible nature, but also popular culture manifestations.

However, it should be clear that we do not intend to reaffirm a narrative about the impact of Aloísio Magalhães on the field of cultural heritage in Brazil, nor to deny it. Our interest is to highlight the way in which his trajectory in the field of heritage policies is explored by academic literature, as well as by IPHAN, to narrate a turning point in heritage policies. This new moment is marked by a change in the project that was being designed by public policy proponents. From a homogeneous Catholic nation with a clearly defined heritage in its colonial heritage, to the idea of a plural, diverse nation, comprising multiple identities and a wide range of cultural regionalisms. More than a critique of the hegemony of a white and Catholic culture, a new narrative and a new project for a Brazilian nation was at stake, built on diversity and pluralism as its foundation. However, beyond the projects, narratives and the role of their protagonists, it will become clear that the changes that shaped intangible heritage policies in Brazil concern the convergence of a multiplicity of social and historical processes, both at the national and international levels.

3 Intangible Cultural Heritage Policies in Brazil

Although the term "cultural assets" emerged in the 1970s, the notion of intangible heritage only appeared on the public scene in the following decade. According to anthropologist Antônio Arantes[4] (2008, 10), until the early 1980s, the discussion

[4]In interviews, Arantes (2008, 2009, 2015) points out that his trajectory crossed at different times with the theme of cultural heritage. The anthropologist highlights his participation in one of the first inventories promoted by IPHAN, through the CNRC, the Ecological and Cultural Survey Project

focused on folklore and popular culture. Despite the emphasis on the popular aspect of culture, the notion of heritage, continued to be conceived almost exclusively in terms of tangible assets subject to preservation. At the time, there was some resistance regarding the recognition that Brazilian culture had been built from the contribution of different social groups. According to Arantes (2009, p. 5), it was only with the emergence of social movements in the 1970s and 1980s that began to claim a series of civil and political rights, that several segments of Brazilian society began to gain recognition for their agendas in Brazilian legislation.[5]

In addition to the large number of social movements in the 1970s and 80 s and their role in claiming new social demands and in building the agenda for expanding rights, the fact is that the category "intangible cultural heritage" appeared for the first time in a legal scope in Brazil only at the end of the decade, with the promulgation of the 1988 Constitution.[6] The Citizen Constitution, as it became known, established pluralism as a guiding legal principle on the part of the Brazilian State, inserting the issue of diversity in the sphere of rights and supporting cultural identities. At the

---

for the region of Lagoas Mundaú and Manguaba (PLEC), in Maceió, carried out in 1976. In 1983, he became head of the Council for the Defense of Historical, Archaeological, Artistic and Tourist Heritage of the State of São Paulo (CONDEPHAAT). Arantes also emphasizes his role as representative of the Brazilian Association of Anthropology (ABA) during the National Constituent Assembly, in which he helped IPHAN technicians to write the chapter on culture, especially in articles 215 and 216. In 2003, he was invited to preside over IPHAN.

[5] Arantes refers to social movements that emerged on the Brazilian political scene during the decline of the military dictatorial regime and the beginning of the country's democratic transition, which played a decisive role in the struggle for social, political and cultural rights. Indeed, the 1980s in Brazil were marked by the mobilization of social movements that broke out on the political landscape at the end of the 1970s. The *Comunidades Eclesiais de Base* – CEBs (Ecclesial Base Communities), influenced by Liberation Theology, gave rise to social movements for transport and housing. Workers set up trade union centers again from the *Associação Nacional de Movimentos Populares e Sindicais* – ANAMPOS (National Association of Popular and Trade Union Movements), and the *Confederação Geral dos Trabalhadores* – CGT (General Confederation of Workers) and the *Central Única dos Trabalhadores* (CUT) (United Workers Front) were created. In the countryside, the *Movimento de Trabalhadores Rurais Sem Terra* – MST (Landless Workers' Movement) emerged (Gohn 2000). There was a significant expansion of debates on the indigenous issue, and NGOs and the indigenous associations were created in various parts of Brazil (Silva 2018a). The period was also marked by several initiatives of the black movement, such as the creation of cultural centers and the strengthening of the black press. In 1978, the *Movimento Negro Unificado* (Unified Black Movement) was founded, contributing to the advancement of the anti-racist agenda (Domingues 2007). The LGBT movement was also present in the second half of the 1970s, after associations and NGOs were created aiming to ensure rights related to free sexual orientation (Facchini 2003).

[6] Article 215 of the section "On culture" stipulates the guarantee, by the Brazilian State, of the full exercise of cultural rights and the access to sources of national culture, providing support and encouragement to the appreciation and dissemination of Brazilian cultural manifestations. The article also establishes the duty of the State to protect "manifestations of popular, indigenous and Afro-Brazilian cultures, and those of other groups participating in the national civilizing process" (Brasil 1988, p. 126). Article 216 establishes for the first time the notion of "intangible heritage," including forms of expression, ways of creating, doing and living that serve as references to the identity and memory of the different groups that form Brazilian society.

same time, this new legal framework stirred a number of groups and associations to incorporate the discourse of social and cultural rights as a form of public action (Montero 2018).

From the 1988 Constitution, therefore, the notion of citizenship built around the idea of diversity gave rise to the emergence of new disputes and claims around civil and cultural rights in the country, creating a space for new political demands in the name of culture. Regarding policies aimed at intangible heritage, the approval of a new Constitution containing a plural concept of nation raised a new problem: the need to create legal mechanisms to implement it (Arantes 2009, pp. 6–7). However, such instruments were only developed in the late 1990s. In 1997, IPHAN promoted an international seminar in Fortaleza to discuss strategies and ways of protecting intangible heritage. The following year, the Ministry of Culture instituted Ordinance no. 37, of March 4, 1998, creating a commission to prepare the guidelines for the regulation of Brazilian intangible heritage. The ordinance also created a Working Group to advise the commission that conducted research on the Brazilian experience and on recommendations, experiences and international legislation on the subject (Arantes 2015, p. 228).

However, the creation of the legal instrument that allowed the development of policies and actions aimed at safeguarding intangible heritage at a federal level, Decree-Law 3551, only took place in 2000 (Brasil 2000a). The decree, which established the registration of cultural assets of an intangible nature, was conceived by IPHAN and the Ministry of Culture (MinC), with the collaboration of specialists from different fields. It was during this time that Arantes received the invitation, from Célia Corsino, museologist and technician at IPHAN, to develop the methodology that was adopted by the intangible heritage inventory. These discussions lead to developing the *Inventário Nacional de Referências Culturais* - INRC (National Inventory of Cultural References),[7] coordinated by Arantes.

According to IPHAN, the INRC focused on the need to democratize the notion of cultural heritage by devising a new instrument based on the instruments and methodologies of social sciences to identify and document cultural assets and, consequently, to preserve these assets. According to Arantes (2015, p. 241), the aim was to adopt the notion of "cultural reference" as a legal-administrative parameter and create the means to apply it. According to the agency:

> We had to analyze previous thoughts and experiences in more depth [...] and evolve towards making new instruments, capable of surveying and identifying cultural assets of a diversified nature, apprehending the senses and meanings attributed to them by social groups and finding appropriate ways to preserve them (Brasil 2000b, p. 7).

[7]Regarding the creation of this new instrument, IPHAN states: "The identification of new cultural assets, representative of different social groups, and the construction of instruments and methods suitable for their research and valorization have been discussed for a long time. Especially after the promulgation of the 1988 Constitution, which incorporates the anthropological (and much more democratic) *vision of culture and the notions of cultural asset, cultural dynamics and cultural reference*, already adopted and experimented by the CNRC and proMemoria" (Brasil 2000b, p. 7, emphasis added).

The goal was, therefore, to develop a specific instrument for the intangible heritage, since, according to Arantes (2015, p. 233) "it was not enough to simply add information of a sociocultural nature to the existing architectural and urban inventory instruments, we had to create others". Specifically, the anthropologist stresses that IPHAN members did not have, until that moment, the technical knowledge that would lead to planning research, writing interview scripts and questionnaires, or the systematizing results that could subsidize programs and policies of this new area of research (Arantes 2015, p. 234).

The INRC was created to meet this new demand in heritage policies. According to the IPHAN's INRC Application Manual, one of the main objectives that determined its design was to identify and document "cultural assets to meet the demand for recognizing assets representative of the cultural diversity and plurality of the groups that form society" (Brasil 2000b, p. 8). In this matter, Arantes (2009, pp. 7–8) states:

> At that time, a team from my office and I worked as consultants and, at the request of IPHAN, we developed the methodology used in Brazil's intangible cultural heritage inventory, which still guides the registration processes. This methodology considers, above all, that the identification of significant cultural practices must start from the values attributed by the social groups involved. [...] And it wasn't us who conceived things this way; it is the new Constitution that articulates the assets that constitute the cultural heritage of the nation to the references of identities of the social groups that form it. Now, the almost unsolvable problem faced is to identify the social groups that make up the nation. This is a serious issue that requires quite complex decisions. Not just decisions of a technical nature, but basically decisions of a political nature. Of course, a dialogue between the State and society is involved. The groups propose recognition processes; but we should check if they are upheld, if they make sense to the wider society and in terms of the current legislation.

Some important points appear in the anthropologist's speech. On the one hand, the parameters stipulated by the Constitution shifted the focus to the actors themselves, their values, practices and knowledge, boosting the production of collective identities. On the other hand, the is the problem of how the claims put forward by these social groups are perceived by the public opinion and by the Brazilian society as a whole, and how these demands are framed under Brazilian legislation. Furthermore, the shift towards the references of the actors and groups themselves highlights an important question about who defines and decides what will be recognized as heritage. This problem leads us to the growing work of a group of specialists from different fields of knowledge in developing criteria and parameters to stablish the practices that could be framed as cultural heritage.

As Fassin (2012) indicates, developing public policies involves stabilizing an institutional analytical framework and establishing procedures and protocols recognized by conventions. This process implies the articulation of a particular set of actors, giving rise to a new lexicon and, consequently, a new horizon of public actions. This procedure is evident in cultural heritage policies in Brazil. In fact, Arantes emphasizes the importance of specialists endowed with "technical knowledge" and also the "sensitivity" required to create procedures for selecting and managing this heritage:

> I was invited to preside over IPHAN in 2003, the year in which, in fact, two important things happened. One was the creation of the Department of Intangible Heritage, bringing together specialists, not only from the traditional areas of architecture, history and archaeology, but also anthropologists, geographers, museologists and people with other backgrounds, holders of specific *sensitivity* and *technical knowledge* for this other type of heritage asset. Another was the implementation of the National Program for Intangible Heritage, with its own funds. Previously people could not work in this area because there was no *legal instrument*, there were no *administrative and technical procedures*, nor *qualified personnel* or even *budgetary resources*, however, in 2003 this began to change (Arantes 2009, p. 9, emphasis added).

Arantes (2015, p. 235) emphasizes that the methodology[8] adopted by IPHAN to carry out cultural inventories referring to intangible heritage was built "in the field," as the result of the "experience, persistence and competence of a group of specially selected researchers" who were part of his team, which included Social Sciences students from undergraduate to doctoral level. According to the anthropologist, it was established that the methodology should not be developed in advance but based on the issues that arose from interactions between researchers and the local population, which provided collaborators to develop the cultural inventory. One can note that, despite the undeniable emphasis given by the public policy proponents to the values and knowledge of social groups, it is evident that this did not exclude the requirement of a group of specialists in charge of developing and defining the technical and administrative procedures that guided the definition of Brazilian cultural heritage.

4 Convergence Between National and International Contexts

Leaving aside for the moment the specificities of the national context, it should be mentioned that heritage policies cannot be understood in isolation from the international context.[9] In light of this, the recent approach adopted by the Brazilian government was part of a set of actions adopted worldwide in recent decades.

[8] According to Arantes (2015, p. 242): "The instrument, as a whole, was conceived from two notions. On the one hand, the notion of totality with regard to social practices, in the Maussian sense of the term; and, on the other hand, the idea of variation, that is, that a structure can assume different configurations in different contexts, with the occurrence of variants being a structural principle of the reality studied, and the various observed phenomena, possible embodiments of these same basic principles."

[9] As Dias (2020, p. 168) points out, the theme of "cultural policies" acquired centrality in the scope of UNESCO, especially from the 1960s onwards, marking the beginning of growing concern to articulate the issues of culture and development. One of the landmarks of this process was the *Declaration sur les droits culturels en tant que droits de l'homme* from 1970, which built an isonomy between the work of the UN and that carried out by UNESCO, postulating the existence of cultural rights and the perspective of its guarantee and defense, supported by an expanded grammar of human rights. According to Dias, there has been, since then, a clear intention by UNESCO to coordinate and expand cultural policies in its member nations.

Among them, it is worth mentioning the UNESCO's Convention for the Safeguarding of Intangible Cultural Heritage (CSICH),[10] ratified in 2003, to which Brazil is a signatory. The CSICH stipulated that the international community should contribute with the signatory States of the convention, working towards increasing "the need to build greater awareness, especially among the younger generations, of the importance of the intangible cultural heritage and of its safeguarding" (UNESCO 2003, p. 3). The Convention attempted, therefore, to define "intangible cultural heritage".

> The "intangible cultural heritage" means the practices, representations, expressions, knowledge, skills – as well as the instruments, objects, artefacts and cultural spaces associated therewith – that communities, groups and, in some cases, individuals recognize as part of their cultural heritage. This intangible cultural heritage, transmitted from generation to generation, is constantly recreated by communities and groups in response to their environment, their interaction with nature and their history, and provides them with a sense of identity and continuity, thus promoting respect for cultural diversity and human creativity. (UNESCO 2003, p. 4).

The notion of intangible heritage developed by UNESCO involves the idea of a set of collective practices transmitted generationally, contemplating feelings of identity and continuity. The convention also calls for respect for cultural diversity, proposing heritage policies that are in line with human rights and the principle of sustainable development. UNESCO's notion of intangible cultural heritage is conceived as something that arises from the interaction between communities and the environment, from an encounter between nature and history. Thus, there is a clear orientation towards valuing the practices of autochthonous societies, reiterating that communities, especially indigenous ones, "play an important role in the production, safeguarding, maintenance and re-creation of the intangible cultural heritage, thus helping to enrich cultural diversity and human creativity" (UNESCO 2003, p. 3). It can be affirmed, therefore, that one of the main outcomes of UNESCO's actions in the field of cultural heritage refers to the strengthening of cultural diversity in the list of human rights, granting it legitimacy and calling for its preservation.

UNESCO's political orientation can be understood as one of the features of a new international conjuncture characterized by a marked acceleration of heritage production, involving new actors and a network of constantly expanding agencies and institutions (Meyer and van de Port 2018, p. 7). This phenomenon has led some authors to speak of a "*heritage craze*." However, Meyer and van de Port opt for the term "*heritage buzz*" to refer to the growing interest in the topic. Despite the conceptual divergence, Meyer and van de Port recognize that there is, in fact, widespread enthusiasm in the attention that the idea of heritage is receiving worldwide. The rapid growth in the number of actors seeking to include new items in heritage agencies' inventory lists, as well as the sheer diversity of objects and practices that are considered eligible for recognition as heritage, indicate that the

---

[10]The Convention established a set of parameters and responsibilities, both on the part of civil society and national States, regarding the recognition of intangible cultural heritage (UNESCO 2003, p. 3).

notion has successfully traveled the world, especially with the rise of UNESCO policies to safeguard "world heritage."

This new landscape has led to the emergence of complex processes of lobbying, consultation, investigation, public debates, fundraising, in addition to bureaucratic procedures for institutionalizing and producing public policies on a global scale. As a result, the emergence of debates about who should be included or not in the list of heritage assets has led social movements, NGOs and interest groups to enter the field of heritage policies, questioning the legitimacy of some heritage assets, as well as developing alternative inventory lists (Meyer and van de Port 2018, p. 8).

This brief outlook on the debate around the patrimonialization landscape in an international context allows us to affirm that the construction of the problem of recognition and the need to preserve intangible cultural heritage, as well as the growing demands for recognition, are not a Brazilian particularity. On the contrary, it seems to be a complex phenomenon that has progressively become a global trend that often goes beyond the borders of national states, encompassing transnational networks of activists and institutions.

Having said that, we understand that, regarding the Brazilian context, the development of intangible cultural heritage policies in recent decades is the result of the convergence of a series of social and institutional processes with different temporalities and characteristics. Among them: the insertion and articulation, from the 1970s onwards, of a set of key actors in government branches, supporting a political project based on the knowledge of social sciences, especially anthropology, to frame a wide range of popular traditions and practices as cultural attributes of the nation; an increase in the mobilizations of various social movements in the context of political reopening and redemocratization that began in the late 1970s; the adoption of a pluralist model as a legal framework in the 1988 Constitution; the actions of international bodies in recent decades and the expansion of heritage processes on a global scale; and the more recent phenomenon of creating legal and administrative procedures, as well as the establishment of a technical team of professionals to develop the parameters for implementing policies on intangible cultural heritage in the country.

It should be clear, however, that it is not simply a matter of describing the emergence of policies on intangible heritage in Brazil, nor of assigning causal explanations. On the contrary, our objective is to underline the convergence of a particular set of processes that made it possible to construct an institutional arrangement forged to develop, within the scope of cultural policies, forms of social recognition directed to popular practices. These legal mechanisms are presented by public policy proponents as part of a democratization project developed to materialize constitutional principles, filling a gap in cultural recognition policies by giving visibility to the demands of social segments that until then were being neglected.

Despite the intentions and goals of its proponents, however, one of the main consequences of this new institutional arrangement is the emergence of a particular form of public policy in Brazil, in which various groups and actors now have an unprecedented legal instrument to render their claims public and dispute the cultural heritage field. This new framework can be seen by the cultural assets and practices already inventoried and recognized so far, which range from popular festivals such as pilgrimages and processions; knowledge, such as the production of *acarajé* (fritter made from black-eyed peas), cheese from Minas Gerais and gourds from the Amazon; artistic expressions, such as *samba de roda* (participants joining in a circle to perform music, dance and poetry), *jongo* (a dance and musical genre of black communities from southeast Brazil), *frevo* (a dance and musical style originating from Recife, Pernambuco), *maracatu* (several performance genres found in Pernambuco), *roda de capoeira* (Brazilian martial art that combines elements of dance, acrobatics, and music), the popular puppet theater from the northeast, *cordel* literature (popular and inexpensive printed booklets containing folk novels, poems and songs); in addition to places, such as the fairs in Caruaru and Campina Grande, among dozens of manifestations encompassed by the notion of intangible heritage of Brazilian culture.

As stated earlier, within this broad universe of practices and expressions, we intend to look specifically at the relation between religion, cultural heritage and law, focusing on the process of patrimonialization of the religious use of ayahuasca as a privileged case study of implementing such policies. As we intend to demonstrate, the processes and disputes that involve implementing a right in the form of public policies are no less complex than those that involve its formulation. On the contrary, these imply several intersections between the academic universe, political activism and legal issues, as well as between a heterogeneous set of actors that articulate, building alliances and disputing the possible directions of public policies concerning the use of ayahuasca in Brazil.

5 The Patrimonialization of the Religious Use of Ayahuasca in Dispute

The use of ayahuasca is currently widespread in Brazil. Ayahuasca consumption is practiced by several Amazonian indigenous ethnic groups, as well as groups recognized by the Brazilian government and academic literature as "Brazilian ayahuasca religions" (Labate and Araújo 2002)—*Santo Daime*, *Barquinha* and *União do Vegetal* (UDV). Furthermore, many contemporary manifestations can be found under the category of "*neo-ayahuasqueiros*" (Labate 2004), referring to new modalities of ayahuasca consumption in urban centers, ranging from artistic to psychotherapeutic use, incorporating elements of Brazilian ayahuasca religions, orientalists, new age, neoshamanic, among other references.

The use of ayahuasca became an object of public policy in Brazil in the 1980s, when the brew was temporarily banned in 1985 by the *Divisão de Medicamentos*—DIMED (Drug Division). At the request of the UDV, the *Conselho Federal de Entorpecentes*—CONFEN (Federal Council on Narcotics) decided to organize a working group to examine the issue. In 1987, after 2 years of research, interviews, bibliographic surveys and participation in rituals, the working group prepared a Final

Report that recommended the suspension of the ban on the religious use of ayahuasca in the country (Brasil 1987). In the following decades, public policies on ayahuasca progressively moved towards the process of regulating the use of the brew, culminating in the creation of parameters on the responsible use of ayahuasca, understood as strictly religious, non-profit and based on the idea of sustainability (Antunes 2019).

From the second half of the 2000s onwards, however, the public debate on ayahuasca underwent a significant change, as its religious use was no longer the object of drug policies and began to be the focus of public policies of patrimonialization. On this matter, the year of 2008 was an important milestone, given the request for recognizing ayahuasca as intangible heritage of Brazilian culture submitted to IPHAN (Acre 2008). The request was the result of a partnership between representatives from *Santo Daime* (CICLU-Alto Santo[11]), *Barquinha*, *UDV*, and representatives from the cultural foundations of Acre, the *Fundação de Cultura e Comunicação Elias Mansour*—FEM (Elias Mansour Culture and Communication Foundation) and the *Fundação Garibaldi Brasil* (Garibaldi Brasil Foundation). In an interview with the anthropologist Beatriz Labate, Marcos Vinicius Neves[12] addressed the discussions that led to preparing the request:

> This process basically started three years ago [2006], when had a meeting with the cultural foundations, both the State Foundation and the Municipal Foundation, and the office of State Representative Perpétua Almeida (PCdoB – Communist Party of Brazil), as well as the leaders and representatives of the more traditional centers here in Acre, specifically *Alto Santo*, *Barquinha* and *União do Vegetal*. So, we decided that the time had come [...] to start an affirmative action in a completely different direction, a new approach, which is to recognize traditional ayahuasca cultures. [...] Affirming not only the cultural expression, but also the historical trajectory of these pioneer and traditional communities that brought hope to the national culture as a whole.[13]

According to Neves, therefore, it was a matter of setting new guidelines for public policies on ayahuasca in Brazil, no longer focusing strictly on the religious aspect, but on affirmative policies to safeguard the history of ayahuasca communities and recognize the use of ayahuasca as a traditional Amazonian cultural expression. Hence, the request should be understood from the background of a specific political moment in Acre, in which some key actors close to ayahuasca groups of Rio Branco

[11]The *Centro Iluminação Cristã Luz Universal* - CICLU-Alto Santo (Universal Light Christian Center) is the first *Santo Daime* church, founded by Raimundo Irineu Serra, in the 1930s. The CICLU-Alto is restricted to its headquarters in Rio Branco.

[12]Historian and archaeologist, he was one of the proponents of the patrimonialization request sent to IPHAN. He integrated the public sector in cultural heritage in the State of Acre, working for 2 years at the *Fundação Garibaldi Brasil* and then, for 6 years, at the Department of Historical Heritage of the State Government and the Cultural Foundation of the State. He has been Director-President of the Municipal Culture Foundation of Rio Branco since 2005.

[13]Interview with Beatriz Labate held on July 10, 2009. Available at: https://www.bialabate.net/texts/ayahuasca-como-patrimonio-imaterial-da-cultura-brasileira, accessed on 05/16/2018.

were inserted in strategic[14] government sectors. This network of key actors marked the beginning of a different approach regarding public policies on ayahuasca, no longer related to drug policies, and inserted in the fields of culture and the environment (Assis and Rodrigues 2017).

Despite this intense political movement, it is important to emphasize that IPHAN refused the initial request to register the use of ayahuasca as intangible heritage of Brazilian culture, based on the argument that food or drinks, as well as philosophies, theologies and beliefs could not be considered cultural assets subject to registration, but references for the production and reproduction of cultural practices. However, there was also an understanding on the part of the Department of Intangible Heritage (DPI) at IPHAN that the agency could face external pressure or future claims, due to the fact that the request did not include several ayahuasca groups, nor the indigenous populations that consume ayahuasca. There was, above all, a concern that indigenous groups would claim the usurpation of their knowledge, if the registration was exclusively linked to certain groups[15] (Iphan *apud* Neves 2017, p. 163).

Despite the initial refusal, IPHAN designated the creation of the *Inventário Nacional de Referências Culturais*—INRC (National Inventory of Cultural References). In September 2011, the started a bidding process to carry out the inventory. The company that won the bid, whose managers are members of a UDV church in Rio Branco, set up a team that included the participation of anthropologists experts in ayahuasca, such as Wladimyr Sena Araújo, Sandra Goulart and Edward MacRae. The team started developing the inventory in 2012 (Labate and Goulart 2016, pp. 7–8).[16]

In addition to the patrimonialization request, it should be pointed out that the Ayahuasca religious groups in Acre have developed other strategies to strengthen their demands, such as the organization of the "Seminar: Traditional Ayahuasca Communities", held in 2010 in the city of Rio Branco. The seminar was proposed by

[14] Among these actors, it is worth mentioning the State Representative Perpétua Almeida from the Communist Party of Brazil (PCdoB); journalist Antônio Alves, from CICLU-Alto Santo, and a member of the Workers' Party (PT) and president of the Elias Mansour Culture and Communication Foundation (FEM); historian Marcos Vinícius Neves (cited above), the federal judge Jair Facundes, a friend of CICLU, among others (Assis and Rodrigues 2017). It is from this narrowing of political alliances that the "Thematic Chamber of Ayahuasqueira Cultures" was created in 2008, whose meetings included representatives from CICLU-Alto Santo, *Barquinha* and *UDV*.

[15] According to IPHAN: "The Advisory Board urged clarification on the cultural expression in question and the inclusion of indigenous people in the process, considering the fact that ayahuasca tea is knowledge originating from indigenous peoples and that, therefore, they could see the registration of tea linked to other groups as a usurpation of their knowledge" (Iphan *apud* Barros 2016, p. 248).

[16] According to Labate and Assis (2018, p. 224): "In October 2014, IPHAN's recommendations on the inventory were sent to its technical team, which proceeded to re-elaborate the report, which in turn corresponds to the first of the three stages of the register process. The Final Report of this stage, with a qualitative analysis that addressed the social, pharmacological, legal and religious aspects of ayahuasca, was completed in 2015, and presented in the city of Rio Branco, Acre on August 22, 2017. However, this has not yet identified which cultural assets would be registered for patrimonialization". So far, we have not had access to the report.

the Thematic Chamber of Ayahuasca Cultures of Acre and the Municipal Council for Cultural Policies, with the presence of representatives of local ayahuasca religious groups, the Ministry of Culture (MinC), IPHAN and the cultural foundations of Acre. On this particular occasion, the ayahuasca groups requested the involvement of the Legislative Assembly and the parliamentarians representing Acre in the National Congress, as well as the municipal, state and federal public authorities, to assist in the processes of shaping public policies for "ayahuasca cultures." According to representatives of Ayahuasca religious organizations in Acre, their claims mainly concerned the recognition of their practices and the fight against religious intolerance and stigma associated with ayahuasca[17] (Acre 2010, p. 1).

Nevertheless, the initiative of these groups to invest in the idea of a shared cultural tradition in order to demand recognition from different sectors of public power does not mean that there is a consensus or a common project for groups that consume ayahuasca. On the contrary, the process of recognizing the religious use of ayahuasca as an intangible heritage of Brazilian culture is full of tensions and disputes. In fact, the early years of the 2010s were marked by articulations and tensions between ayahuasca groups and public institutions to participate in the cultural inventory. These articulations mainly refer to the question of defining which cultural references would constitute the common core between the different ayahuasca segments (Labate and Coutinho 2014).

Tensions on this issue were highlighted at different occasions, such as at the *I Encontro da Diversidade Ayahuasqueira* (I Meeting on the Cultural Diversity of Ayahuasca), held in Rio de Janeiro in 2011. The meeting was organized by various groups previously excluded from the debate, among them the *Igreja do Centro Eclético da Fluente Luz Universal*—ICEFLU (Church of the Eclectic Center of the Fluent Universal Light)—the first dissident of the Santo Daime and the main group responsible for its expansion in Brazil and internationally –, in addition to other ayahuasca groups and representatives of indigenous ethnic groups in Acre. The event was supported by MinC and IPHAN. The meeting is seen by the academic literature as a reaction and a response to the "Seminar: Traditional Ayahuasca Communities"[18] (Assis and Rodrigues 2017). According to the organizers, the purpose of the event was to identify and register "ayahuasca diversity," enabling an expansion of the request for ayahuasca patrimonialization undertaken by ayahuasca groups in Acre. The event was marked by strong criticism of the request sent to

[17]It is not uncommon for policies on intangible heritage to involve processes of social legitimation through the symbolic positivization of stigmatized practices, such as the practice of producing and selling *acarajé* in Bahia. Historically persecuted and marginalized until the mid-twentieth century, it has become a Brazilian intangible cultural heritage, and symbol of Bahian cuisine and traditional culture (Reinhardt 2018). Similarly, the use of ayahuasca moved between different stigmas, from macumba and charlatanism in the first half of the twentieth century, to its association with drug consumption in recent decades (Goulart 2008).

[18]The Ayahuasca groups from Acre that organized the seminar were invited to the meeting in Rio de Janeiro, but refused to participate.

IPHAN, mainly for not including the Indigenous Peoples that use ayahuasca in the request (Labate and Goulart 2016, pp. 8–9).

In this context, it is important to highlight two documents that resulted from the meeting: the *Manifesto da Diversidade Cultural Ayahuasqueira* (Ayahuasca Cultural Diversity Manifesto) and the *Carta para o Encontro da Diversidade Cultural Ayahuasqueira* (Letter to the Ayahuasca Cultural Diversity Meeting) signed by Alex Polari, member of the ICEFLU doctrinal council. The "Manifesto"—signed by Santo Daime groups, independent ayahuasca organizations and representatives of Indigenous Peoples—reaffirmed the importance of the religious use of ayahuasca in Brazilian religiosity and culture, highlighting the need for broadening the diversity that characterizes the ayahuasca universe. According to the document:

> What we can call the ayahuasca field nowadays went beyond the Amazon forest during the twentieth century, since its beginnings, being implanted in the capitals of practically all Brazilian states. They are the most diverse symbolic expressions that, beyond their immediate cataloging, express the Brazilian religious and cultural ethos, whose cradle can be found in the miscegenation of the Brazilian people, in its indigenous, Afro-descendant, Eastern and European expressions and manifestations. [...] The I Ayahuasca Cultural Diversity Meeting is the expression of the richness of this movement (Rio de Janeiro 2011, pp. 1–2).

On the other hand, the letter sent by the ICEFLU representative presented a harsher tone in relation to the ways in which the patrimonialization process was being conceived at that time. The initial criticism mentioned the non-inclusion of representatives of Indigenous Peoples, ancestral holders of this heritage according to Polari, and condemned the exclusion of groups considered relevant to the tradition of the religious use of ayahuasca without any prior consultation or debate. Furthermore, Polari rejected the classification given to ICEFLU, framed under the "eclectic" category.[19] According to the ICEFLU representative, it was not a matter of affirming the position of "traditional" or of denying the classification of "eclectic", but of problematizing the way in which the construction of "a 'theory of the 3 fields' (originators, traditional and eclectic) represents more the attempt at a political solution, than properly raising a methodological rigor that could face the difficult issue of ayahuasca diversity" (Alverga 2011).

[19] According to Labate and Goulart (2016, p. 7) the creation of a new classification arrangement is an important novelty in this debate, initiating a distinction between "originators," "traditional" and "eclectic" segments. The category "originators" encompasses the various indigenous ethnic groups that consume ayahuasca. The "traditional" category concerns the "three founding masters" of the three "ayahuasca branches," *Santo Daime* (CICLU-Alto Santo), *Barquinha* and UDV, which express traditional Amazonian culture, however, adopting a markedly Christian stance. The "eclectic" category, on the other hand, refers to the *Santo Daime* group ICEFLU—which vehemently rejects such a notion—and also include other expressions, such as institutions classified under the "neo-ayahuascans" rubric. According to Marcos Vinícius Neves, the idea of this classification emerged in a meeting in 2007, in which leaders of the ayahuasca groups of Acre discussed with Federal Deputy Perpétua Almeida (PCdoB) about the possibilities of creating public policies focusing on ayahuasca (Neves 2017, p. 176).

For ICEFLU, the State should begin by inventorying the indigenous and pan-Amazonian ancestral origin of ayahuasca, moving on to forms of *pajelança* (a religious manifestation focused on treating physical and spiritual diseases) and then to contemporary developments, "covering both traditionalist and eclectic elements, contained in the urban and genuinely Brazilian religious phenomenon of the *Santo Daime* Christian religions". According to Polari, ICEFLU considers "the sacramental brew the primary fact of the ayahuasca culture" and "along with its ritualized nature, authentic sacred alchemy, with an elaborate system of symbolic prescriptions and the beauty of its ceremonial, as the core of 'designating it as historical heritage'" (Alverga 2011).

In response to criticisms about the non-inclusion of Indigenous Peoples, the actors who elaborated the request sent to IPHAN argued that the request did not require the consultation of Indigenous Peoples, because the indigenous use of ayahuasca constitutes a distinct phenomenon, associated with international Pan-Amazonian identity and culture, while the use made by ayahuasca religions were part of the national culture. Regarding the excluding groups classified as "eclectic," the proponents of the request stated that the request sent to IPHAN focused solely on the cultural traditions associated with the founding masters of the three Brazilian ayahuasca religions, but not on later developments.[20]

Other disagreements about possible projects for ayahuasca patrimonialization can be observed in Marcos Vinícius Neves' speech, when interviewed by anthropologist Beatriz Labate about the specific focus of the request developed by the ayahuasca religious groups of Acre. According to Neves:

> Our focus is cultural, our focus is historical, not religious. [...] We cannot forget that the founding masters of the most traditional branches of ayahuasca had a common historical process. [...] They were very successful in inserting it into the local society, making an impressive transposition of expressions that were traditionally indigenous [...] to Brazilian society. This is the project, this is the focus. It is an affirmative action that does not seek to deny anything that exists today [...] only the affirmation, the more precise delimitation of the social phenomenon that happened in the western Amazon, and the recognition of this as part of national culture. [...] And it seems to us, to all who participate in this movement, that this is what was relegated to the background, as ayahuasca began to be discussed in other areas.

Hence, there is an obvious dispute regarding the possible paths for the patrimonialization of ayahuasca between the ayahuasca religious groups themselves. Other points of tension were evident at the II World Ayahuasca Conference, held in Rio Branco, in October 2016. As in the first conference, the event was organized by the Spanish NGO ICEERS, and was attended by representatives of various indigenous ethnic groups of Acre, of ayahuasca religious groups, IPHAN representatives,

[20] MacRae (in press) understands this categorization as an arbitrary attempt from the Acre groups, who claim the notion of "traditional" in order to exclude ICEFLU from the patrimonialization process. ICELFU is portrayed, according to MacRae, as a rupture with the original church founded by Raimundo Irineu Serra, despite its founder, Sebastião Motta de Melo, having been a direct follower of Irineu Serra and a member of the CICLU-Alto Santo between 1965 and 1975.

as well as therapists, sociologists, anthropologists, physicians, politicians and local authorities (Labate and Assis 2018).

Regarding the IPHAN's position, there were questions regarding the expected directions for the process. According to Gusmão, who works at DPI/IPHAN-Brasília, the suggestion of an object to be registered with the INRC did not fit in any of the existing records in Brazil.

> Ayahuasca registration is not possible. What we can think, considering the registration, is some cultural expression related to what we call a cultural system linked to the use of ayahuasca. So, a celebration? It would be possible! A specific knowledge that is suddenly related to preparing the brew or preparing the ceremony? We can register this. But the brew itself cannot be registered. It doesn't fit in any of those little boxes. It doesn't fit in any of those books (Gusmão *apud* Santos 2018b: 107).

The IPHAN representative refers to the four intangible heritage domains: knowledge, celebrations, forms of expression, places. Thus, ICEFLU's request that the registration should begin with the beverage itself did not fit the current legislation, as ayahuasca was not subject to registration, only the practices associated with it. In Gusmão's view, there was, therefore, a bigger problem to be faced. According to the member of IPHAN, until that moment, a specific frame had not been defined that could fit the normative stipulated by the Brazilian legislation. Thus, the challenges faced in implementing public policies surpassed the difficulties of equating a multiplicity of voices and different demands. The need to consider the claims of actors within a pre-established legal and institutional framework required, therefore, an articulation and negotiation process between state actors and the interested parties to define which practices should integrate the cultural inventory.

In addition to the problem raised by the IPHAN representative, it is worth noting that the organizers of the event called a meeting closed to the public to discuss proposals on recognizing ayahuasca as a cultural heritage of humanity by UNESCO. The universalist tone of the proposal was criticized mainly by representatives of Indigenous Peoples. According to Labate and Goulart (2017), the problematization by indigenous leaders of the "authenticity," "originality" and "traditionality" or lack thereof of religious groups was also worthy of note, as an indigenous representative claimed that "while *Mestre* (Master) Irineu is a hundred years old, we are millenary" (MacRae in press).

The discontent of indigenous peoples was reaffirmed in the "Open Letter of the Indigenous Peoples of Acre / Brazil to the II World Ayahuasca Conference" (Acre 2016). According to the document, despite the considerable number of indigenous participants, they did not feel that they were included in envisaging and organizing the event. Among the main points, the letter emphasized the need for an active participation of Indigenous Peoples in the ayahuasca patrimonialization process. The letter also recommended holding indigenous meetings with the presence of the government agencies responsible for the process, even suggesting the constitution of an ethics council "to discuss the issue of origin and define criteria on the use and patrimonialization of Ayahuasca" (Acre 2016). Undoubtedly, the event was an important milestone in the debate, as, from that moment on, various Indigenous Peoples from Acre began a different strategy, no longer associated with the neo-ayahuasca and religious groups in the Southeast of Brazil. Therefore, the questioning of the "authenticity" and "originality" of the ayahuasca religions and the attempt to develop a political agenda of their own mark a distance from the groups in question. From then on, it was a matter of seeking an exclusively indigenous alliance to dispute the patrimonialization process.

By and large, this context of debates, disputes and negotiations, observed throughout the conference, explains the complexity of the political processes that involve the issue of recognizing intangible heritage in Brazil. Regarding the case of ayahuasca, this process reveals a redefinition of the debate, as well as the emergence of new alliances and of new demands for recognition. In this new landscape, the more incisive presence and growing protagonism of Indigenous Peoples have become key elements responsible for blurring the categories and classifications previously established in the public debate on the use of ayahuasca in Brazil. Indigenous Peoples began to organize themselves as a new force in the dispute for the patrimonialization of the religious use of ayahuasca. As we will see below, their views and claims not only question the authenticity of the Ayahuasca religious groups, but also the legitimacy and capacity of the Brazilian State to contemplate their demands.

6 The Ayahuasca "Guardians:" Original Rights and Political Protagonism of Indigenous Peoples

Despite the fact that indigenous peoples entered the public debate on the patrimonialization policies of the religious use of ayahuasca starting in the 2010s, their presence into urban ayahuasca scene—hitherto predominantly occupied by ayahuasca religions and neoayahuasca groups—dates back to the early 2000s. Their activities included multicultural festivals, held in Acre villages, workshops in large cities in Brazil, as well as retreats and ceremonies promoted for middle-class groups and foreigners[21] (Labate and Coutinho 2014).

Regarding public policies, the first significant appearance of indigenous groups in the debate on patrimonialization occurred approximately 4 months after the "Seminar: Traditional Ayahuasca Communities" was held. According to Labate and Coutinho (2014), in August 2010, representatives of the *Pano* peoples met with the executive secretary of the Ministry of Culture, Alfredo Manevy, to emphasize the need to include indigenous peoples in the patrimonialization process of the religious use of ayahuasca.[22]

---

[21] For an analysis of ayahuasca's emerging status as a commodity in international trade networks and the global economic system of the early twenty-first century, see Tupper (2017).

[22] Despite the fact that Indigenous Peoples were included at a later date in the public policy process on the religious use of ayahuasca, we should emphasize that the political action of the former is not a recent phenomenon. Its political role in the Brazilian public space dates back to the 1970s and, later,

Notwithstanding this first initiative, the protagonism of indigenous peoples gained strength, especially after the II World Ayahuasca Conference. As we pointed out in the previous section, the event generated a series of reactions from members of indigenous ethnic groups in the Amazon region, who contested the ways in which the patrimonialization process was being conducted, demanding a larger role in this debate.

Many of these criticisms were reaffirmed at the I Yubaká Hayrá—Ayahuasca Indigenous Conference, held from December 14 to 17, 2017, in the Poyanawa Indigenous Land, in Acre. The conference was organized under the coordination of the *Organização dos Povos Indígenas do Rio Juruá*—OPIRJ (Organization of Indigenous Peoples of the Juruá River), *Organização dos Povos Indígenas de Taraucá*—OPITAR (Organization of the Indigenous Peoples of Taraucá), *Organização dos Povos Indígenas do Rio Envira*—OPIRE (Organization of the Indigenous Peoples of the Envira River) and the *Associação dos Seringueiros Kaxinawá do Rio Jordão*—ASKARJ (Association of Kaxinawá Rubber Tappers of the Jordão River) (Silva 2018b). It was mainly an indigenous event, in which various leaders from the Juruá River and Alto Purus region participated, in addition to a few public authorities, among them members of IPHAN. The event featured artistic exhibitions and ceremonies with ayahuasca. According to its organizers, the conference was conceived in response to the II World Ayahuasca Conference, and the supporting role assigned to Indigenous Peoples in the event.

Among the agendas of the conference, several points should be mentioned, such as the importance of ayahuasca as a foundation of indigenous cultures in Acre, the experiences of exchanging and disseminating ayahuasca as an indigenous medicine within Brazil and abroad, the traditions of the use of ayahuasca, sustainability management of plant species, the implications of the National Council on Drug Policies (CONAD) resolutions for indigenous communities and the heritage process (Dias 2018). The conference was opened with reading a letter written by Dedê Maia, of which an excerpt below is transcribed:

> I heard on several occasions from the organizers of the event (II World Ayahuasca Conference), the Spaniards, responding to our insistence on placing indigenous representations on some Western scientist roundtables, that "the conference was not indigenous. The conference was scientific." Or, they argued, arrogantly, that "the Indigenous people were only invited guests." But we understood otherwise. We understood that the indigenous representatives were the hosts. These guys were coming to our land. A land from where this seed of scientific knowledge of the forest, known worldwide as Ayahuasca, a hundred years ago flew like a *samaúma* seed, across this world. We considered that the issues addressed by Western scientists concerned Indigenous Peoples, guardians of this knowledge for centuries. But the arrogance and western scientific elitism, led by some "doctors," did not allow them to give in to the academic format of their conferences. [...] Here you are free to speak, to

to the period of redemocratization in the 1980s (Silva 2018a). However, its focus was mainly on the context of the struggle for the demarcation of lands. The insertion in the field of heritage is a recent move, which encompasses only part of the indigenous populations, mainly the ones from the Amazon.

dialogue, to think about possible paths with the sacred and ancestral knowledge of Indigenous Peoples (Maia 2018).

Maia's letter presented an explicit criticism of the way in which the II World Ayahuasca Conference was held. The letter also made several tensions explicit between a "science of the forest" and "academic science," and between who are the guests and hosts in this debate. In addition to the problem of the legitimacy of the academic universe to talk about (and on behalf of) ayahuasca, the event also raised a series of questions regarding the patrimonialization process and the role of IPHAN. These problematizations were explicit in Benki Pianko's speech, one of the main indigenous leaders of Acre and an *Ashaninka* representative. Benki questioned the role of IPHAN in the ayahuasca heritage process, discussing the legitimacy of the agency to produce a policy that would meet the interests of Indigenous Peoples.

Who do these council participants think they are in conducting an evaluation process that is being provided to defend the right to the indigenous use of ayahuasca? Are we interested in getting this resource? [...] We are the original people, experts on this plant, that today is being transmitted to other peoples of the world. [...] So that they can know the way we use it, as a tradition, and also see the way people today are willing to use it, as a church (Benki Pianko *apud* Santos 2018b, p. 134).

In addition to questioning the role of IPHAN, Benki's speech emphasized the notion of "original people," highlighting the central role of Indigenous Peoples in expanding the use of ayahuasca, especially to religious groups. It is also worth noting the way in which the indigenous leader established an opposition and a distance between "tradition," understood as something intrinsically indigenous, and "church." One can note that, according to Benki, the use of ayahuasca by religious groups is not understood as a tradition *per se*, but a new configuration of ayahuasca consumption originating from indigenous traditions.

On the other hand, the leader of the *Nova Esperança* village, Biraci Júnior Yawanawá, recognized the use of religious groups as one of the traditions of ayahuasca use. Similar to Benki, Biraci criticized IPHAN's role in the patrimonialization process, questioning the lack of an indigenous representative at the organization. The Yawanawá leader even considered the possibility of making different registrations for ayahuasca use according to each tradition.

Who analyzes this? Is there a *pagé* (shaman) there to analyze it with these people? In fact, the request for registration did not come from Indigenous Peoples, it came from religious groups. Then, during the process, they remembered: the Indigenous Peoples also use it. [...] So, there are riverside communities, rubber tappers, there are Indigenous Peoples, there are ayahuasca religions. Each one has its own way of using it, has its own path, has its tradition. [...] What are the possibilities of having different registrations? (Biraci Júnior apud Santos 2018b, p. 132).

Biraci Júnior's speech highlighted the difficulty of stipulating general parameters for patrimonialization processes, as well as the obstacles in delimitating common features that encompass the various forms of ayahuasca consumption. Biraci criticized the fact that the process refers to diffuse rights, which involve not only indigenous peoples, but also riverside communities and religious groups. The questioning of the legitimacy of the ayahuasca patrimonialization process in relation to the indigenous people and the proposal to seek independent recognition from other ayahuasca groups was also evident in other statements. According to Francisco Pianko, Ashaninka leader:

> The issue about the origin of *Kamarãmpi* [ayahuasca]; this shouldn't be a doubt for anyone, it belongs to the Indigenous Peoples. Because we know more than anyone about it. [. . .] The widespread use that they are trying to put in place is also not up to Indigenous Peoples. This is a matter of regulation, of putting indigenous people in the same framework [as other groups], which also weakens our struggle, our achievements, our rights. [. . .] We have to have our own way, our own right (Francisco Pianko *apud* Santos 2018b, pp. 133–134).

Once more, the claim for its own recognition process is explicit. It is also worth mentioning Pianko's argument that indigenous knowledge was appropriated by other groups and that the possibility of considering the most diverse manifestations in the same process would diminish indigenous demands. Daiara Tukano[23] also expressed this, and even suggested developing an indigenous conception of the notion of "heritage."

> To what extent do we really need to adapt to this whole system of recognizing cultural heritage? [. . .] We fought a battle for decades to recognize indigenous rights as original rights. This means that original rights are prior to anyone who has set foot on this earth, to say that their science is better, that is comes first, that it precedes ours. [. . .] Is it worth getting into this process or creating our own process of recognizing what our heritage is? What is heritage in the indigenous view? Because those who have to define the concept, the idea of heritage, are not white people. We have to have our own science, our own policy, our own definitions (Daiara Tukano *apud* Santos 2018b, pp. 132–133).

It is clear that, despite the contrasts in the speeches, questioning the legitimacy of IPHAN and its registration instruments, as well as the need for a particular patrimonialization process regarding indigenous peoples, were recurring points in the criticisms made by the leaders present at the event. It is also worth noting Daiara's questioning about the limits of a notion of "white" heritage, stating the need for an indigenous definition of its own. This criticism can be read as a radicalization or even a rupture with the registration project developed by IPHAN, which calls for plaintiffs to participate, but which maintains the prerogative of delimiting the heritage in the hands of its technicians and specialists.

In addition, when analyzing the indigenous leaders' speeches, it is clear that there is no single position in relation to ayahuasca religions. However, the defense of a clear separation between the indigenous use of ayahuasca and religious groups is recurrent, confirming our hypothesis that a new front of dispute was formed by Indigenous Peoples. This new coalition progressively starts to oppose the religious groups of Acre and, to a lesser extent, the neoayhuasca and other religious groups excluded from the original request sent to IPHAN. Thus, there is a clear intention to set an agenda that would meet indigenous interests. This fact is demonstrated by the

[23] Daiara Hori Figueroa Sampaio is part of the Tukano indigenous people of the Alto Rio Negro in the Brazilian Amazon. She holds a Master's degree in Human Rights from the University of Brasília.

recurring claims of a patrimonialization process focused exclusively on the indigenous use of ayahuasca. Furthermore, indigenous leaders are the first to criticize IPHAN's legitimacy, condemning the lack of dialogue with Indigenous Peoples and questioning the agency's ability to meet their demands.

One of the main results of the discussions held during the I Ayahuasca Indigenous Conference was writing the *Carta de Recomendação Interna*—CRI (Internal Recommendation Letter), signed by representatives of the different indigenous ethnic groups present at the event. The document presents a critique of the notion of "diffuse right,, which "weakens indigenous rights, placing indigenous ayahuasca on the same level as churches and other diverse non-indigenous groups" (Acre 2017, p. 2).

The letter proposed a series of actions. Regarding the specific issue of patrimonialization, the letter suggests the presence of *pagés* in the IPHAN commission in charge of the ayahuasca INRC. The document recommends assessing the possibility of a recognition process aligned with the vision of Indigenous Peoples. The letter also proposed setting up a Working Group "to monitor IPHAN's work and other research related to traditional medicines" (Acre 2017, p. 3).

The document outlines the concern about alleged inappropriate uses of ayahuasca by ayahuasca religions and other groups, especially regarding commercializing the brew. There are also accusations of disrespect from regulatory bodies regarding the circulation of ayahuasca by indigenous peoples. Finally, the letter suggested the registration of indigenous associations (*Cadastro Nacional da Pessoa Jurídica*—CNPJ—in Portuguese) so that ayahuasca could be shipped in the country. The issue of transiting with ayahuasca is extremely important, as, according to CONAD's deliberations, a CNPJ as a religious institution is mandatory to receive and send shipments, as well as to transport ayahuasca. Thus, as the Indigenous Peoples of the Amazon become ever increasingly present in the urban circuits of ayahuasca in Brazil, they were faced with the problem of circulating with the beverage.

Regarding this point, Gusmão highlighted, in a speech at the I Indigenous Conference, that registration as intangible cultural heritage would not solve the problem related to transporting ayahuasca. According to the IPHAN representative, the agency has no control over the cultural assets that are registered. For Gusmão, the problem of ayahuasca circulation does not concern IPHAN, but the National Anti-Drug Secretariat and CONAD, the public bodies with the power to decide on this issue (Gusmão *apud* Santos 2018b, p. 108).

Specifically, the possibility of being registered as religious institutions, as stipulated by CONAD, is also the focus of controversy among indigenous leaders. On the one hand, there are leaders who argue that the use of ayahuasca is an *a priori* indigenous religion. In this regard, the main problem is the need to institutionalize something that is already seen as an intrinsic part of indigenous religiosity. Biraci Brasil, who was prevented from traveling with ayahuasca and barred from airports in Acre on more than one occasion, makes this clear.

> Authorization? How that's outrageous! Like traditional and ancient knowledge, Christians put their bibles all over the world (inside hotels, on planes, in churches...). Muslims and the

> Quran, they are respected all over the world. What about our religion? (Biraci Brasil *apud* Santos 2018b, p. 136).

However, there are leaders who take a different stance and a more radical approach on the instruments created by CONAD and the regulatory procedures of the Federal Police. In fact, some of the speeches even questioned the legitimacy of the legal mechanisms established by public bodies regarding the uses and circulation of ayahuasca by Indigenous Peoples. Such criticism is clear in Francisco Pianko's speech:

> If we are going to use the instruments, creating organizations to be able to use our ayahuasca, we will be giving in, undermining ourselves. I think we need to look into it more closely and see these instances to educate these "bullies" [Federal Police]. [. . .] This is clearly not solved just by writing it on paper. This is an in-depth process (Francisco Pianko *apud* Santos 2018b, p. 138).

These statements make it clear that indigenous leaders' claims regarding the use of ayahuasca go beyond the scope of heritage policies. Their demands verge on the domains of drug policies and public bodies responsible for regulating the religious use of ayahuasca in Brazil. Therefore, there is not a specific agenda directed to IPHAN and another to CONAD. On the contrary, it seems that there are overlapping claims that concern diverse interests, which go beyond the limits and objectives of heritage policies. This overlapping is made explicit, for example, in Daiara Tukano's testimony at the end of the I Ayahuasca Indigenous Conference:

> There was also a discussion about the patrimonialization of ayahuasca as a cultural heritage of Indigenous Peoples. It was a very important conversation because we came to the conclusion that this medicine is from our origins. That Brazilian and international legislation, international treaties, already recognize the indigenous right as an original right. And the most important indigenous right is their cultural practice, which is their identity. So, our practice with the medicine, our ceremony, our transit, is an original right, and the original right in Brazil is an entrenched clause. The original right supersedes other laws, because we are the original peoples of this land. So, we came, because of this concern, to discuss on how to carry out this dialogue with the competent authorities, with the Brazilian government, but also with other institutions in the world, such as UNESCO, and even other countries, to make it clear what indigenous right is.[24]

Daira's speech is two-sided. On the one hand, the mention of UNESCO and international treaties demonstrates the mobilization of instruments developed by international law. This resource inserts indigenous claims into a broader and more universalist set of rights that goes beyond the jurisdiction of the nation-state model. On the other hand, the notion of "original right" highlights the specificity of the status of indigenous peoples under Brazilian legislation and the limits of their legal instruments to deal with indigenous demands. Furthermore, Daiara's stance in relation to UNESCO refers to the ways in which the policy-making process has an increasingly transnational scope. In this new context, global policy models end up exercising increasing normative power over national legislation.

[24] Available at https://www.youtube.com/watch?v=9QidmaDBEHA. Accessed on 19/05/2020.

Undoubtedly, the I Ayahuasca Indigenous Conference was a milestone in terms of gaining visibility of the political agenda regarding the indigenous use of ayahuasca. However, the recent insertion of Amazonian Indigenous Peoples in the patrimonialization process of ayahuasca should not be seen as a ready-made project, nor as something that is limited to ayahuasca and its uses. On the contrary, this new movement seems to mark the initial steps of a process of developing a broader political agenda focused on indigenous rights inside and outside their lands. This new agenda has been shaped through tensions, disputes, participation in academic and legal forums, as well as creating its own channels of visibility, whether to question governmental bodies and international agencies, or to organize its own events and conferences.

7 Conclusion

In order for a right to take form and materialize, many social processes need to take place at various levels, fostering public debate and creating norms. This construction involves a convergence of processes and opportunities, such as the visibility of a certain issue at a given historical moment, developing state bureaucracy, as well as the mobilization of multiple actors around the theme. This is the case of intangible cultural heritage policies in Brazil, materialized through the convergence of various social and institutional processes at different levels and with particular temporalities.

In retrospect, the consolidation of policies aimed at intangible heritage enabled the multiplication of actors demanding recognition and the developing of new forms of affirmative policies. On the other hand, the question arises of who decides, how they decide, who is or is not part of the cultural heritage, that is, the problem of disputes and alliances that involve the processes of naming and defining what will be considered in public policies. Furthermore, there is still the broader issue, which goes beyond the legal scope and concerns the ways in which a claim is made public.

All these elements are in dispute and are contextually defined, as we have seen in the case study presented. The initial proposal presented by the ayahuasca religious groups in Acre, requesting the recognition of traditions linked to the three founding masters of *Santo Daime*, *Barquinha* and UDV, was considered too narrow, not only by IPHAN, but by other groups that consume ayahuasca, who were excluded from the process. Therefore, the rejection of the original request led to an expansion in the scope of the debate and, consequently, of the patrimonialization process, increasing the number of actors involved, as well as the disputes, questioning classifications and proposing new directions for recognizing ayahuasca use as intangible cultural heritage.

It is worth remembering, as Meyer and van de Port (2018, p. 11) point out, that although actors may not reach a consensus on what constitutes heritage, they are increasingly well versed in their vocabularies. We would say that, in addition to heritage, they are also becoming well versed in the vocabulary and grammars of law. However, we must escape the trap of considering its uses and appropriations as erroneous. Likewise, we should avoid *a priori* conclusions, as the tangibility of a right is not prior to the network of interactions that implement it but implies a set of articulations and disputes that often go beyond the limits of the legal domain.

We hope to have demonstrated throughout the analysis that the patrimonialization process of ayahuasca does not establish a consensus or a common project among the actors. Nor are claims, interests and values given in advance, but they emerge contextually. Legal demands do not precede interactions; on the contrary, the interactions and disputes between actors shape the interests and claims. On the other hand, agendas, arguments and categories can also change according to the forms of mobilization, as they reverberate and cause (or not) friction.

Furthermore, when looking at implementing rights and public policies, we should point out that we are not necessarily talking about personal interactions. Processes do not take place on the same level or arena. Most of the time they are parallel processes that occur in different arenas and that at a given moment meet, articulate, overlap, putting into dispute discourses, categories and actors. When looking at such processes, we do not see "religions," nor the "State", in their monolithic sense, but a series of actors that, in their multiplicity of trajectories and positions, produce alliances and disputes. Representatives of ayahuasca religions, indigenous leaders, international NGOs, technicians from IPHAN, cultural foundations, parliamentarians, as well as specialists from different fields such as anthropologists, historians, sociologists, among others, are constantly mobilized, disputing and shifting the meanings of the patrimonialization process of the religious use of ayahuasca in Brazil.

From this perspective, one can conclude that the logics developed to shape policies to recognize intangible cultural heritage start from an aporia: the demand for clear definitions, at the expense of reifying social practices and groups that multiply, divide and renew, in a scenario that is always fluid, porous, inconstant and that resists classifications. This aporia explains some of the gaps between the creation of a right as a norm, the development of legal mechanisms to regulate it, and the processes of implementing such a right through public policies.

References

Acre (2008) Carta de solicitação para o processo de reconhecimento do uso da ayahuasca em rituais religiosos como patrimônio imaterial da cultura brasileira. http://www.bialabate.net. Accessed 10 Dec 2019

Acre (2010) Carta das Comunidades Tradicionais da Ayahuasca Rio Branco – Acre. http://www.bialabate.net. Accessed 10 Dec 2019

Acre (2016) Carta Aberta dos Povos Indígenas do Acre / Brasil a II Conferencia Mundial da Ayahuaska (Nixi Pae, Huni Pae, Uni Pae, Kamarãbi, Kamalanbi, Shuri, Yajé, Kaapi. . .). http://www.bialabate.net. Accessed on 10 Dec 2019

Acre (2017) Carta de Recomendação Interna - 1ª Yubaka Hayrá Conferência Indígena Ayahuasca. http://www.bialabate.net. Accessed on 10 Dec 2019

Alverga AP (2011) Comunicado da Igreja do Santo Daime (Igreja do Culto Eclético da Fluente Luz Universal. Patrono: Padrinho Sebastião Mota). Carta Enviada ao Encontro da Diversidade Ayahuasqueira
Anastassakis Z (2017) A cultura como projeto: Aloisio Magalhães e suas ideias para o Iphan. Revista do Patrimônio Histórico e Artístico Nacional 35:65–77
Antunes HF (2019) O uso da ayahuasca como problema público: um contraponto entre os casos do Brasil e dos Estados Unidos. Universidade de São Paulo, Tese
Arantes AA (2008) Entrevista: Antônio Augusto Arantes. [Entrevista concedida à] Lilian de Lucca Torres. Ponto Urbe 3:1–17
Arantes AA (2009) Ayahuasca - from dangerous drug to national heritage: an interview with Antonio A. Arantes. [Entrevista concedida à] Labate, Beatriz C. & Goldstein, Ilana. Int J Transpers Stud 28:53–64
Arantes AA (2015) Trajetória e desafios do Inventário Nacional de Referências Culturais (INRC): Entrevista com Antonio Arantes. [Entrevista concedida à] Sara Santos Morais e Rodrigo Martins Ramassote. Revista CPC 20:221–260
Assis GL, Rodrigues JA (2017) De quem é a ayahuasca? Notas sobre a patrimonialização de uma "bebida sagrada" amazônica. Religião e Sociedade 37(3):46–70
Barros GC (2016) Tradição e modernidade no campo ayahuasqueiro: uma análise dos processos de regulamentação e patrimonialização da ayahuasca no Brasil no período de 1985/2016. Universidade Federal de Campina Grande, Tese
Brasil (1987) Conselho Federal de Entorpecentes (CONFEN). Relatório Final do Grupo de Trabalho 1987. Brasília. http://www.bialabate.net/wp-content/uploads/2008/08/Relatório-Final-GT-Confen-1987.pdf. Accessed 23 Nov 2018
Brasil (1988) Constituição da República Federativa do Brasil. Senado Federal: Centro Gráfico, Brasília
Brasil (2000a) Decreto-Lei 3551. Presidência da República: Casa Civil. Brasília
Brasil (2000b) Inventário nacional de referências culturais: manual de aplicação. Instituto do Patrimônio Histórico e Artísitico Nacional (IPHAN), Brasília
Chuva MRR (2009) Os arquitetos da memória: sociogênese das práticas de preservação do patrimônio cultural no Brasil (Anos 1930–1940). Editora UFRJ, Rio de Janeiro
Desvallées A (2003) De la notion privée d'héritage matériel au concept universel et extensif de patrimoine: retour sur l'histoire et sur quelques ambiguïtés sémantiques. In: Martine C (ed) Médias et Patrimoine, Université de Laval / Unesco, Chaire patrimoine culturel, pp 19–35
Dias CG (2020) Ordem do dia: Uma análise do trabalho da Unesco em torno das políticas culturais (1979-82). Novos Estudos 39(1):165–184
Dias M (2018) 1ª Conferência indígena da ayahuasca yubaka-hayra no Acre a sabedoria dos antigos. https://www.bialabate.net/news/1a-conferencia-indigena-da-ayahuasca-yubaka-hayra-no-acre-a-sabedoria-dos-antigos. Accessed 19 Nov 2018
Domingues P (2007) Movimento negro brasileiro: alguns apontamentos históricos. Tempo 12(23): 100–122
Facchini R (2003) Movimento Homossexual no Brasil: recompondo um histórico. Cad. AEL 10(18/19):83–123
Fassin D (2012) On humanitarian reason: a moral history of the present. University of California Press, Los Angeles
Freitas MBAP (1999) Mário de Andrade e Aloísio Magalhães: Dois personagens e a questão do patrimônio cultural brasileiro. Revista Do Programa De Pós-Graduação Em Arquitetura E Urbanismo Da FAUUSP 7:71–93
Gohn MG (2000) 500 anos de lutas sociais no Brasil: movimentos sociais, ONGs e o terceiro setor. Mediações 5(1):11–40
Gonçalves JRS (1996) A retórica da perda: os discursos do patrimônio cultural no Brasil. Editora UFRJ/IPHAN, Rio de Janeiro
Goulart SL (2008) Estigmas de grupos ayahuasqueiros. In: Labate BC et al (eds) Drogas e cultura: novas perspectivas. EDUFBA, Salvador, pp 251–288

Labate BC (2004) A reinvenção do uso da ayahuasca nos centros urbanos. Mercado de Letras/ FAPESP, Campinas
Labate BC, Araújo WS (eds) (2002) O uso ritual da ayahuasca. FAPESP/Mercado das Letras, São Paulo/Campinas
Labate BC, Assis GL (2018) Genealogia do processo de patrimonialização da ayahuasca no Brasil. In: Labate BC, Policarpo F (eds) Drogas: perspectivas em Ciências Humanas. Gramma/Terceiro Nome/NEIP, Rio de Janeiro
Labate BC, Coutinho F (2014) "O meu avô deu a ayahuasca para o Mestre Irineu": reflexões sobre a entrada dos índios no circuito urbano de consumo de ayahuasca no Brasil. Revista de Antropologia USP 57(2):215–250
Labate BC, Goulart SL (2016) Religião, Política e Cultura: o uso da ayahuasca como patrimônio cultural. 30a Reunião Brasileira de Antropologia, João Pessoa
Labate BC, Goulart SL (2017) Da Amazônia ao Norte Global e de Volta: As Várias Ayahuascas da II Conferência Mundial da Ayahuasca. V Congreso de la Asociación Latinoamericana de Antropologia - XVI Congreso de Antropologia en Colombia, Bogotá
Lins P, Gomes E, Machado C (2017) Editorial: Religião, patrimônio e modernidades plurais. Religião e Sociedade 37(3):9–16
Londres C (2000) Referências Culturais: Base Para Novas Políticas de Patrimônio. In: Instituto do Patrimônio Histórico e Artísitico Nacional (IPHAN) Inventário nacional de referências culturais: manual de aplicação. IPHAN, Brasília
MacRae E (in press) Eu brilho na floresta. Editora Yagé, São Paulo
Maia D (2018) Conferência Indígena da Ayahuasca: longe é um lugar que não existe. Xapuri Socioambiental https://www.xapuri.info/sagrado-indigena/conferencia-indigena-ayahuasca/. Accessed 10 Jan 2020
Meyer B, van de Port M (2018) Introduction – heritage dynamics: politics of authentication, aesthetics of persuasion and the cultural production of the real. In: Meyer B, van de Port M (eds) Sense and essence: heritage and the cultural production of the real. Berghahn Books, New York, pp 1–39
Montero P (2018) Syncretism and Pluralism in the Configuration of Religious Diversity in Brazil. Mecila Working Paper Series, 4, São Paulo
Neves, AC (2017) Reflexões sobre a patrimonialização da ayahuasca: conquistas, disputas e tensões. Dissertação, Universidade Federal da Bahia
Reinhardt B (2018) Intangible Heritage, Tangible Controversies: The Baiana and the Acarajé as Boundary Objects in Contemporary Brazil. In: Meyer B, van de Port M (eds) Sense and essence: heritage and the cultural production of the real. Berghahn Books, New York, pp 75–111
Rio de Janeiro (2011) Manifesto da Diversidade Cultural Ayahuasqueira. http://www.bialabate.net. Accessed 10 Dec 2019
Sala D (1990) Mário de Andrade e o Anteprojeto do Serviço do Patrimônio Artístico Nacional. Revista IEB 31:19–26
Santos CR (2018a) O patrimônio de Mário de Andrade: tirando o pedregulho da botina para não manquejar. Revista CPC 13(25):11–47
Santos FL (2018b) "Índio não usa droga, ele usa medicina": a criminalização da ayahuasca indígena. Dissertação, Instituto do Patrimônio Histórico e Artístico Nacional
Silva DB (2018b) Yubaka Hayrá: Notas sobre a Conferência Indígena da Ayahuasca. Campos 19(1), jan.jun:183–194
Silva ECA (2018a) Povos indígenas e o direito à terra na realidade brasileira. Serviço Social e Sociedade 133:480–500
Tupper KW (2017) The economics of ayahuasca: money, markets, and the value of the vine. In: Labate BC et al (eds) The world Ayahuasca diaspora: reinventions and controversies. Routledge, New York, pp 183–202
UNESCO (2003) Convention for the Safeguarding of the Intangible Cultural Heritage. http://www.unesco.org. Accessed 10 Jan 2020

Part II
Human Rights as Language

Controversies in Brazil's Supreme Court over When Human Life Begins

Lilian Sales

Abstract This chapter analyzes two cases that went to the Supreme Federal Court (SFC) related to "when human life begins" aiming to reconstruct the controversies surrounding them in the Brazilian public arena during the first decade of the 2000s. The first case refers to research that was published on embryonic stem cells and the second to the possibility of anticipating the delivery of anencephalic fetuses. In this chapter, we will initially review the context prior to the trial of these cases. In other words, we will briefly review the positions and actions taken by federal governments from the 1990s onwards, which enabled these two themes to be the subject of public debate in Brazil in the 2000s. Then, we will identify the central actors in the two controversies and the ways in which categories related to human rights and bioethics are mobilized and disputed by the actors who antagonize each other in the two cases.

1 Introduction

This chapter examines two cases that went to the Supreme Federal Court aiming to analytically reconstruct the public controversies related to the "defense of human life" that they aroused. The first case concerns the Direct Action of Unconstitutionality 3510, carried out by the Prosecutor General of the Republic, Cláudio Fonteles, reacting against the fifth article of the Biosafety Law, which allowed the use of embryonic stem cells (ESC) in scientific research. The case was judged by the Supreme Federal Court in May 2008. The controversy surrounding this case was marked by a constellation of arguments that was also explained in the public hearing convened by the SFC in April 2007.

The second refers to the trial of the case that allowed the right to interrupt a pregnancy of an anencephalic fetus (Claim of Non-compliance with Fundamental Precept 54). In 2004, Supreme Court's justice Marco Aurélio Mello issued an injunction that allowed the therapeutic anticipation of birth in cases of anencephaly.

L. Sales (✉)
Federal University of São Paulo, Unifesp, Guarulhos, SP, Brazil
e-mail: lilian.sales@unifesp.br

P. Montero et al. (eds.), *Religious Pluralism and Law in Contemporary Brazil*, Law and Religion in a Global Context 4, https://doi.org/10.1007/978-3-031-41981-2_7

This injunction was revoked in less than 4 months, and the case went back to trial in 2012, preceded by a public hearing in 2008.

The two trials were preceded by intense public debates, mobilizing agents from different areas in the two poles of the discussion: in favor or against publishing research on embryonic stem cells and/or the early induction of labor of anencephalic fetuses. In addition, the two trials were preceded by public hearings at the Supreme Court, in which Civil Society, represented by scientists or institutions (movements, representative class institutions, religious institutions, among others), expressed their positions and arguments about this theme in the trial.

The defense of human life from conception is the argument around which groups opposed to the two cases were organized, among which the leading role of groups and actors linked to the Catholic Church was observed. The "defense of life" argument is strong in both cases, as it has been widely disseminated, appearing repeatedly in multiple scenes of these controversies: in public hearings, newspaper and magazine articles, talks on radio and television networks and even in documentaries (Sales 2015, 2020).

The justifications present in these multiple scenes, especially in public hearings, indicated that the antagonistic sides were supported by elements of science and rights. These were the two grammars that permeated the justifications, activated by the actors in the two poles of the cases. In this aspect, even the actors representing religious institutions did not mention elements conventionally understood as religious or theological on the basis of their justifications. On the contrary, the argument followed the "strategic secularism" structure (Vaggione 2017), relying on elements of science and rights, especially in bioethics references as guidelines in its statements.

We chose to analyze the antagonistic sides in these two actions, classifying them as pro-choice and "pro-life", in the case of the anencephaly trial, and pro-research and "pro-life" in the embryonic cells case. This division anticipates the dispute over rights present in the scenes of these controversies, especially in public hearings: the rights of women and people with disabilities, on the one hand, and the rights of fetuses and embryos, on the other. The actors opposing the two cases defend the presence of life in the human fetus and embryo, stating that it is a matter of defending the primordial human right: the right to life. Actors in favor of the cases, on the other hand, defend the right to freedom of choice and human dignity for women or those who might benefit from the research. The dispute arises from categories and classifications of rights, more specifically human rights.

However, elements of awareness are added to the grammars of science and rights in the justifications of the antagonistic sides. They use real stories, images and videos that demonstrate suffering, joy, relationships, and emotions. Personal narratives are an important part of the justifications and indicate that moral values and symbols are also in dispute and are part of the grammar of these controversies.

According to the theoretical approach adopted, controversies have a configuration, which are established around problems of public interest. There is a first moment of crisis, in which an issue or a topic would begin to be debated, put into question, generating a series of discussions, polarizations, positions and debates about them. This movement and mobilization surrounding an issue lead to it being seen as a problem of public interest. Controversies are established from public problems.

Following this interpretative key, Cefäi and Pasquier (2003) emphasize that, in parallel with the emergence of a problem of public interest, there is the constitution of a public. Groups, actors, organizations emerge from the discussions around a particular problem, interact, state their opinions and positions, transforming this issue into a public problem. This public is formed throughout the discussions and mobilizations on a given issue. From this perspective, the public and the public problem are constituted simultaneously, in the conflicting process of debates and positions on issues on which there is no consensus, or on which consensus is interrupted.

Controversies would be a second moment of the crisis. A moment in which the crisis would already be slightly stabilized, already constituted in a public problem and leading to a series of positions and debates around it. Although there is no consensus, the problem is on the verge of being defined. The conflict remains, but it has a less chaotic form.

From this perspective, the two themes were constituted as controversies in the Brazilian public arena during the legal proceedings. Using embryonic stem cells in scientific research and the permission of abortion in the case of anencephaly were issues that became part of the national public debate when these cases were being heard at the Supreme Court. They are often themes addressed in the media and debates, mobilizing a range of institutions and actors around them. These two cases went beyond the borders of the judicial sphere where the trial took place, sparking a public debate and replicating (or constituting) multiple scenes: in the media, in newspapers and websites, in the public hearing, in documentaries (e.g., about anencephaly), and also in others demonstrations "in defense of life."

Another aspect that characterizes an issue as problem of public interest is the fact that the State is asked to take a stand. In our analysis, the judiciary is called upon to give a verdict on each of the themes: using embryonic cells in research and interrupting a pregnancy of an anencephalic fetus. In the cases analyzed, therefore, there was already a constituted public problem, the controversies were already established and the arenas of dispute relatively fixed.

In this chapter, we are interested in identifying the public mobilized throughout the controversies (in the second moment of the crisis, when the public problem is already established), and the strategies and arguments used to defend the antagonistic causes around the two public problems mentioned. To do this, in the first part of the chapter, we will briefly review the positions and actions taken by Brazilian federal governments, from the 1990s onwards, which contextualize the fact that these issues were placed on the agenda judged by the Supreme Court during the first decade of the 2000s.

Then, in the second part of the chapter, we will focus on the description of the public's controversies, describing the antagonistic sides in the two cases, emphasizing the role of actors linked to Catholicism in opposing the two actions. Finally, in the third section, we will analyze the utterances made and the way in which the categories are managed in the speeches and presentations during the audiences. We will demonstrate ways in which categories related to science and human rights are disputed by actors linked to antagonistic blocks in the two cases, and the strategies used to confer potentiality on arguments for or against the trials.

To write this chapter, we watched hearings on anencephaly and the use of embryonic cells on a Brazilian television channel called *Canal Justiça* and we followed their repercussion in the media, identifying actors and arguments discussed in these two scenes.[1] The two controversies have repercussions in several other scenes, for example on television and in newspapers, especially in moments close to the trials of the cases. The public debate that took place in the scenes enabled us to identify prominent arguments and actors. Some of the actors who stood out in the media appear again in public hearings at the Supreme Court and in other scenes. These data were also used to write this chapter, By carrying out cross checks, we identified actors who appeared in multiple scenes: public audience speakers, authors who wrote articles in the media, interviewees in debate programs, and justifications made in defense of their positions.

Although we analyzed these two controversies more broadly, for this chapter we will focus on the scene of public hearings, in which the disputed positions were already crystallized and organized in sides: against or in favor of the cases.

2 The 1990s and 2000s: Human Rights and the Inclusion Paradigm

Actors linked to the Catholic Church interfering in the political or judicial arenas is not a novelty in Brazil. It usually happens when changes in the legislation on "the beginning of human life" are discussed in this arenas. An example of this was the dispute over abortion, established between the feminist movement and the *Conferência Nacional dos Bispos do Brasil*—CNBB (the National Conference of Bishops) during the discussions about the new Constitution in Brazil in 1988. The Conference of Bishops wanted the phrase "defense of life from conception" to be included in the Constitution[2] (Dalmolin 2011; Rocha 2005). Despite not having managed to insert the phrase into the Brazilian Constitution, abortion remained a

[1]We used the Atlas TI qualitative data analysis program to identify the main arguments in the secular and religious media. Articles and reports from two widely circulated Catholic channels were systematized: and the National Conference of Bishops (CNBB) and *Rede Canção Nova* websites, a community linked to the Charismatic Renovation movement, and also widely circulated national newspapers: *Folha de São Paulo* and *O Globo.*

[2]The attempt to intervene in the constituent processes was repeated in Colombia, in 1991, and in Argentina, in 1994. In all three cases, actors linked to Catholicism defended that the phrase "defense of life from conception" be inserted in the Constituents of these countries. It was during this period that the subject gained considerable dimensions in Latin American countries (Ruibal 2014).

crime in Brazil, with only two exceptions in the period: in the case of rape and in the case where the mother's life was at risk.

There have been significant changes in Brazil since then. In the last two decades, until 2016, the Brazilian State drew closer to social movements, such as during the government of Luiz Inácio Lula da Silva (2003–2010), when feminists were called to take on state jobs, and influenced sexual and reproductive health and rights policies. In this context, the debate around abortion has returned to the national public sphere, especially when the Third National Human Rights Plan (PNDH in Portuguese) was launched in 2009, which addressed very different issues, including decriminalization of abortion.

According to Adorno (2010), this latest update of the National Human Rights Plan proposed more mechanisms for expanding rights, addressed decriminalization of abortion, civil unions between people of the same sex, the right for same-sex couples to adopt, the prohibition of religious symbols in public establishments of the Union. It addresses a list of rights that, until that moment, had not been prioritized by the Federal Government.

Public actions and policies aimed focused on Human Rights have a recent history in Brazil, and gained momentum during the governments of Fernando Henrique Cardoso (1994–2001). During this period, the promotion of human rights in Brazil was aimed at defending civil and political rights (Gonzalez 2010). Actions to repair the violations of individual rights, which occurred during the dictatorship, and the fight against State violence were prioritized. In this context, the first National Human Rights Planwas conceived and approved in 1996.

In Lula da Silva's governments (2003–2006 and 2007–2010), a new orientation of action concerning Human Rights emerged: cultural, environmental, sexual and reproductive rights started to occupy a prominent role in programs and policies. The agenda of the Secretariat for Human Rights (created during the Fernando Henrique administration) adopts the policy of diversity rights, based on dialogues established with the demands of the LGBT, feminist, black and indigenous movements.

The third National Human Rights Plan represents this agenda and can be considered the culmination of a process that began in the 1990s, when the inclusion paradigm, which considers society from a wide range of differences—ethnic and racial, gender, beliefs—began to become more prominent in Brazil. This paradigm is based on the notion of Brazilian internal diversity and justifies the necessity for including this diversity. The process of inclusion has to be made, according to this standpoint, by public policies aimed at valuing diversity and the inclusion of minorities—sexual, gender, racial, ethnic, religious. In this scenario, universalist policies lose their centrality, and public policies which consider the specificities of each group, are valued.

However, this paradigm shift and the valorization of pluralism, as well as investing in actions in favor of diversity rights are the backdrop for demands related to sexual and reproductive rights and bioethics, that concerns the two case studies analyzed in this chapter. The theme of diversity and the rights associated with it is becoming increasingly present in Brazil, and also increasingly disputed by groups.

In parallel and simultaneously to actions in defense of the expansion of Sexual and Reproductive Rights (and of Human Rights more generally), the reaction of sectors of society to these new policies have been constituted, with the organization, for example, of anti-abortion movements (in Civil Society) and Parliamentary lobbies in Congress (political sphere). As pointed out by Maria das Dores Machado (2012), the various initiatives in favor of reproductive and sexual rights carried out during the years of the Lula da Silva government led to a collective reaction from segments in the National Congress, especially those linked to Churches and Religions, but not only those. This reaction was also observed in Civil Society, with the organization of anti-abortion movements, such as the *Movimento Nacional da Cidadania pela Vida* (National Citizens Movement for Life): *Brasil sem Aborto* (Brazil without Abortion) and the National Association of *Pró-Vida e Pró-Família* (Pro-Life and Pro-Family) (Resende 2016).

3 Actors and Alliances

In this section, we will analyze the controversies around the two cases presented in the introduction: using embryonic cells in research and the possibility of interrupting a pregnancy of an anencephalic fetus. We will start this analysis by presenting the actors who mobilized these cases, dividing them into two sides: against and in favor of the cases in the trial.

3.1 Actors and Alliances: The "Pro-Life" Block

The pro-life block is not a watertight group, but a group that acquires a specific configuration throughout each of the trials. It is a configuration organized around arguments and positions shared among actors against those actions. The same is considered related to favorable actors: they have a specific configuration that is based on the issue confronted in the legal arena.

We identified the actors against and in favor of the subject of the trials based on the positions that they have taken publicly, especially at the two public hearings. In the case of the "pro-life" block, "the defense of human life" is the common frame that gather groups, actors and institutions contrary to the trial. These actors conceive the acts in the trial as an attack on human life.

There were agents linked to the Catholic Church, more specifically to the CNBB, in both cases. In the ADI 3510 trial, the CNBB was accepted as an *amicus curiae* [3] in the process, acting as a lawyer for the trial and appointing more than half of the those

[3] An *amicus curiae* or literally "friend of the court" is an expression used to designate an institution whose purpose is to provide support for court decisions.

who gave statements at the public hearing. In the trial on anencephaly, the CNBB was not accepted as an *amicus curiae*, and had the same participation time in the hearing as other civil society institutions.

Nevertheless, the CNBB participated in the two trials, jurists and scientists linked to the Catholic Church in Brazil gave statements against the actions in the two public hearings. The defense of the conviction that human life begins at fertilization, prevailing in catholic doctrine, is made by actors who master the language in the arenas in question: bioethics, science and rights.

In addition to them, the anti-abortion movements had participated of the public hearings. These movements call themselves "lay people" or "non-religious," but they have branches of CNBB among their ranks, such as the *Pastoral da Família*, which is part of the National Citizens Movement for Life: Brazil without Abortion and the National Association of Pro-Life and Pro-Family. The standpoints of these two anti-abortion movements were represented at the public hearing on the anencephaly case called by the Supreme Court.

The relationships and links between those who gave statements at public hearings and Catholic entities and institutions were observed. We will focus on some examples of these connections. The first speaker of the "pro-life" side at the public hearing on embryonic cells was Lenise Aparecida Garcia. She is a professor and researcher in Biology at the University of Brasilia (UnB) and often participates in events, congresses and lectures promoted by the CNBB, such as the Bioethics Symposium, held during the 2010 National Eucharistic Congress in Brasília. This symposium was organized by Garcia, and other speakers at this public hearing also participated, such as researcher Cláudia Batista, the second speaker of the pro-life block at the public hearing on embryonic cells. Participation in events promoted by Catholic entities is not restricted to the CNBB, Garcia also takes part in radio programs on *Rádio Maria*, a catholic channel, in Brasília, for example.

In addition to her academic connections and active participation in events related to the Catholic Church, Lenise Garcia is also a militant in anti-abortion movements in Brazil, and president of the *Citizens Movement, Brazil without abortion*, considered the largest anti-abortion movement in Brazil, whose members include Catholic religious institutions. The positions of these two anti-abortion movements were represented in the public hearing on anencephaly (but not in the hearing on embryonic cells, exclusively for scientists). In the hearing on embryonic cells, Lenise spoke as a scientist, in the second hearing her participation was as a member of civil society, representing the *Citizens Movement, Brazil without Abortion*. The same happened with the doctor and professor at the Federal University of Rio de Janeiro (UFRJ), Rodolfo Acatuassu Nunes, who spoke at the two public hearings. In the first, about embryonic cells, as a scientist and in the second, as a spokesperson for the National Association for Pro-Life and Pro-Family. The fact that both were actors and speakers at the two public hearings is the link that points to the connection between the two controversies, as well as between the Catholic Church and the anti-abortion movements active in Brazil. When certain themes, such as the use of embryonic cells in research and the abortion of anencephalic cells, are discussed in the judicial arena, these movements and actors articulating themselves around the generic argument of the "defense of life". Both situations are considered as "attacks on human life", as we will demonstrate later.

Another example of the actors and their links with a Catholic institution is noted by Dr. Elizabeth Kipman Cerqueira's participation, who is also a speaker at the two hearings. She was also responsible for preparing the text for the CNBB Fraternity Campaign in 2008, whose theme was "Fraternity and defense of life", that demonstrates once again the connection between the scientists at the two public hearings and the Catholic Church. This text for the Fraternity Campaign points to the centrality of bioethics as an academic field that provides a scientific foundation for the frameworks "in defense of life" disseminated by the CNBB, justifying its position against abortion, euthanasia, using embryonic cells in research, assisted human reproduction, among others.

The link between actors and institutions linked to the Catholic Church in Brazil is clear. In fact, in previous analyses we found that, based on the material produced and the events held by the CNBB on bioethics, a theme that permeates the two trials, the connections are repeated. Participants/spokespersons/authors/speakers circulate at congresses and lectures promoted on the themes "Bioethics" and "Life" by this institution and those from the pro-life block at public hearings (Sales 2020). In other words, speakers circulate at congresses on bioethics held by the CNBB and produce materials on this topic for this institution, such as the text for the Fraternity Campaign.

When we observe the way in which Catholic actors act on issues related to the "beginning of life", we see changes over time. Until the eighties, as in the Constituent Assembly process, this intervention took place directly through the CNBB. It participated in the public debate and tried to interfere in the decision-making process, defending the inclusion of the "defense of life from conception" in the text of the Brazilian Constitution (Rocha 2005). More recently, its position is defended through jurists, scientists and movements, as observed in public hearings. In the ADI 3510 case, in which the CNBB was accepted as *amicus curiae*, jurists (at the trial) and scientists (at the public hearing) spoke on its behalf. Its role in justifying the position "in defense of life" involves the mediation of actors who dominate the grammars at play in the arenas in question: science and rights.

Bioethics has become the scientific field that supports the positions of the Episcopal Conference and actors linked to Catholicism in disputes involving the beginning or end of human life. Since the 1990s, Bioethics has become an area of knowledge that has gained special attention from the Vatican. Scientific advances in the field of Biomedicine, as well as victories of women's movements in the UN conferences of the 1990s led Pope John Paul II to establish the Pontifical Academy for Life, in 1994, aiming at "defending and promoting life considering advances in medicine and law".

The defense of Vatican positions and convictions by scientists and doctors, who use scientific terms and methodology, is not exactly a novelty in the Catholic Church. Some authors have already demonstrated that since the confrontation with scientism in France in the nineteenth century, the Catholic Institution, from Vatican, utilizes doctors and scientists to defend its positions using scientific language (Claverie 2003; Harris 2001).

However, the use of science by Catholic actors in the cases on the "beginning of life" is related to a specific fields: bioethics and sexuality. The centrality given to these issues at the Vatican dates back to the 1960s and gained even more emphasis in the pontificate of John Paul II, during which the reproduction of life, sexuality and the complementarity between the sexes gained prominence (Carnac 2013).

Furthermore, the opposition to these themes acquired a sense of urgency in the Vatican in the 1990s, in reaction to the victories of the women's movement at the UN Conferences in Cairo (1994) and Beijing (1995).[4] The defeat of the Vatican is decisive for the consolidation of the Catholic Institutions' position on Bioethics, starting a reaction to confront policies recognizing reproductive rights and bioethics in international debate forums and in National States.

Bioethics has become the field of knowledge in which the confrontation of the expansion of sexual and reproductive rights takes place, which is why it gains centrality in the Catholic hierarchy. Thus, the Vatican has produced a series of texts on human reproduction, which encompass issues of bioethics. The Encyclical Letter *Evangeliun Vitae* is especially important, addressing issues of bioethics, especially those that take into account the beginning or end of life, such as abortion, Assisted Human Reproduction, Euthanasia and using embryonic cells in scientific research.

However, this Encyclical Letter is not just about doctrine, it also establishes new Institutions into the Catholic structure, like the Pontifical Academy for Life, which, from 1996 onwards, brought scientists and jurists together who defend the doctrinal convictions of the Vatican. In the institutional offensive of the Vatican in the field of bioethics, the background of experts, scientists and jurists is crucial. In this regard, one of the first actions of the Vatican, after creating the Pontifical Academy for Life, was to create the Institutes for Bioethics in all the Pontifical Universities in Europe and Latin America (Irrazabal 2010). Scientific Institutes were first created in European Catholic universities and were given the task of allocating and training specialists, who played a central role in the scientific and legal defense of the Vatican's convictions. The Bioethics Institute of the *Università Cattolica del Sacro Cuore*, founded by Elio Sgrecia, and the Bioethics Institute at the *Universidad de Navarra* are two major references in the formulation of the academic-scientific and legal discourse on bioethics of the Catholic Institution. These institutes were also occupied with training scientists and experts who disseminated and defended the Vatican's views on bioethics.

Since then, the presence of actors linked to the Catholic Church in public controversies related to bioethics and sexual and reproductive rights has been

[4]This would have been the trigger for the reaction of the Catholic Church on issues of bioethics, gender and human reproduction: the UN conferences held in the 1990s, in which the Vatican suffered major defeats in its positions on policies to control reproduction and sexual rights and from which feminists emerge victorious, obtaining recognition of sexual and reproductive rights as human rights (Correa 2018; Garbagnoli and Prearo 2017).

observed in several countries in Latin America and Europe, and they are becoming more prominent in the first decade of the 2000s. Some authors even classify the manifestations of lay Catholic movements or those linked to the Catholic Church as "Catholic activism" (Béraud and Portier 2015; Turinna 2012) or even as "Catholic militantism" (Garbagnoli and Prearo 2017), because, in many cases, this presence involves mobilizations and public manifestations contrary to the legislation that regulates issues related to bioethics and the expansion of sexual and reproductive rights in countries with a Catholic tradition on both continents. This confrontation is also observed in Brazil, in the controversy over the use of embryonic cells in research and in the controversy over anencephaly. Evidently, these mobilizations have specific consequences and characteristics in each country, however, it is important to draw attention to this effort from the Vatican to publicize their convictions on these issues.

In the case of Brazil, we found that Catholic institutions, such as the CNBB, incorporated a new form of political action since the redemocratization period. First, by the presence of actors who publicly take a stand in defense of the Vatican's convictions. Furthermore, if during the Constituent Assembly the mobilization against abortion was led by the CNBB, from the 1990s onwards, with the organization of pro-life movements in Brazil, the CNBB became part of these movements and organizations, who are also connected with international pro-life activists and networks, as demonstrated in this section.

3.2 Actors and Alliances: The Pro-Research and Pro-Choice Blocks

In the ADI3510 case, the speakers in favor of using embryonic cells in research circulated mainly in the academic environment, participated in congresses and lectures, and many of them were members of the Brazilian Academy of Sciences. During the period of controversy over embryonic cells, some of them were in contact with movements and organizations that represent people with disabilities and their families. An example of this was the Non-Governmental Organization (NGO) called *Movitae*[5] and the *Projeto Ghente*,[6] both active defenders of liberalizing the use of embryonic cells in scientific research. Organizations representing people with disabilities were also key agents in this controversy, because using embryonic cells in research would represent a possibility of treatment and eventual cure for disabilities. Researchers and potential patients were united in defending the case, forming a single bloc in the audience.

[5] Pro-life movement in defense of embryonic stem cell research. The NGO filed a request with the Supreme Federal Court to join as an interested party that discusses the constitutionality of Article 5 of the Biosafety Law.

[6] Project in defense of research with the ESC comprising people with disabilities and their families.

Researcher, Mayana Zatz, represents this connection between scientists and movements. She was considered throughout the controversy as the main spokesperson in defense of ESC research, bridging the gap between the scientific community and civic organizations. As only "scientists" were able to speak at this hearing, civil organizations defending the rights of people with disabilities and religious entities were represented by "scientists".[7]

On the other hand, ADPF 54, which claimed the "therapeutic anticipation of birth" in the case of pregnancy of an anencephalic fetus, was proposed in 2004 by the *Confederação Nacional dos Trabalhadores da Saúde*—CNTS (National Confederation of Health Workers). [8] Many of the institutions present at the public hearing were related to health professionals, such as professional bodies, for example.

Several institutions linked to health professionals sent representatives to speak in favor of this case, constituting the largest group in the audience. Among them, we can highlight: the Federal Council of Medicine, the Brazilian Federation of Gynecology and Obstetrics Associations, the Brazilian Society of Medical Genetics, among other similar institutions. Associations linked to human rights, especially those related to women's rights, also stood out in the defense of the therapeutic anticipation of birth of anencephalic patients, such as the Anis Bioethics Institute, Human Rights and Gender and the National Feminist Health Network, Sexual Rights and Reproductive Rights. The main alliance in favor of the case in this trial was between institutions that defend the rights of women and class representative bodies in the health sector.

Medical-scientific elements were observed at the two public hearings and were brought up by speakers representing the two poles of the debate. In the case of the hearing on anencephaly, when we observed the professional category of the speakers, we noticed the predominance of physicians; 16 among the 27 exhibitors. These professionals appeared as representatives of scientific associations, professional associations and religious institutions linked to the two blocks. In this aspect, despite the favorable position for the action by professional associations in the health area, there were also doctors who represented civil society and religious institutions that took a stand against the case.

[7]The value given to the scientific dimension of the public hearing is evident since its convocation, which aimed to "scientifically" clarify the moment in which life would begin. In addition, all speakers should start their talks by presenting their professional qualifications, titles and academic standing. These elements were fundamental for the legitimacy of the exhibitors and their speeches. (Sales 2014; Luna 2010).

[8]Having this action, the CNTS sought to enable pregnant women, in cases of anencephaly, to interrupt their pregnancy without the need for judicial authorization or permission from the State.

4 Arguments and Classifications: Opposition Between a Mother's Rights and the Rights of Fetuses and Embryos

The *rapporteur's* speech in the ADPF 54 case summarizes the fundamental question of the public hearing on anencephaly: would the anencephalic fetus be a human being? Or, in other words, would the fetus with anencephaly be a living human being? The disputed issue at the two hearings is based on the presence of human life in fetuses/embryos. To prove the humanity of these beings is vital for the constitution of their rights, in particular the "right to life."

At both poles of the controversies, "lives" were being defended and in dispute. On the one hand, embryos and fetuses are considered human persons and subjects of rights, and the State must defend their life and human dignity. On the other hand, the human life and dignity defended are those of people already born, possible beneficiaries of research with embryonic stem cells, in the ADI 3510 case and pregnant women with anencephalic fetuses, in the ADPF 54 case.

The academic-scientific device is central to both controversies, however, Moral elements are also present, as well as those related to human rights and modern individualism. The argumentative effort of supporters and opponents of the cases was aimed at constituting one of the figures—pregnant women or anencephalic fetuses, in vitro embryos or people benefiting from research with embryonic cells—in subjects with rights. A series of categories related to human rights—the right to life, freedom of choice, freedom of conscience, human dignity—is triggered by actors in both poles of the controversies. The attribution of the right to life for anencephalic fetuses and in vitro embryos is the central element of the discursive strategy of the anti-abortion block in both actions, while the blocks in favor of the actions insist on the human dignity of women and people with disabilities. The grammar of human rights is fundamental, in which its lexicons and *modus operandi* are often used and serve as a source of legitimacy for the arguments and positions in defense of two causes: the cause of "defense of human embryos and fetuses" and the cause the "defense of human dignity" of people with disabilities and women.

However, symbols and values are utilized as a background for the reasons mentioned. The sensitization elements, through telling real stories, images and videos that demonstrate suffering, joy, relationships, emotions, and personal narratives, are an important part of the attempts to convince. Thus, on the one hand, there is a distance from personal cases, a generalization through justifications based on legal, scientific and human rights elements and terms. On the other hand, these same justifications are full of personal accounts, stories of suffering and joy from real people, incorporated into speeches through the use of photographs and stories reported in letters and videos. In the next sections, we will analyze the justifications and persuasion strategies that comprise these controversies.

4.1 Therapeutic Anticipation of Birth x Abortion

The defense of the human life of fetuses and embryos was evident in the hearing on anencephaly, in which the opponents classified the act at trial as "abortion", or even as "eugenic abortion". On the other hand, the supporters of the case did not use this classification, calling it "therapeutic anticipation of birth" or "therapeutic interruption of pregnancy".

One of the main strategies of the "pro-choice" block was to escape the classification of "abortion" for the case in the trial, emphasizing its therapeutic dimension: a medical treatment for pregnant women with anencephalic fetuses. On the contrary, the "pro-life" block's strategy was to classify this act as murder. These two forms of classification demonstrate what would be in dispute at the two public hearings: the right to life and human dignity, incorporated in the arguments of each of the blocks in dispute.

By defending the presence of human life in anencephalic fetuses, pro-life speakers portray the anticipation of childbirth closer to murder. This term was an important part of the strategy used by the "pro-life" block, launching the legal dispute into the field of morality. The classification of this block as "pro-life" is significant, highlighting the notion that the antagonistic group encouraged death.

The recurrent use of the abortion category in the multiple scenes of this controversy contributed to this association. This recurrence was noted during the public hearing, for example, in which several presentations about anencephaly stated that the case in the trial was about "abortion". As in the following speech, which emphasizes the "murder" of fetuses with anencephaly and its "eugenic" character.

> The only way a doctor can know the date someone is going to die is if he/she sets the date and time to kill this person. [...] And undoubtedly the abortion of an anencephalic patient, because he/she has no life expectancy, is characterized as a eugenic abortion. [...] Every woman wants to have a perfect, healthy child, but if he/she is not perfect, healthy, then shall I kill him/her? It's really an abortion, let's stop using euphemisms.] The anencephalic fetus is deficient, it is not the undead. [...] So, the anencephalic fetus is alive until it dies. The anencephalic fetus dies. And it only dies because it is alive, if it were not alive it would not die.[9]

Abortion, murder, execution by an arranged time and date. Extermination of the lives of people with disabilities, all these ideas appear together in the speech. Associating the act in the trial with abortion, understood as murder, is an important argument used by the anti-abortion block, which seeks to reiterate the negative moral characterization that abortion has on Brazilian society. The disputed issues in the two controversies—the anticipation of anencephalic birth and the use of embryonic cells in research—refer to this broader and more forceful moral issue in Brazil: decriminalization and/or legalization of abortion.

[9]Speech given by Lenise Aparecida Garcia. Public Hearing on Anencephaly, Part 4: https://www.youtube.com/playlist?list=PLippyY-19Z47vGsw8_FF1gBWqzkSv7njE2. Accessed on: 16/09/2014.

The emphasis on classifying the act as abortion is aimed at convincing against the trial. This is a powerful device, even more evident when compared to data from the Pew Forum survey, carried out in 2006, according to which 79% of Brazilians agree with the statement that abortion is not justifiable in any situation (Pew Forum, 2006: 36–8). This data shows the degree of rejection of this procedure by Brazilian society, and, consequently, the strength of this argument used against the possibility of anticipating the delivery of anencephalic fetuses.

On the other hand, the block that defends the liberalization of the act attempts to minimize this procedure, classifying it as "therapeutic anticipation of birth." Thus, the emphases is in its clinical and therapeutic character: it is portrayed as a medical procedure (a therapy) to be performed in women suffering from this physical condition (the pregnancy of an anencephalic fetus). They reinforced the importance of this therapy to stop the disease and expunge the enormous suffering experienced by pregnant women of an anencephalic fetus, to whom the maintenance of the gestation would result in giving birth to a stillborn child or to a newborn with no life expectancy.

Thus, using this category (abortion) triggers a long-term Christian/Catholic morality in Brazilian society. It touches on one of the great "controversial moral issues" of Brazilian society, as classified by Luiz Fernando Dias Duarte (2013), which disputes the morality of a group and/or society.

The group in favor of action, on the other hand, triggers a value that is important to the contemporary world: that human suffering is something to be eliminated. There is an increasingly prevalent tendency to get rid of pain from the horizon of experiences. The group in favor of the action seeks, in this respect, to humanize women who choose to practice abortion in the case of anencephaly (while the opposing actors seek to humanize the fetus). They would be suffering from a disease and in a state of physical and psychological suffering and would be deserving of a dignified and adequate treatment (therapy) for this disease, which would help their situation of suffering: therapeutic abortion.

4.2 *Obscuration of the Mother and the Autonomy and Uniqueness of Fetuses and Embryos*

Another strategy used by the "pro-life" block to demonstrate the presence of human life in fetuses and embryos was to assert its specificity and autonomy to develop:

> To take the discussion to the *in vitro* environment, we can observe that the embryo grows by itself. After the fifth day, if this embryo is not transferred to the mother's uterus, it dies, but its development until this day is autonomous.[10]

[10]Public hearing on embryonic stem cells. See part 2: https://www.youtube.com/playlist?list=PLippyY19Z47vGsw8_FF1gBWqzkSv7njE2. Accessed on: 16/09/2014

> Right after fertilization, when the embryo is three millimeters long, and you can already see its little heart beating. Do you think I need size to recognize a living being? Not for the mother. (...) It has the potential to develo, follows a process of self-construction and self-development. Its ontogenesis belongs to itself. The human being is a whole through each of its self-construction stages. Biology defines human life as a dynamic process. One that ontologically has a movement that is its own, that comes out of itself, a movement of development.
>
> At first, during fertilization, the unique characteristics of an individual are already defined. All its genetic characteristics are joined, therefore the embryo is already an individual, with no equal copy. [11]

The autonomous development of the embryo, even in the *in vitro* environment, is emphasized by the speakers. This ability to develop independently is presented as evidence of the presence of human life in embryos. The idea is that of movement, a path, and autonomy, self-construction. From fertilization, through all the stages, the exhaustively repeated words are self-construction, ontogenesis, and the main focus is to prove that human life exists in *in vitro* embryos.

Furthermore, the demonstration of the uniqueness and specificity of the *in vitro* frozen embryo was also constant at the hearing on embryonic cells. Speeches mentioning the unique and unrepeatable *genome* of each *in vitro* embryo, using data and scientific elements, were common, and accompanied by images that showed each stage of embryonic development, from fertilization to birth, emphasizing that that newborn baby (showing the baby's image) would be the continuation of a process initiated in fertilization. The *in vitro* embryo would have a "specific genetic identity" that could only develop into a "specific" baby.

The speeches were reinforced by images representing the autonomy and uniqueness of the human embryo in its development. Throughout the two hearings, slides, photos and films were used to show the stages of human development that ended with images of beautiful newborn babies. The images demonstrate the development of a unique, specific child, who develops autonomously, independent of the maternal body. The gestational process is not mentioned, only the development of the embryo and fetus can be seen in the images, which recurrently, in the various speeches, was completed with the image of a baby.

The strategy of using images presenting the embryo or fetus as specific and autonomous beings is not exclusively present in the public hearings. It is repeated in the broader controversy. An example of this is the images used throughout the 2008 Fraternity Campaign, whose theme was "Fraternity and in Defense of Life", in a reference to the defense of human life according to Catholic principles: from its beginning to its natural end. In this Fraternity Campaign, the image of a pregnant

---

[11][17]Public hearing on embryonic stem cells. See part 2: https://www.youtube.com/playlist?list=PLippyY19Z47vGsw8_FF1gBWqzkSv7njE2. Accessed on: 16/09/2014

[18]Speech by Elisabeth Kipman Cerqueira. Public hearing on embryonic stem cells. See part 3: https://www.youtube.com/playlist?list=PLippyY19Z47vGsw8_FF1gBWqzkSv7njE2. Accessed on: 16/09/2014

[19]Public hearing on embryonic stem cells. Part 3: https://www.youtube.com/playlist?list=PLippyY19Z47vGsw8_FF1gBWqzkSv7njE2. Accessed on: 16/09/2014.

woman's body, in profile, focusing on the presence/existence of a fetus in her womb, circulated widely in Brazilian parishes. In this image, the focus is on the fetus, the woman is in the background, as a faceless figure, not presenting any elements that could identify her. It is the life of the fetus that is highlighted in the image, and, more broadly, defended in the 2008 Fraternity Campaign.

These imagery strategies demonstrate the individuation of the embryo, more specifically its autonomous character. Another specific, but emblematic example, was observed in some parishes in Rio de Janeiro during the period of the 2008 Fraternity Campaign. Parishes are free to create strategies to disseminate the conceptions of the Campaigns. In the case of the 2008 Fraternity Campaign, one strategy particularly caught our attention: the Archdiocese of Rio adopted a little fetus doll in the shape and size of a 3-month-old fetus as its symbol. Some churches, such as *Santa Margarida Maria*, in *Lagoa*, and *São Judas Tadeu*, in *Cosme Velho*, in the South Zone of Rio, left the doll on display on the altar. The tiny doll had a sign on it saying: "*I already have life*". Thus, the association between the fetus and human life, its autonomy and specificity, gain materiality.[12]

This effort to demonstrate the specificity and autonomy of the human embryo is part of the humanization and individuation strategy carried out by anti-abortion actors, in order to turn it into a subject of rights. We note that this effort is operationalized through several strategies, which combine and complement each other: using the scientific academic *modus operandi* is one of them, as mentioned above. However, the materialization of fetuses into small dolls and the use of images of babies strengthen the humanization of embryos. They gain corporeality and have a specific face, an image that reminds everyone that those beings can become newborns, and therefore human beings.

Furthermore, this strategy of personalizing fetuses and embryos places them at the top of a hierarchy of humanity/individuality. They are the humans who must be taken into account in the trial, according to anti-abortion actors. The mother figure is almost non-existent, and when she is present, as in the images mentioned beforehand, she has no defined identity (unlike embryos and fetuses, defined as "unique", specific), she is just a shadow, a figure. The images expose the embryo and fetus disconnected from the mother, an obscured figure without identity, as opposed to the focus on a single, specific, individual identity of the embryo.

[12] The strategy of distributing small dolls in the shape of fetuses at 12-week pregnancy was also observed in the controversy over the decriminalization of abortion. At the public hearing on ADPF 442, which discussed the decriminalization of abortion up to the 12th week, held in August 2018, these dolls were distributed by groups of Catholics at the entrance to the Supreme Court hearing.

4.3 The Dispute over Conscience and the Right to Choose

Another strategy used by agents against actions to prove that embryos and fetuses are individuals and subjects of rights is to attribute the presence of consciousness in fetuses and embryos. The debate about conscience took place at the public hearing on anencephaly. The pro-life block speakers insisted on demonstrating the presence of consciousness in the anencephalic fetus. According to some speakers, the anencephalic fetus has a "primitive conscience." Others claimed that a fetus with anencephaly possess part of the brain, and although the presence of consciousness cannot be proved, it certainly cannot be asserted that it does not exist. As noted in the following speeches:

> Prudence guides this action of organ donation (from anencephalic fetuses) due to the possibility of a "primitive conscience".[13]

> Consciousness is the foundation of being. The high brainstem is the substrate of consciousness, related to the individual's ability to choose. Every anencephalic fetus has a trunk. It is the entrance and exit door of the mind. (...) The consciousness of a fetus is similar to that of a human being (...)[14]

"Primitive consciousness" could exist, according to these speakers, because anencephaly does not represent the complete absence of the brain, but a partial one. Slides, which have many bibliographical references as their source, illustrated this statement and point out the exact location of primitive consciousness in the part of the brain that the anencephalic fetus has.

The defense of conscience is important in the individualization strategy used by pro-life actors in this controversy, constituting one of the foundations of the fetus' humanity. Once more, the discourses bring references to the values of the modern person, that characterize the individual as endowed with awareness and ability to choose. Freedom of conscience is one of the central foundations of individuality, as well as specificity/uniqueness and autonomy, mentioned above.

The strategy of attributing characteristics of the modern person to fetuses and embryos also makes use of sensitization devices, such as the use of documentaries and photos that portray babies who were diagnosed with anencephaly and who survived after delivery. An emblematic example, and much cited in the public hearing about anencephaly, was the case of the girl Marcela de Jesus,[15] reported in the documentary "*Flores de Marcela*". The documentary has many images that demonstrate the interaction between Marcela and her mother, the girl had crying

[13] Public Hearing on Anencephaly, Part 2: https://www.youtube.com/playlist?list=PLippyY-19Z47vGsw8_FF1gBWqzkSv7njE2. Accessed on: 16/09/2014.

[14] Public Hearing on Anencephaly, Part 4: https://www.youtube.com/playlist?list=PLippyY-19Z47vGsw8_FF1gBWqzkSv7njE2. Accessed on: 16/09/2014.

[15] Marcela was diagnosed with anencephaly within weeks in her mother's womb, and her mother decided to not interfere with the pregnancy. She lived an exceptional time for a fetus diagnosed with anencephaly, 1 year and 8 months old, and a documentary about her life was made when the girl was 1 year and 2 months old.

or happy reactions when her mother was there, which were interpreted as the girl's ability to communicate with her mother. Marcela is treated, then, as the example that fetuses diagnosed with anencephaly have conscience, that they are humans with the capacity for interaction and communication. The ability to relate to the mother, to respond to her stimuli, is presented as an affective evidence that completes the argument for the presence of consciousness in anencephalic fetuses.

Scenes from this documentary, as well as photographs of babies with anencephaly interacting with the family, in typical scenes of family happiness, were used in the audience, showing that those babies were alive, interacting and bringing happiness and fulfillment to their families. The existence of those children represented the counterpoint of the abortion-murder rhetoric: these mothers had "let her be born," in the words of Marcela's mother, and therefore enjoyed the family happiness generated by the presence of a child.

The humanization strategy mobilized by the pro-life bloc was completed by activating elements that touched the affections and emotions, which were fundamental for the public to adhere to its cause, contrary to the anticipation of birth in the case of anencephaly.

At the other pole of this controversy, the strategy of defending values related to the human person (and human rights) is also present, as in the public hearing on anencephaly in which it was emphasized the disrespect for freedom of conscience and to the human dignity of women who did not wish to maintain an anencephalic pregnancy. For the block defending the action, the conscience to be considered is that of the pregnant woman, it is the human dignity of women that should be guaranteed. This device can be detected in several speakers' rhetoric:

> Many pregnant women with anencephalic fetuses have their dignity destroyed. Those who decide to not interrupt the pregnancy despite knowing how to carry an anencephalic fetus have their decision respected, but those who do not wish to maintain this pregnancy have their right denied. (...) Forcing this woman to maintain this pregnancy is torture.
>
> What is intended is to guarantee the dignity of the human person. Today, the penal code obliges women, knowing their diagnosis and prognosis, to carry the pregnancy to the end.[16]

Pre-trial legislation would "force" women to maintain an anencephalic pregnancy, ignoring human dignity and freedom of choice. Conscience, freedom of choice and human dignity emerge as fundamental rights of women, they would be the subjects of rights to be defended. The maximum example of disrespect for the freedom and dignity of these women would be to force them to maintain the gestation of a fetus with no potential for life.

The dispute over the category of conscience and individualization of one of the groups by using human rights' references, such as the right to life, human dignity, and individual freedoms, gain embodiment in public hearings by reports and images of real people—pregnant women, children diagnosed with anencephaly and people with disabilities, such as the aforementioned example of Marcela de Jesus.

---

[16] Speech by Débora Diniz. Public Hearing on Anencephaly, Part 2: https://www.youtube.com/playlist?list=PLippyY-19Z47vGsw8_FF1gBWqzkSv7njE2. Accessed on: 16/09/2014.

At the other pole of this controversy, the block in favor of the action presented Severina's example, a woman from the countryside on a low income, who went a long way in court in an attempt to interrupt the pregnancy of an anencephalic fetus but did not obtain the right to anticipate the labor and her child was born dead. During the case, a documentary was made about the history of Severina, in which excerpts were shown during the hearing. Severina, according to the speakers, was forced to bury her stillborn child, not having her right of choice and conscience respected. She would represent, in terms of this block, hundreds of women whose freedom of conscience is restricted.

These real-life experiences were brought to the public hearing through the stories of these women. One scene from the documentary called *Uma História Severina* is remarkable. It shows the day on which Severina obtained court authorization to terminate her pregnancy. The scene shows her leaving the house with her maternity bag at 1.30 pm. The suitcase that she had just packed when she got the "document", the judicial authorization for the termination of pregnancy. In her maternity bag, there were no baby clothes and no layette. The next scene shows Severina in a baby clothing store, before arriving at the maternity hospital. She is buying the baby a little outfit. She tells the sales assistant, who insists on showing her other items from the layette: "No, it's just this outfit, because he won't survive anyway...". She was shopping for her son's funeral clothes. The seller doesn't really know what to do, she looks helpless when Severina replies. The camera zooms in on Severina's expression showing pain.

The image reminds viewers of the universe of objects and symbols that are associated with expecting a baby. Severina is a pregnant woman in a shop that sells layettes, and it is expected that she will be interested in various items. The scene dialogues with the metaphor used by actors in favor of the ADPF 54 case: replacing the crib with a coffin, women like Severina prepare the funeral of their children right after birth. Setting up the crib and layette, which mark the arrival of a child, is replaced by the preparation of the coffin and funeral. That is what Severina did in the layette shop: she prepared the burial of her son, still with him in her womb.

Another example is when a letter is read out written by a woman who was forced to maintain the pregnancy and had to bury her daughter. In addition to the disrespect for her freedom of choice, the letter is an account of the suffering experienced by this woman, with details that portray her pain, her daughter's coffin, the fetus that would have no chance of survival moving in her womb, among other elements that reiterate her painful experience in spite of her decision to anticipate the birth.

This suffering is expressed in the documentary scenes, just as it is expressed in the public hearing on anencephaly. The block "pro-choice" created an image of these women as victims, and the use of images and documentaries is crucial in this process. The documentary scenes and the reports from the audience portray the pain, express the suffering of women who had to maintain an anencephalic pregnancy. In so doing, they make this suffering intelligible, almost palpable, in this controversy.

The construction of a person as a victim is a way of giving social recognition to suffering and it is an important element in the fight for rights. This construction, in the case analyzed, is carried out by expressing emotions, affections and sufferings. For certain groups—pregnant women or anencephalic fetuses—to be perceived as victims is necessary to give intelligibility to their sufferings or their joys. Documentaries, letters and reports of pain and violence experienced by women (in this case, state violence to hinder the possibility of interrupting the pregnancy) are important. They show pain and feelings and, by expressing them, make them intelligible (to the other, or to the public that is constituted throughout the controversy).

5 Final Considerations

The values expressed in the two controversies come from different grammars, science, rights, especially human rights, and the values of the modern person. The agents' discourses, at the two poles of the debate, appropriate the academic-scientific grammar, as well as the legal grammar and also the values of a modern person. We observed that the use of scientific terms and elements, as well as the activation of categories of human rights and modern individualism, was recurrent in the justifications produced, articulating the lines at the two poles of the debate. Using these categories was constant in the justifications for and against the actions, serving as a legitimization strategy for the arguments about the use of embryonic stem cells in research and about the anticipation of anencephalic birth.

Several elements were connected in the same speech/justification. They mingled and overlapped in the speeches at the two public hearings. In addition to the use of science and rights grammars, awareness raising strategies are added, by telling real stories, images and videos that demonstrate suffering, joy, relationships, emotions. Drama, especially through images, videos and narratives, is an important part of convincing strategies. Thus, on the one hand, there is a distancing from personal cases, a generalization through justifications based on legal, scientific, human rights and modern individualism elements and terms. On the other hand, these same justifications are full of personal accounts, stories of suffering and joy from real and concrete people, personally brought to the speeches through their photographs, their stories documented in letters and videos. The sum of these elements, often present in the same speech, seems to be fundamental for creating persuasion in the public arena in which these controversies took place.

In the case of the pro-life block, in the dispute between individuals and subjects of rights, embryos and fetuses are placed at the top of the hierarchy of rights. The superposition of the fetus/child over the mother/woman appears above all in the hearing on anencephaly. It is a model that has historical depth in Catholicism. When the speakers trigger elements of this pattern in their justifications (through speeches or images) they are triggering a long-lasting morality in the Catholic Church, which has great convincing power.

Among the blocks favorable to the actions, there was the construction of possible beneficiaries of the actions—pregnant women with anencephalic and people affected by diseases possibly treatable with the use of embryonic cells—in figures of victims.

This construction of the victim's figure is in the sense of building a socially intelligible way of expressing and having the suffering recognized, legitimizing demands. It is the way to recognize the suffering imputed and to consolidate rights, and that is why the demonstration of the suffering imputed to these people is recurrent. According to Janine Barbot and Dodier (2011), the current context is marked by the growing attention given to the fight against suffering in the public space, and the production of figures of victims in this context would bring even more legitimacy and strength to their demands—in the case analyzed, claims for rights.

References

Adorno S (2010) História e desventura: o 3° Programa Nacional de Direitos Humanos. Novos Estudos CEBRAP 86(5–20):2010

Barbot J, Dodier N (2011) De la douleur au droit. Ethnographie des plaidoiries lors de l'audience pénale du procès de l'hormone de croissance contaminé. In: Cefaï D, Terzi C (eds) L'expérience des problèmes publics. EHESS, Paris, pp 289–322. Collection «Raisons Pratiques, 22

Béraud C, Portier P (2015) Métamorphoses catholiques. Acteurs, enjeux et mobilisations depuis le mariage pour tous. Éditions de la Maison des sciences de l'homme, Paris

Carnac R (2013) S'adapter pour mieux résister: la théologie de la sexualité de Jean-Paul II. In: Rochefort F, Sanna ME (eds) Normes Religieuses et Genre. Armand Colin/Recherches, Paris, pp 97–108

Cefäi D, Pasquier D (2003) Les sens du public. PUF, Paris

Claverie E (2003) Les guerres de la Vierge: une anthropologie des apparitions. Gallimard, Paris

Correa S (2018) A "política do gênero": um comentário genealógico. Cadernos Pagu 53:e185301

Dalmolin A (2011) Aborto, Igreja Católica e movimento feminista nos anos oitenta: uma cruzada de valores. X Seminário de Estudos Históricos. FEEVALE, Rio Grande do Sul

Duarte LFD (2013) Aonde Caminha a Moralidade. Cadernos Pagu 41:19–27

Garbagnoli S, Prearo M (2017) La croisade anti-genre. Du Vatican aux manifs pour tous. Editions Textual, Paris

Gonzalez RS (2010) A política de promoção aos direitos humanos no governo lula. Rev Debates 4(2):107–135

Harris R (2001) Lourdes. Jean Claude Lattes, Paris

Irrazabal G (2010) Bioethica e Catolicismo. Dificultades en torno de la constitucion de una Identidat Colectiva. Relig Soc 30(1):101–116

Luna N (2010) Embriões no Supremo: Ética, Religião e Ciência no Tribunal. Teoria Soc 18:168–203

Machado MDC (2012) Aborto e ativismo religioso nas eleições de 2010. Rev Bras Ciên Polít 7:25–54

Resende PG (2016) Movimentos Sociais e Contramovimentos: mobilizações anti aborto no Brasil contemporâneo. Dissertação Mestrado em Ciências Sociais - Universidade Federal de São Paulo

Rocha, M. (2005) Discussões políticas e decisões no parlamento. In: Ávila, M, Ferreira, V, Portella, A (ed). Novas legalidades e democratização da vida social: família, sexualidade e aborto. Garamont, Rio de Janeiro

Ruibal A (2014) Feminismo frente a fundamentalismos religiosos: mobilização e contramobilização. Rev Bras Ciên Polít 14:111–138

Sales L (2014) A controvérsia em torno da liberação de pesquisas com células-tronco embrionárias no Brasil: posições e argumentos dos representantes da Igreja Católica. Rev Antropol 57(1): 179–213

Sales L (2015) Em defesa da vida humana': moralidades em disputa em duas audiências públicas do STF. Relig Soc 35:143–164
Sales L (2020) Emoções e Afetos na controvérsia sobre a Anencefalia. Rev Bras Ciên Soc 35(103): 1–19
Turinna I (2012) Le Magistere post-conciliare face au Biopouvoir. In: Béraud C, Gugelot F, Saint-Martin I (eds) Catholicisme en tension. éd. de l'EHESS, Paris
Vaggione J (2017) La Iglesia Católica frente a la política sexual. Cadernos Pagu 50:e175001

Quilombola Communities and the Right to Land Ownership: Notes on a Legal Controversy in the Supreme Federal Court

Sabrina Soares D'Almeida

Abstract The Federal Constitution of 1988 granted hitherto unforeseen rights to ethnic and cultural minorities in previous constitutional charters and was responsible for providing new treatment to these collective subjects who were historically pushed to the margins of the civic and legal world. Among them, we can mention the right to land ownership occupied by the remaining members of the quilombo communities, guaranteed by art.68 of the *Ato das Disposições Constitucionais Transitórias*—ADCT (Temporary Constitutional Provisions Act). This right led to a series of controversies that resulted in a request for an *Ação Direta de Inconstitucionalidade*—ADI (Direct Action of Unconstitutionality) in 2004 asking for the declaration of unconstitutionality of the presidential decree that regulated the procedures for the titling of these lands. This chapter aims to analyze the judgments of this ADI in the Supreme Federal Court, focusing on the actors involved, their alliances and oppositions, as well as the positions defended. Among the actors, we attempt to underline the role of a religious institution that is very active in debates on the agrarian issue, the *Conferência Nacional dos Bispos do Brasil—CNBB (*National Conference of Bishops of Brazil). By doing this, we intend to demonstrate the important role played by the CNBB in defining some categories and formulating certain arguments. The empirical material that supported this analysis consists of legal documents, including requests for admission as an *amicus curiae*, requests for public hearings, reports, oral arguments, public motions, notes and ministers' votes.

1 Introduction

The Brazilian Federal Constitution of 1988 granted hitherto unforeseen rights to ethnic and cultural minorities in previous constitutional charters and was responsible for providing new treatment to these collective subjects who were historically pushed to the margins of the civic and legal world. Article 68, responsible for

S. S. D'Almeida (✉)
Brazilian Center of Analysis and Planning, São Paulo, Brazil

Department of Anthropology, Federal University of Minas Gerais, Belo Horizonte, Brazil

P. Montero et al. (eds.), *Religious Pluralism and Law in Contemporary Brazil*, Law and Religion in a Global Context 4, https://doi.org/10.1007/978-3-031-41981-2_8

recognizing the territorial rights of *quilombola* communities, can be understood as an effort in this direction.

In doing so, it also raised a question of complex resolution that has been discussed in the academic, legal and political spheres, producing a legal controversy that will be analyzed in this chapter and concerns the way in which this constitutional provision (Article 68)[1] could be concretized.

Since then, some impasses have arisen regarding the procedures to guarantee this right and the definitions of the categories in the wording of article 68, among which we can mention a few: which groups would correspond to the so-called remaining members of quilombo communities? What would be the most suitable criteria for land demarcation to be titled? Should this titling be done in the name of a community or in individual lots, borrowing the model adopted for agrarian reform? In cases where private properties overlap these territories, what solutions—administrative and legal—should be adopted to resolve these conflicts?

With the aim of answering these questions and regulate the process for recognition, identification, delimitation, demarcation and titling of lands occupied by the remaining members of quilombo communities provided for the Article 68, President Luiz Inácio Lula da Silva enacted a decree—Decree 4887/2003. However, in 2004, an *Ação Direta de Inconstitucionalidade*—ADI (Direct Action of Unconstitutionality) was filed by the *Partido da Frente Liberal*—PFL (Liberal Front Party)[2] aiming to declare the unconstitutionality of decree 4887. The *ADI Quilombola*, as it became known, appears, then, intending to question the constitutionality of some procedures and definitions that were established by Decree 4887/2003. It went to trial at the Supreme Federal Court in 2012, 2015 and 2018[3] when the final decision was finally handed down that declared the constitutionality of the decree that regulates the phases of the titling process of *quilombola* territories. In addition to the ministers of the Supreme Federal Court, the Attorney General of Brazil, the Public Prosecutor's Office and the Attorney General's Office, a group of state actors and organized civil society who requested admission as an *amicus curiae* took part in it, and therefore were able to express their arguments before the court on this issue.

This chapter aims to describe how the various actors who participated in this legal controversy[4] faced the issue of how to concretize article 68 of the Federal Constitution, through which, as already mentioned, the right to land ownership of the remaining members of the quilombo communities to the land they occupy. Considering this, the actors who were involved in this controversy will be described—

[1]Temporary Constitutional Provisions Act. "Final ownership shall be recognized for the remaining members of the quilombo communities who are occupying their lands and the state shall grant them the respective title deeds."

[2]Currently called Democrats.

[3]These interruptions in the trial are due to the ministers' requests for view.

[4]The controversy that arose around Article 4887/03 extended to the media, political and academic arenas, however, within the scope of this work, we will focus on its development in the legal arena, although it is necessary to recognize that all of them are interconnected.

focusing on their alliances and oppositions—as well as the justifications formulated by them (Boltanski and Thevénot 2006).

In this chapter, we also intend to highlight the participation of the *Conferência Nacional dos Bispos do Brasil—CNBB (*National Conference of Bishops of Brazil) as an *amicus curiae* in this controversy, a condition that, in itself, already points to its interest and representativeness in taking a stand on the subject. As we will see, its importance is related to it having been involved in the agrarian issue in Brazil since the 1950s. Since then, it has been formulating arguments and strategies in defense of the right to land, having contributed, according to Reis (2012), to producing the idea of access to land as a human right.

Empirical material collected and analyzed consists of legal documents that are available for consultation on the Supreme Federal Court's website, including requests for admission as an *amicus curiae*, requests for public hearings, reports, public motions, notes and ministers' votes. In addition to this documental survey, we resorted to recordings of the trial in which the *amici curiae* made their oral arguments.

2 Article 68 and Attempts to Regulate It

The legal category "remaining members of quilombo communities" was created in the context of the national constituent assembly and inaugurated with the Federal Constitution of 1988 which, through Article 68 of the *Ato das Disposições Constitucionais Transitórias*—ADCT (Temporary Constitutional Provisions Act), recognized the ownership rights of these groups to the land they occupy for the first time. Members of social movements linked to the black and *quilombola* cause consider this article as an advance in the right of conquest of this segment by recognizing, for the first time in the country's history, the ownership right of the remaining members of quilombo communities over the lands they occupy. This conquest could be seen from two aspects. The first concerns the objective of promoting racial equality and social justice. The second is a reparation measure as it seeks to repair a historic debt of the nation with Afro-descendants considering the oppression suffered during and after slavery.

From the promulgation of the Constitution to the first attempt to discipline this constitutional provision, 13 years passed, when the then President Fernando Henrique Cardoso promulgated Decree 3912/01, whose validity lasted only 2 years and was the target of numerous criticisms by social movements and defenders of the rights of quilombo communities. According to these actors, this decree restricted, rather than expanded, the exercise of this right as it had requirements that would make it difficult to recognize an area as a *quilombola* territory. Among them was the requirement that only ownership of lands that: (1) were occupied by quilombos in 1888 could be recognized; (2) were occupied by remaining members of quilombo communities on October 5, 1988. This requirement became known as the "political-legal timeframe thesis" and, to this day, it has been the object of divergences and disputes in different arenas.

Using this timeframe thesis, communities claiming the title of their lands are required to have been occupying them for a 100 years, that is, from the abolition of slavery to the promulgation of the Federal Constitution of 1988. According to the statement of the organizations *Terra de Direitos*, *Centro pelo Direito à Moradia Contra Despejos* (Center on Housing Rights and Evictions), *Centro de Justiça Global* (Center for Global Justice), *Instituto Socioambiental e Instituto Polis* (Institute for Studies, Education and Assistance in Political Sciences), as *amicus curiae*.

> [...] demand that it be proven – and it is unknown how this could be done as they never held titles to their land – that they remained in the same place for more than 100 years as the abolition of slavery (1888) was not only a restriction measure on the full enjoyment of constitutionally guaranteed rights, but also of historical and social injustice. (Petition for admission as an *amicus curiae*, 2004)

Another criticism about the decree referred to the fact that the competence to carry out the process of identification, demarcation and titling of *quilombola* territories was reserved for the *Fundação Cultural Palmares* (Palmares Cultural Foundation) as this institution did not have the structure to carry out highly complex processes such as these, as they required, in addition to anthropological reports, the preparation of technical reports identifying the territory—which involved knowledge from the most diverse areas, such as: agronomy, biology, topography, sociology, economics, among others (Petition for admission as an *amicus curiae*, 2004). Moreover, according to these civil society organizations, very few communities obtained the title to their land during the years that Federal Decree 3912/01 was in force, precisely because of these weaknesses.

Giving rise to the dissatisfaction of the *quilombolas* and defenders of their rights, in 2003, at the request of the newly elected president Luiz Inácio Lula da Silva, an inter-ministerial working group was formed aiming to review the provisions contained in the decree of its predecessor. Furthermore, also in 2003, the new decree was edited and promulgated, which started to regulate the matter and became known for innovating, compared to the previous one, in the following points:

1. the competence to carry out the whole process was transferred from the Palmares Cultural Foundation to Incra (except for certifying *quilombo* communities). This body became responsible for producing the identification, delimitation and demarcation reports of the territory to be recognized and titled; for expropriation of private properties when incident on these areas and their subsequent title.
2. suspending the "political-legal timeframe thesis".
3. adopting the criterion of self-demarcation of lands to be titled.
4. adopting the self-declaration criterion to identify the remaining members of the *quilombo* communities.

Let us now look at each of these items in detail. Regarding the first one, the 2001 decree did not mention any expropriation procedure, determining that ownership rights would only be recognized in situations of unambiguous possession and maintained for a long period of time, in which the possession requirements were prolonged, peaceful and continuous. This premise can be found in article 1, in which the normative understanding of the lands that could be recognized and titled is explicit: "only ownership of lands that: I—were occupied by quilombos in 1888 and; II—were occupied by remaining members of *quilombo* communities on October 5, 1988".

As mentioned above, the 2003 article suspends the "political-legal timeframe thesis " (item 2) and begins to define the lands occupied by the remaining members of the quilombo communities referred to in article 68 as those "used for the guarantee of its physical, social, economic and cultural reproduction", without any mention of the requirement of occupation for a prolonged and continuous period.

The aforementioned decree goes even further and innovates in relation to the previous one by establishing that, at the time of land demarcation, the territoriality criteria indicated by the *quilombolas* themselves (item 3) must be taken into account, as well as the recognition of the legitimacy of the criterion of self-declaration in the definition of these groups (item 4).

Until then, there was a silence in the 2001 decree regarding what would be the criteria to define the *quilombola* communities, mentioning only that the administrative process for identifying the remaining members of the quilombo communities and for recognizing and titling their lands would be initiated by request from the interested party[5] and that this administrative process should include a technical report containing the ethnic, historical, cultural and socioeconomic aspects of the group; investigating the chain of title; delimitation of lands considered susceptible to recognition and demarcation. In other words, the new decree added some elements that were not in the previous decree: it provided criteria for defining a *quilombola* community (self-declaration accompanied by an anthropological report); and criteria for defining the area of the territory (self-demarcation, indicating that it should be appointed by the *quilombolas* themselves).

Contrary to what is observed in the 2003 decree, the 2001 decree does not explain the nature and degree of participation and intervention that should be granted to these groups throughout the stages of identification, recognition, delimitation and demarcation, determining only—and generically—that their participation in all stages of the administrative procedure should be ensured. When comparing them, one can see the important role that the decree of 2001 reserves for government institutions throughout all stages of the process. In 2003, the leading role of state institutions remained, but it advanced compared to the previous decree by providing details on the nature of *quilombola* participation, as observed by the self-demarcation and self-declaration criteria which, as we shall see, will be questioned by the ADI.

Not a year has passed since the recently enacted Decree 4887/03 for the *Partido da Frente Liberal*—PFL (Liberal Front Party) to file a Direct Action of Unconstitutionality (ADI 3239/04) questioning its constitutionality, giving rise to the legal controversy that will be analyzed in this chapter.

---

[5]Decree 3912/2001, article 2.

3 Actors

The ADI *Quilombola* brought together a multiplicity of actors who, roughly speaking, were divided between those who defended the validity of Decree 4887/03 and its maintenance and those who judged it to be unconstitutional. The first will be designated as those in favor of *quilombola* rights and the second as those against these rights.

Among the actors are civil society organizations (in greater numbers),[6] the State Prosecutor's Office, the Public Prosecutor's Office, the Attorney General of Brazil (representing the author of the objection, in this case, President Luiz Inácio Lula da Silva) and justices of the Supreme Federal Court. Among the organizations that represented organized civil society are those recognized for working in defense of human rights and ethnic and cultural minorities; employer class entities; residents' associations, as shown in Table 1.

The table shows 3 sets of actors: those who represent the State and are called to take a stand (in the case of the Attorney General of Brazil, Attorney General's Office and Public Prosecutor's Office); Supreme Federal Court ministers (responsible for judging the ADI); *Amici Curiae* (joining government and civil society entities).

The admission of *amici curiae* in trials aims to provide technical and scientific support to judges promising to increase the quality of court decisions. This is a legal mechanism provided for in the Brazilian legal system so that governmental and civil society entities that prove their representativeness in the matter can be manifested in proceedings in which the constitutionality of governmental laws and acts that threaten or violate the rights or interests of collectives that they represent are discussed. Among the motivations of the *amici curiae* is the intention to influence a certain decision. The choice of those who are admitted to this condition falls on the rapporteur of the process, who uses some criteria defined by law to grant or deny the request for admission, among which is the one related to the requirement of affinity with the subject in question and its representativeness with people who may be affected by the court's decision (Almeida 2019).

Due to this requirement to demonstrate affinity with the theme and representativeness vis-à-vis groups whose rights are being violated, the *amici curiae* petitions reserve most of their pages to prove this representativeness. In the petition asking for admission to this condition (Brasil 2010), the CNBB, which interests us more directly in this chapter, presents itself as a Catholic institution "whose mission is to constructively collaborate to promote integral human development and the greater good of the country". In the same text, seeking to give legitimacy to its role and, consequently, to demonstrate that it has a certain prestige in the courts, the following is stated:

> In carrying out its mission (...) it usually addresses public authorities on matters that are of interest to the **common good** and the saving mission of the church, as expressly determined in Articles 4 and 5 of the Canonical Statute. (...) The representativeness of the CNBB is, for

[6] They participated in the condition of an *amicus curiae*.

Table 1 Actors who participated in the trial of the ADI Quilombola

In favor of maintaining Decree 4887/03	Against maintaining Decree 4887/03
State	
Attorney General of Brazil	
Attorney General's Office	
Public Prosecutor's Office	
Supreme Federal Court	
Ministers	
Amici Curiae[a]	
Pro Bono Institute	Pará State
Conectas Human Rights	Santa Catarina State
Brazilian Public Law Society	The Brazilian Confederation of Agriculture and Livestock—CNA
Center on Housing Rights and Evictions—Cohere	The National Industry Confederation
Global Justice Center	Brazilian Pulp and Paper Association (Bracelpa)
ISA	Brazilian Rural Society
Instituto Polis	
Terra de Direitos	
Federation of Agricultural Workers of the State of Pará—Fetagri-Pará	
Popular Legal Advice Center Mariana Creole	
KOINONIA Ecumenical Presence and Service	
United Quilombos Association of Barro Preto and Indaiá	
Quilombola Residents Association of Santana—Quilombo de Santana	
Coordination of Black *Quilombola* Rural Communities of Mato Grosso do Sul	
The National Institute for Colonization and Agrarian Reform (INCRA)	
Paraná State	
CNBB	
Institute for Racial and Environmental Advocacy—IARA	
Palmares Club of Volta Redonda	

[a]Some *amici curiae* were highlighted, each with a color, to indicate those who jointly applied for this condition

> these reasons, recognized by public authorities [because it relates to the different segments of cultural, economic, social and political reality] in view of its relevant role in **the defense of solidarity, charity, common good and less privileged**, which demonstrates its legitimacy to contribute to the formation of the understanding of judges in the course of this action" (Request for admission as *amicus curiae*, 2010, bold type added by author).

Later in the text, the organization also discusses the "undeniable affinity" between the matter under discussion—Decree 4887—and its institutional mission. According to what has been presented in this petition, it claims that it meets the representativeness criterion, as its role in collaboration for the common good and in charity towards people oppressed by poverty or injustice would be common.

It can be observed, from the above, that in order to prove its representativeness and affinity with the topic, the CNBB aims to highlight both the regularity with which it positions itself in relation to the authorities ("it usually addresses public authorities on matters that are of interest to the common good") and for its role in promoting the common good, more generally, and in its defense of *oppressed people* and the *less privileged.*

It is worth noting that, at the *ADI Quilombola*, the CNBB and KOINONIA Ecumenical Presence and Service were the only religious actors to be admitted as *amicus curiae*, as well as the only ones from this field to request admission into the process in this condition. Despite there being two religious actors, we focus only on the role of the CNBB in this chapter. This is due to two reasons. Let us look at each of them.

The first is related to its participation in other legal controversies that have gained public visibility in recent years, such as those involving sexual and reproductive rights. It is important to highlight that these controversies differ from the case we are analyzing in this chapter, as research by Sales (2015), Santos Costa 2014 and Luna (2013) on legal controversies surrounding abortion and embryonic stem cell research[7] pointed out, the topic of sexual and reproductive rights has kindled interest and provoked the manifestation of various religious segments, participating in these Catholic, Evangelical and Spiritist controversies, which did not occur with *ADI Quilombola.*

Mapping the controversy surrounding the ownership rights of the remaining members of the *quilombo* communities leads us to affirm that other religious segments are not disputing land-related issues in the public arena, indicating that, at least for the time being, this issue remains a monopoly of the Catholic Church.

Another aspect that stands out in its role in the case of *quilombola* rights, compared to the aforementioned legal controversies, is the fact that the CNBB takes a stand against sexual and reproductive rights (Steil and Toniol 2012; Luna 2013; Sales 2015; Santos Costa 2014), while demonstrating in favor of the territorial rights of *quilombolas*. This means that depending on the rights at stake (whether sexual and reproductive or territorial), the institution is positioned in favor of or against these rights, which indicates a non-uniformity of its position in terms of rights.

In the controversy over the *ADI Quilombola*, the CNBB allied with civil society organizations that had sound experience in guaranteeing and promoting human rights and social justice (nationally and internationally) and, together with other state representatives, showed they were in favor of the constitutionality of Decree 4887/2003, that is, in favor of the right to ownership of *quilombola* communities, presenting very similar arguments to defend their positions.

[7] On such topics, according to Sales in this volume.

This role of the Catholic Church in the defense of human rights is not recent and, according to Steil and Toniol (2012), incorporating Human Rights as a guiding paradigm for the actions of individuals and governments appears in the institution's encyclicals and official documents as early as 1960, during the pontificate of Pope John XXIII. The same happened, according to the authors, with the CNBB when publishing documents and *communiqués* from bishops and dioceses that acted as sources of legitimization of the speech in defense of Human Rights.

The second reason that justifies the choice of focusing only on the CNBB's role is related to its history of action in the agrarian issue in Brazil.[8] According to Bandeira (2010), bishops from the Northeast who participated in the founding of the CNBB already acted in defense of agrarian reform even before the Second Vatican Council, even though at that time the right to land was not yet established as a human right. According to Reis (2012), the production of the idea of access to land as a human right would only occur in the 1970s, as a result of the interaction between the progressive Catholic Church, peasant movements and a transnational human rights network.

There are also numerous documents, booklets and other forms of dissemination prepared by the CNBB, elements that show its public commitment to the issue of agrarian reform and land rights. As an example, we can mention the Pastoral Land Commission foundation, in 1975; the CNBB publication, from 1979, in which it defends agrarian reform; a CNBB document entitled "The Church and Land Problems", 1980; the 1986 Fraternity Campaign, whose motto was "God's Land, Land of Brothers", among others that could be mentioned.

4 ADI Quilombola

As seen above, the legal controversy surrounding the ownership rights of remaining *quilombo* members involved a variety of actors, among which we are interested in analyzing the CNBB in detail. For the sake of clarity, we decided to present, in most cases, the positions of the actors together, to the detriment of a presentation that takes individuals as a unit to be described.

The legal controversy revolved around 4 specific points of Decree 4887/03 that were presented by the author of the petition as the reasons that led to the request for a declaration of unconstitutionality. As we shall see, it was around these 4 points that the debate was polarized and, based on them, the justifications for the two positions (in favor and against) were produced.

[8]CNBB was founded in 1952, and Koinonia in 1994.

4.1 *Formal Unconstitutionality: Is Article 68 a Norm of Full Effectiveness and Immediate Applicability?*

As previously mentioned, Decree 4887/03 was the second attempt by the executive branch to concretize article 68 of the ADCT of the Federal Constitution of 1988. This decree aims to regulate "the procedure for identification, recognition, delimitation, demarcation and titling of the lands occupied by the remaining members of the quilombo communities referred to in art. 68 of the Temporary Constitutional Provisions Act".

The fact of directly regulating a constitutional provision (art. 68) was presented by the ADI applicant as the first reason to allege its unconstitutionality. According to the author's argument of the petition, there would be no previous law that would give validity to Decree 4.887/03. From the perspective of this legal interpretation, decrees have the nature of a secondary normative instrument (their validity depends on the formal law), that is, their function would be to execute previously existing laws. Thus, a presidential decree, intending to directly regulate a constitutional provision, would no longer need the mediation of a law and, for this reason, would be unconstitutional. It can be concluded, that, in the case of Decree 4.887, there is no previous law that could be regulated by the aforementioned decree, and that would mediate between the decree and the Federal Constitution. In other words, there would be an impediment to a decree directly regulating a constitutional article. Among the actors in the legal controversy that supported this idea are, in addition to the author-party, the *amici curiae* gathered in those in favor of the annulment of Decree 4887. Among the ministers, only Cezar Peluso, who also held the position of rapporteur of the process in the beginning, and Gilmar Mendes, embraced this argument and argued that this is a formal unconstitutionality as article 68 is not a norm of full effectiveness and immediate applicability, and the head of the executive is not authorized, therefore, to regulate this constitutional command (article 68) by regulation (presidential decree).

The other pole of the controversy, which joins the largest number of actors (among which the CNBB), uses two different arguments to defend the constitutionality of Decree 4887/03. The lawyer who represented the CNBB in the process, in his oral argument, stated (supported by Article 5 of the General Law) that Article 68 is a rule that enshrines a fundamental right and, therefore, has an immediate and self-applicable effect. That means the executive is authorized to regulate it.

Due to its nature, this norm would be related to the principle of human dignity. In defending the constitutionality of the decree, the Catholic entity sets out the reasons described below. The first is that, in the understanding of the Catholic institution and other actors who hold this position, the decree finds its foundation of validity in Article 68, which, in turn, is configured as a self-applicable constitutional norm. Self-applicable constitutional norms are those that, since the admission into force of the Federal Constitution of 1988, produce, or have the possibility to produce, all the essential effects as they are a fundamental right. That is, article 68, as it enshrines a fundamental right, would be self-applicable, which means that it would not need a law to regulate it. According to the Catholic institution, this would have been a sensible choice by the constituent, as it would prevent the legal uselessness of norms central to human dignity, in this case, the right to land held by *quilombola* communities. Citing the work of Minister Gilmar Mendes to support this position, he also argues that this concern on the part of the constituent would be linked to the need to overcome the concept of the State of Formal Law in which fundamental rights only gain expression when regulated by law.

To provide even greater support for its position, the CNBB cites excerpts from decisions rendered in other judgments of Regional Federal Courts in which it was decided by recognizing the self-applicability of the constitutional precept contained in art. 68.

In addition to defending that Decree 4887/03 finds its constitutional and legal basis in Article 68, which, in turn, has full effectiveness and immediate applicability, the Catholic institution argues that the rights of *quilombo* communities are subject to protection by international treaties of human rights, invoking ILO Convention 169. In this regard, and similarly to what the other actors who hold this position of controversy expressed, the norms of international law that protect or extend human rights would have been raised to the status of constitutional norm. Edson Facchin, for example, argues that we are dealing with a fundamental right that, although it is not included in the list contained in Title II of the constitutional text ("On Fundamental Rights and Guarantees"), "also carries with it the fundamental note, for ensuring to an ethnic minority the right to ownership and, by doing this, the recovery of the exercise of other citizenship rights, including respect for their community identity" (Acórdão 2018: 194). The same position is inferred from the vote of Minister Luiz Fux, who makes an equivalent reservation, but ends up concluding that, despite not being present in Title II of the Federal Constitution, it does not mean that it does not have this nature, as the rights expressed in the magna carta do not exclude others arising from the regime and principles adopted by it, or from international treaties to which Brazil is a signatory. This argument is equally defended by the CNBB which, to support it, finds inspiration in the formulations of attorney Daniel Sarmento, reproducing an excerpt from his work in which he states that "the main criterion for the recognition of fundamental rights not included in the catalog is its connection to the principle of the dignity of the human person" (p. 19). This was also the understanding expressed by the Public Prosecutor's Office, through its assistant attorney Deborah Duprat, on her oral argument.

Similar to the CNBB, other actors that held the position in favor of the constitutionality of the Decree, we can say that most of them made constant reference to Convention 169 of the International Labor Organization (ILO).[9] This was not only observed about this specific point of the controversy, but also to others that we will

[9]The Inter-American Convention on Human Rights was also mobilized by ministers Luís Roberto Barroso and Rosa Weber as an international instrument in which the decree would obtain its foundation of validity, as it provided for the right to ownership, as well as its subjection to the social function.

address below, which points to the relevance of this international treaty as an important source of legitimacy for the objected Decree and, more than that, because it fills the Constitutional silence on which new rights could be considered fundamental. According to the Public Prosecutor's Office report, prepared by Daniel Sarmento (Regional Prosecutor of the Republic), this is an open catalog that may incorporate other rights provided for in international treaties. As already pointed out, the main criterion for recognizing a fundamental right not included in the catalog is its connection to the principle of human dignity. It would be the case of article 68, which, according to the assistant attorney, refers to the right to housing that integrates the existential minimum, being, therefore, an important component of the principle of human dignity. She goes even further by stating that:

> Deprived of land, the group tends to disperse and disappear, absorbed by the surrounding society. Therefore, it is not only the land that is lost, as the collective identity is also in danger of succumbing. Thus, it is no exaggeration to say that when land is removed from a *quilombola* community, it is not just violating the housing rights of its members. Much more than that, it attacks the ethnic identity of these people. This is why the right to land for remaining quilombo members is also a fundamental cultural right (art. 215, CF) (Public Prosecutor's Office Report, 2008)

According to those in favor of Decree 4887, the territory is important not only because it guarantees a place to live and work, but also because it supports collective ethnic identity. Guaranteeing access to and permanence on the land means, therefore, guaranteeing a place of residence and identity.

Another aspect highlighted by most ministers, referring to what had already been pointed out by prosecutor Daniel Sarmento on another occasion who spoke in defense of the self-applicability of the decree, was the fact that it contained all the necessary elements for its effectiveness, once that there the object of the right (land), the condition for its recognition ("that they are occupying"), its titleholder ("remaining members of *quilombo* communities"), the taxable person (State) and the specific obligation (issuance of bonds) are found. It would be these indications that would eliminate the need to enact a law to enable the protection of the right to ownership. Barroso, for example, claims that the requirement of infra-constitutional laws to implement art. 68 would be a way of hindering the exercise of the right guaranteed therein.

The other group of actors of those who defend the constitutionality of the Decree follows a different argumentative path to reach the same conclusion, namely, that Decree 4887/03 is constitutional. They argue, along the lines of the Attorney General of Brazil, that the aforementioned instrument is based on two laws: Law 7.668/88 and Law 9649/98. The first creates the Palmares Cultural Foundation and the second gives the Ministry of Culture the competence to approve the delimitation of the lands of the *quilombola* communities and, according to its defenders, they would be responsible for directly regulating the Constitution, implementing it in the first degree. Following this reasoning, the Decree would be in the second stage of implementing the norms of articles 215 and 216, as well as article 68, all from the Federal Constitution. This would be proof that this is not an autonomous decree, as the author of the petition suggests.

Luís Roberto Barroso and the Public Prosecutor's Office present a position that combines these two arguments, as they argue that the decree finds its first foundation of validity in art. 68 (self-applicable, as it enshrines a fundamental right) and its second basis of validity in Convention 169, in the Inter-American Convention on Human Rights and in the laws of 1988 and 1998. The minister therefore concludes that the right of *quilombola* communities to ownership in their territory it would be provided for in a self-applicable constitutional norm (art. 68), in two international treaties to which Brazil is a signatory, and in two federal laws. Considering this, it would not be an autonomous decree, as it would discipline a set of primary norms on the issue.

4.2 New Expropriation Modality

Considering the repeal of the Decree of 2001 and the promulgation of Decree 4.887 of 2003, it was established, through art. 13, that titles of private domain that applied to territories occupied by the remaining members of *quilombo* communities would be subject to expropriation. The National Institute for Colonization and Agrarian Reform (INCRA) would have to assess these properties and regulate hypotheses susceptible to expropriation.

The author-party of the Direct Action of Unconstitutionality (ADI) in question argued that this article of Decree 4887 that provides for expropriation would be unconstitutional. In their reading of article 68, it would be incumbent on the Public Authorities to expropriate the area, as ownership would result directly from the Constitution, as the constitutional text would attest by stating that "definite ownership is recognized", that is, as in the case of indigenous, the lands would already belong to the *quilombolas*, and the State would only issue the titles. The author claims that:

> There is no need to talk about other people's ownership to be expropriated to be transferred to the remaining members of *quilombos*, much less promoting public expenditure to cover future compensation. The lands are, from the outset, by virtue of the Major Law itself, of the remaining members of the *quilombola* communities that have settled there since October 5, 1988. The role of the State is limited, according to article 68 of the *Ato das Disposições Constitucionais Transitórias* – ADCT (Temporary Constitutional Provisions Act) to merely issuing the respective titles (ADI 3239, 2004: 6).

From the transcribed statement above, we would like to extract two points that will be discussed in the controversy. The first, which we will go into further in this topic, concerns the issue of expropriation itself and the argument that this mechanism would not fit in cases involving the lands of the remaining members of *quilombos*, as ownership would already be assured by article 68 itself, with the State only the issuance of the respective titles. Thus, any rule that determines the expropriation of the area would incur in what is known in the legal world as "unconstitutionality vice" any rule that determines the expropriation of the area, as well as "the use of public resources for the subsequent transfer to the holders of the original right of definitive ownership" (ADI 3239 2004a: 7).

The second point, which will be addressed in the next topic, points to a requirement that, if met, would guarantee ownership rights. It concerns the requirement of having been occupying the lands claimed on the day of the promulgation of the Federal Constitution. Briefly stated, the requesting party's argument consists of the following: expropriation is not applicable in these cases, as the ownership of the remaining members would already be assured since the promulgation of the Constitution, attributing the responsibility to issue the titles to the State. However, only those communities that were occupying them at the time of the promulgation of the Constitution, in 1988, would only have their ownership rights assured. As already seen, this formulation was called the "political-legal timeframe thesis". We will return to this later.

As a basis for his assertions, the author resorts to the work of some jurists, including Claudio Teixeira da Silva, who has an excerpt of his article transcribed in the petition: "the constitutional command requires the State to act only in issuing ownership titles, being prohibited to it, in respect of the principle of legality, to carry out expropriations on the grounds of compliance with article 68 of the ADCT" (ADI 3239 2004a: 7). Moreover, the expropriation referred to in Decree 4887, in addition to incurring a defect of unconstitutionality for the reasons set out above, would not fit into any of the modalities provided for in the constitutional text (art. 5, XXIV).

Among the ministers, Cézar Peluso was the only one who agreed that the expropriation would be unconstitutional. He argues that the lands that should be titled are those whose ownership is secular, showing himself to be a supporter of the timeframe thesis. It also agrees with the statement that the expropriation referred to in Decree 4887 does not fall under the modalities of "public necessity or utility" (a) or "social interest" (b), as defended by some actors who are pro-constitutionality. He disputes the adequacy of the second modality because the case of *quilombola* lands would be associated with the preservation of historical monuments and cultural heritage which, in turn, would be provided for in the modality of "public utility". Added to this is the fact that in these cases, private ownership should be transferred to the public domain and not, again, to private individuals.

In his vote, the minister presents excerpts from a series of articles published in newspapers that have a large circulation to reinforce his argument that the decree would have provoked a latent conflict in Brazilian society and a growing number of *quilombola* communities that would have emerged after it. In the reports presented by the minister, the role attributed to anthropologists as "creators" of non-existent *quilombola* communities calls our attention, in addition to their supposed influence (negative, from this point of view) in defining the extent of land to be recognized.

As a member of those that defend the unconstitutionality of expropriation and representative of the position of the actors that comprise it, the Brazilian Rural Society states that the decree produces legal uncertainty when confronting private ownership, protected by the Constitution, and that this process cannot be done at the expense of the right to ownership. A conflict between individual and collective rights can be observed in this group. Individual rights, more specifically ownership rights, must supersede collective rights, revealing the hierarchical framework that this group grants to rights.

The actors in the other group did not manifest at any time against private ownership, but they were against the fact that the right to ownership and the individual overlap and often even annihilate collective rights. They argue that, as well as rights related to the individual, rights of a collective order (right to have their own way of life, right to communal possession of land, right of a group to have a decent life in which their values are respected, etc.) must also be worthy of recognition, respect and legal protection.

Regarding expropriation, these actors argue that recourse to it is legitimate because the legal basis for such action is "social interest", that is, the preservation of Brazilian cultural heritage. From this perspective, *quilombola* communities are conceived as cultural heritage of the nation and liable to be respected and preserved.

It is important to highlight that this point is the one that draws the most comparisons with the indigenous people. This is because the applicant grants an interpretation similar to *quilombola* lands to that granted to indigenous lands in the Constitution, which can be seen in the use of the term "original right owners" in the written petition. These are considered an original right of these peoples and any private title incident on them is considered null or void, excluding the right to any type of indemnity for the bare land, except for improvements. For those who are acting in defense of the decree, article 68, contrary to what the applicant would believe, does not invalidate existing ownership titles, as was done with indigenous lands.

In the *Quilombola* case, there is a Constitutional silence regarding the way to be used to resolve these conflicts. In the opinion of most ministers, this silence would give rise to endless discussions, were it not for the decree that offered, through expropriation, an adequate solution to accommodate the legal assets at stake, referring to the right to ownership guaranteed in the Constitution and the rights of *quilombola* communities. The conclusion is that, if the Constitution does not invalidate the titles, recourse to expropriation in these cases becomes legitimate.

The expropriation modality that is defended both by ministers and by organizations of those in favor of the Decree—among them the CNBB—is that of social interest,[10] defined as that which aims, among other objectives, "to condition land use to its social function". The hypothesis that would best fit for expropriation in the *Quilombola* case, among those provided for in Law 4504/1964, would be the one that authorizes this procedure for "the establishment and maintenance of colonies or cooperatives for settlement and agricultural work".

In order to reinforce the legitimacy and constitutionality of the recourse to expropriation, the argument that Article 216 of the Federal Constitution puts forward for expropriation in order to protect Brazilian cultural heritage is often used in this legal controversy. It is worth recalling that the Federal Constitution expanded the

[10] Luiz Fux, Rosa Weber, Dias Toffoli, Edson Fachin and Luís Roberto Barroso. Its legal content is given by Law 4504/1964.

concept of heritage other than monuments, including in this category "the ways of creating, doing and living".

Some of the actors who defend decree 4887 argue that article 68 must be understood in conjunction with article 216, which authorizes expropriation for the protection of Brazilian cultural heritage, remembering that its genesis took place within the discussions on cultural heritage Brazilian during the constituent assembly.

The CNBB endorses this point of view by defending the complementarity and dialogue between article 68, article 216 and the expropriation instrument. For the Catholic institution, this resource would be the most appropriate administrative procedure also against ILO Convention 169, establishing that governments must adopt the appropriate measures to guarantee the protection of ownership and possession rights of tribal peoples and determining that procedures must be instituted within the national legal system to resolve the land claims made by these peoples. In summary, the CNBB argues that the expropriation is supported not only by the national legal framework (Law of 1962 and art. 216 of the CF), but also by international human rights treaties, such as the aforementioned Convention.

Some actors who are opposed to the idea of including *quilombola* lands in the law that provides for expropriation for agrarian reform purposes—unsystematically expressed in the arena being analyzed, but widely discussed in other periods and other arenas—under the justification that individual title, as in agrarian reform, would be inadequate for an ethnic group whose regime of appropriation of space is not organized on this basis. The CNBB is one of these actors and maintains that land tenure regularization must respect the plurality of forms of land occupation resulting from the Brazilian sociocultural and ethnic diversity and emphasizes that the existing instruments in private law do not consider the multiple forms of land appropriation of these other groups. Individual holders, as is done in agrarian reform, would mean, in the understanding of the Catholic institution, the end of their existence as a community, condemning them to the loss of their values, customs and cultural standards and thus affronting the constitutional principle enshrined in the articles 215 and 68 of the ADCT.

Another argument put forward by some members of this group who, as can be seen, took a more conciliatory position, is that the expropriation would be able to "pacify the controversy", by providing a response to the territorial dispossession suffered by the *quilombolas* and, at the same time, promoting the recomposition of assets of the eventual holders of rights over the disputed land. According to them, the advantage of Decree 4887 would lie in the fact that it protected *quilombola* ownership without neglecting the eventual rights of individuals: "Thus, both constitutional interests were respected in a line of tension, harmonizing and balancing them in the interior of the Brazilian legal system" (Acórdão 2018: 300).

They point out that many of these titles are valid and purchased in good faith. Deborah Duprat, in her oral argument representing the Federal Public Ministry, defends that the recognition of the lands of the *quilombola* communities is "a burden and a bonus of the whole Brazilian society", as it should interest all Brazilians to have these groups forming part of the diversity that would characterize us. For this reason, the deputy prosecutor emphasizes that the indemnities must be fair, as it would not be correct for only one owner to pay for it. Along the same lines, minister Luiz Fux expresses himself, using the principle of social solidarity[11] as the second constitutional foundation that grants legitimacy to expropriation and justifies the collective sharing of the costs inherent to guaranteeing and enforcing the right to land for *quilombola* communities. His speech is also illustrative in this regard: "It would not be in the least fair or reasonable for the burdens arising from the preservation of Brazilian cultural heritage (CRFB, arts. 215 and 216) to fall exclusively on the former owners of territories occupied by the remaining groups of *quilombos*. Considering this, the attribution to the State of the duty to indemnify them constitutes an adequate instrument for dividing the costs of implementing art. 68 of the ADCT" (Acórdão 2018: 301).

4.3 Demarcation Procedure: Self-Demarcation x Temporal Criteria

What is in dispute in this specific point of the controversy are the criteria foreseen in Decree 4887 for the delimitation of the land area to be destined to the remaining members of *quilombo* communities (1); and the definition that this provision grants to the term "land occupied by the remaining members of *quilombo* communities" (2). Let us see what paragraphs 2 and 3 of article 2 of Decree 4887, which was the object of contestation, say:

> § 2 Lands occupied by the remaining members of *quilombo* communities are those used to guarantee their physical, social, economic and cultural reproduction.
>
> § 3 For the measurement and demarcation of lands, the territoriality criteria indicated by the remaining members of the *quilombo* communities will be taken into account, in which the interested community is entitled to present the technical pieces for the procedural instruction.

Regarding paragraph 2, the ADI applicant claims that it is "excessive breadth" to define the lands that will be recognized as those on which the remaining members had their physical, social, economic and cultural reproduction. For the author of the request, the economic activities and physical reproduction of the *quilombola* communities do not necessarily correspond to the areas where the *quilombos* would actually have been located, arguing that only the areas where it can actually be proven should the existence of *quilombos* in the past be recognized: "the area whose ownership must be recognized is only and solely the territory in which, during the imperial phase of Brazilian history, the *quilombo* was demonstrably formed" (ADI 3239 2004b: 11). These would be the areas to which the Constitution would refer.

Concerning paragraph 3, the use of "criteria of territoriality indicated by the remaining members of *quilombo* communities" is questioned to define the lands that will be recognized, that is, self-demarcation. According to the petition,

[11] Article 3, I, of the Federal Constitution.

"subjecting the demarcation of lands to the indications of the interested parties does not constitute a reputable, moral and legitimate definition procedure" (ADI 3239 2004b: 11).

The criticism by the formulators of the ADI request consists precisely in what supporters of the *quilombola* cause recognized as an advance of Decree 4.887 compared to the previous decree, from 2001. The Interministerial working group that was formed to discuss the wording of Decree 4.887 used the concept of territoriality and defined the areas of cultivation, extraction, farming and forestry, as well as the areas of recreation and perambulation, as subject to claim. This represented an advance for the *quilombola* movement, as the previous decree only allowed the claim for areas of effective occupation, that is, the areas of housing and production that were being used by residents at the time of the claim. Added to this, the requirement that this space actually occupied corresponds to the same space that would have been occupied during the imperial phase. These requirements for the demarcation and titling of the territory in the decree of 2001 would prevent all those communities that, for some reason, have moved to other areas, from having this right guaranteed.

Among the ministers, only Cezar Peluso cast his vote in accordance with what was argued by the ADI applicant on this issue. In his interpretation, the lands to be titled must be those whose ownership is secular, arguing that the constituent would have opted for the historical meaning of *quilombo*. He demonstrates that he is aware of the recent process of resemantization that the *quilombo* category went through, however, he believes that "the respectable works developed by jurists and anthropologists", with the intention of modernizing this concept, would have a meta-legal nature and, therefore, would not have, and they should not have a commitment to what he apprehends from the constitutional text.

The CNBB is at the other pole of the debate regarding "occupied lands", the criterion of self-demarcation and the concept of *quilombo*. Its speech demonstrates his knowledge and alignment with recent discussions that this topic has raised in the field of Anthropology. Regarding the concept of *quilombo*, it shows its agreement in relation to its resemantization, opposing the historical meaning of the term. It radically disagrees with the interpretation that limits lands to be allocated to *quilombola* communities today to those existing in the imperial period, claiming that it does not matter where they are located today, as the imperative is that culture, identity, ways of creating, doing and living of the *quilombolas* are preserved, wherever they are. Their argument points to the need to question and overcome the requirement of occupying the claimed lands, as it must be considered that these are vulnerable populations and, therefore, victims of processes of invasion and expulsion.

It can be observed that the institution defends a broad concept of territory, similar to the other actors in this group, understanding it not only in its physical and geographic dimension, but as maintaining an inseparable link with the cultural and identity plan of a group. This concept of territory that extrapolates its physical and geographic dimension is what explains a very common argument among them, namely, that the ownership right of the remaining members of *quilombola* communities to the land they occupy is not reduced to a right to housing but encompasses their right to a particular culture and identity. In the words of the lawyer who represented the CNBB, "the *quilombola* territory cannot be understood as a mere externalization of the right to ownership, as it acquires meaning from the recognition of the right to cultural survival of a certain ethnic group" (Request for admission as *amicus curiae*, 2010).

Minister Celso de Mello reinforces this interpretation by stating that land titling of the remaining members of *quilombo* communities is closely related to the postulate of human dignity, for two reasons: to guarantee the right to housing and to integrate the existential minimum of a dignified life (1); for preserving the ethnic and cultural integrity of these groups. For this reason, the members of this group, which we are describing here through the CNBB, understand that article 68 must be understood together with arts. 215 and 216 of the Federal Constitution, responsible for protecting the cultural rights of the groups that form the nation.

As other actors, the support of this group on this theme tends to oppose what would be the Western conception of land to that of traditional communities; the first would reduce it to a mere instrument to be exploited economically, while among the latter, the land, in addition to being an instrument for its physical reproduction, would be related to the maintenance of an identity and a culture. Citing attorney Daniel Sarmento, the CNBB lawyer argues that, due to this relationship that traditional communities have with the land, the original constituent would have considered it a fundamental cultural right under the terms of art. 215. It also qualifies the negligence in protecting these lands as ethnocide.

This formulation in which we find this close link between territory/culture/identity is widely disseminated within this group and one of its important sources of inspiration is ILO Convention 169, which defends that the land category should include the territory concept. This means to say that not only the areas used for their physical reproduction, but also those used for their social, economic and cultural reproduction, along the lines of what we find in Decree 4887 must be considered. For them, both the definition of land present in the Decree and the self-demarcation criterion are supported by ILO Convention 169.

We have seen so far that the characterization of the lands to be allocated to *quilombola* communities raises two divergent positions concerning the actors involved in this legal controversy. Those in favor of Decree 4887 defend the use of the concept of territory, which means that they are in favor of recognizing and titling lands that are necessary for the physical, economic, social and cultural reproduction of *quilombola* communities, abolishing the temporary thesis as a criterion to define them. Those against Decree 4887, on the other hand, maintain that this definition would be too broad and argue that only those where a *quilombo* had been established in the imperial period and in which its remaining members were from 1888 until 1988, the year of promulgation of the Federal Constitution, would be worthy of recognition.

The ministers who defended the constitutionality of the self-demarcation criterion expressed a very similar argument among themselves, as they stated that this criterion is not the only parameter to be considered, accompanied by countless others throughout the process of recognizing the lands to be titled.[12] All of them considered the idea wrong of the author-party that demarcation is subject to *quilombola* interest, for the simple reason that the Decree is clear in stating that the territoriality criteria indicated by the *quilombolas* "will be taken into account", which means that they are not absolute. They also emphasize that the process generally follows 14 steps[13] until it is finally titled.

The fact that it is provided for by INCRA's Normative Instruction that any interested party may file an objection—showing that the adversary system and the broad defense of all interested parties are guaranteed—would be one more element that would allow us to state that the demarcation is not subject to the indications of the interested parties themselves. Moreover, there is a requirement to prepare studies and anthropological reports that may corroborate or displace the alleged territoriality and its area, thus minimizing the chances of abuse by interested parties.

4.4 Self-Attribution: Who Would Be the Holders of the Right to Ownership?

The subjects of law in article 68 are the remnants of *quilombo* communities, however, the article itself did not specify which collectives would fall into this category, a factor that triggered this dispute for the most appropriate criterion to define who would be the remaining members of the *quilombo* communities. Faced with this silence in the Federal Constitution, and having as inspiration ILO Convention 169, decree 4887/03 elected self-attribution as the criterion for identifying these groups.[14]

According to article 2:

> [...} the remaining members of *quilombo* communities are considered, for the purposes of this Decree, to be ethnic-racial groups, according to self-attribution criteria, with their own historical trajectory, endowed with specific territorial relations, with a presumption of black ancestry related to the resistance to the historical oppression suffered.

The ADI applicant considers it a "mere expression of the interested party's will", pointing to the risks of fraud that could result from its request as land ownership could be attributed to "persons who effectively have no relationship with the inhabitants of communities formed by runaway slaves, at the time of slavery in the country" (ADI 3239 2004c: 10).

For those who defend the unconstitutionality of Decree 4887, self-attribution would be a subjective, broad and lacking criterion. Due to these attributes that impute to the criterion, the reminiscence of those who identify themselves as

[12] This understanding was also expressed by Incra and the Attorney General of Brazil.

[13] This understanding was also expressed by Incra and AGU. These steps are contained in INCRA's Normative Instruction No. 57/2009.

[14] This decree recognized the remaining members of *quilombo* communities as ethnic groups.

quilombolas needs to be proved. By "remaining members" these actors understand those individuals who are descendants of slavery who, necessarily, were inhabitants of *quilombos*. Thus, they differentiate between reminiscence and descent. The remaining members would be those descendants of slaves who fled during slavery and became residents of the *quilombos*. On the other hand, descent would only indicate that a certain person is a descendant of slavery, without proof that they had constituted or were members of a *quilombo*.

The logic of the debate around the self-attribution criterion is largely similar to that observed in the previous topic about self-demarcation. First, because the actors in favor of Decree 4887 converge on the idea that self-declaration is the first step on the path to the recognition of a *quilombola* community and, although fundamental, it does not represent an absolute criterion. They draw attention to the other items that must be accompanied by this criterion and that are described in the aforementioned decree, among which the presumption of black ancestry related to resistance to the historical oppression suffered; the specific territoriality; and its own historical trajectory, which, as a rule, are presented in the anthropological reports that support requests for recognition and titles.

They claim that the process, like the demarcation process, comprises several steps, among which self-attribution would be just the first. The internal regulations of the Palmares Cultural Foundation would also prove to invalidate the applicant party's argument that self-attribution would be disconnected from any factual support. To this end, the possibility for the agency to carry out technical visits to communities that are seeking recognition to gather information and resolve doubts, as well as the requirement to prepare an anthropological report, were mentioned.

The pro-constitutional side of the decree, supported by advances in the field of Anthropology in studies on ethnicity, defends that identity is not a mere matter of desire and interest, given that belonging to an ethnic group means recognizing oneself and being recognized by other members. For Deborah Duprat and also for Carlos Frederico de Souza Filho (Prosecutor for the State of Paraná), it is an act of unfounded power to allow people outside the group to say who is or is not a *quilombola*. Duprat cites the sociologist Pierre Bourdieu to support his assertion, stating that, according to this author, establishing borders is an act of power and, for this reason, it is not possible to say who is a *quilombola* or even to say which area each community should claim.

This group as a whole defends that *quilombola* communities should be recognized as ethnic groups, whose borders must be defined by the interested parties, following the understanding inaugurated by Anthropology.[15]

Anthropology, as scientific knowledge, is not the only source that lends legitimacy to the criterion of self-declaration. Alongside it, the actors of the block that

[15]For this argument, anthropologists Eliane Cantarino and Alfredo Wagner Berno de Almeida are often cited. I suggest referring to the year of the work here and inserting the complete reference in the list at the end, so that international audiences have a chance to consult something more specific about the authors.

defends constitutionality extract the legitimacy of this criterion from ILO Convention 169, which enshrined the "awareness of one's own identity" as a criterion for determining ethnic groups, thus, there would be compatibility between the decree and the Convention, which is why it would not be unconstitutional.

The CNBB, as a member of this group, adds, in addition to the arguments listed above, that this is a methodological divergence and, therefore, should be the object of scientific and not legal analysis. The Catholic organization, following the arguments initiated by the Attorney General of Brazil, emphasizes that this is a "scientific criterion" adopted at the international level—the object of intense discussions at the time of the ILO General Conference in 1989—and that it has already been internalized in the Brazilian legal system. It argues that this is a discussion of the scientific field that has been internalized by the Brazilian regulatory system and at the international level and, therefore, does not lack constitutionality. For this reason, it claims that the court would not be the space where scientific criteria should be discussed. As the other members of this group, the CNBB extracts the legitimacy of the self-attribution of Anthropology, which, according to its reading, uses it as an "essential defining element of the condition of an ethnic group" (request for admission as an *amicus curiae*, 2010: 26) and international treaties regulating human rights.

5 Final Considerations

In this chapter, we sought to map the legal controversy that formed around ADI 3239/2004, describing the actors involved, their alliances and the justifications produced to defend their positions.

Among these actors, the CNBB stood out, which, in this specific controversy, joined forces with civil society organizations recognized for acting in defense of human rights. As seen, the action of the Catholic institution in defense of these rights and the right of access to land is not limited to this controversy which, it can be said, is only one of the fronts of its action. Since its foundation, CNBB has been preparing documents, booklets, texts, books, among other materials in which it explicitly defends the right to land ownership they occupy, while helping, together with other actors, to produce the meanings of the categories that circulate in this field.

In the case of the controversy analyzed here, we described the position of the Catholic institution through its request for admission as an *amicus curiae* in the process and its oral support in the plenary of the Supreme Federal Court. However, since its founding in 1952, it has been presenting itself as an engaged and prominent actor in the defense of the right of access to land, having contributed, as shown by Reis (2012) to the production of the idea of access to land as a human right, alongside national peasant movements and international human rights organizations. This shows, for example, how it helped to guide the debate and helped to construct the meaning of some categories included in this controversy. Thus, we chose to focus on their participation in the controversy, without, however, failing to mention their role in other arenas where the issue of land rights has been discussed.

The analyzed material also reveals the strategic importance of the Human Rights category to innovate the understanding of what is constitutional. The argumentative constructions of those that defended the validity of Decree 4887/2003 point in this direction.

References

Almeida EM d (2019) Capacidades institucionais dos amici curiae no Supremo Tribunal Federal: acessibilidade, admissibilidade e influência. Rev Direito Práx 10(1):678–707

Bandeira M (2010) Dom Távora: um exemplo de trabalho social no Brasil (entrevista a Patricia Fachin). Revista IHU On-Line 341

Boltanski L, Thevénot L (2006) On justification: economies of worth. Princeton University Press, Princeton

Brasil. Supremo Tribunal Federal. ADI 3239, 2004a. Disponível em www.stf.jus.br

Brasil (2004b) Pedido para ingresso como amicus curiae na ADIN 3239: Instituto Pro Bono. Conectas Direitos Humanos e Sociedade Brasileira de Direito Público

Brasil (2004c) Pedido para ingresso como amicus curiae na ADIN 3239: Terra de Direitos. Centro pelo Direito à Moradia Contra Despejos, Centro de Justiça Global, Instituto Socioambiental e Instituto Polis

Brasil. Pedido para ingresso como amicus curiae na ADIN 3239: Conferência Nacional dos Bispos do Brasil, 2010

Brasil. Supremo Tribunal Federal. Acórdão da ADI 3239, 2018. Disponível em www.stf.jus.br

Luna N (2013) O direito à vida no contexto do aborto e da pesquisa com células-tronco embrionárias: disputas de agentes e valores religiosos em um Estado laico. Relig Soc 33(1): 71–97

Reis RR (2012) O direito à terra como um direito humano: a luta pela reforma agrária e o movimento de direitos humanos no Brasil. Lua Nova 86:89–122

Sales L (2015) 'Em defesa da vida humana': moralidades em disputa em duas audiências públicas do STF. Relig Soc 35(2):143–164

Santos Costa I (2014) Os bispos nordestinos e a criação da CNBB. Interações 9(15):109–143

Steil CA, Toniol R (2012) A trajetória dos Direitos Humanos na Igreja Católica no Brasil: do discurso político ao discurso moral. In: de Oliveira PR, de Mori G (eds) Mobilidade religiosa: linguagens, juventude, política, vol v, 1st edn. Paulinas, São Paulo, pp 75–88

Human Rights and Their Policy-Visibility in Producing a Public Islam in Brazil

Helena de Morais Manfrinato Othman

Abstract Since the September 11, 2001 attacks, Muslim communities in Brazil have been associated with "religious terror", "intolerance" and "gender oppression". In view of this, local Islamic organizations have mobilized some visibility strategies aimed at disassociating the image of Islam as a violent religion, mainly using the narrative of "human rights". In this chapter, I will analyze institutional initiatives that, through this language, aim to control the proliferation of negative images (Latour 2004, p. 24) of Islam. The aim is to normalize them based on parameters determined by them, circulating information about the religion, to project a positive public image of Islam in Brazil.

I will analyze initiatives of three Sunni Islamic organizations, *União Nacional das Entidades Islâmicas*—UNI (the National Union of Islamic Entities), the World Assembly of Muslim Youth—WAMY and the *Centro de Divulgação do Islã para a América Latina*—CDIAL (Islam Dissemination Center for Latin America) in the city of São Paulo. My focus will be on their outreach material, the participation of sheikhs in interfaith events, interviews and political events, and the creation of a legal framework to defend Muslims from Islamophobic attacks. Finally, I will discuss a case of Islamophobia against a young Muslim woman who had the support and visibility of this institutional network.

I start from the hypothesis that "human rights", in their various forms, constitute a kind of "lingua franca" that enables actors to speak and circulate in different public spaces and form connections with networks that go beyond the scope of the religious community, contributing to the formation of a public Islam in Brazil.

H. de Morais Manfrinato Othman (✉)
Brazilian Center of Analysis and Planning, São Paulo, Brazil

P. Montero et al. (eds.), *Religious Pluralism and Law in Contemporary Brazil*, Law and Religion in a Global Context 4, https://doi.org/10.1007/978-3-031-41981-2_9

1 Introduction

"Human rights" seem to be ubiquitously present on Brazilian[1] Sunni and Shia Islamic entity websites, on the shelves in the halls of their headquarters, on the improvised benches next to the café at their courses, events and interreligious forums, alongside news about wars in the Middle East and philanthropic actions in their bilingual newspapers, in printed color brochures and in the sheikhs' public speeches. They are a recurrent language when it comes to defending Islam and its practitioners in the face of interpellations that associate the religion with "terror", "intolerance" or "gender oppression".

The circulation of these themes in the narratives about Islam grew significantly after the 9/11 attacks in 2001,[2] consolidated as a media event (Moreira 2004), that is, having a continuous agenda on world television networks and in print media, and reinforced on the Internet and the first opinion blogs. These media narratives poured out into an orientalist imaginary of Islam and the Arab peoples in Brazil (Pinto 2010), which described them as barbaric and exotic, and evoked a feeling of aversion to religion, but also of interest. This mediatized event would create a "cascading effect" (Appadurai 1996) that would erupt with each new international event, creating new waves of Islamophobic attacks.[3]

The ripple effect materialized in an intense search by Islamic organizations and mosques for "official" statements to the press, an influx of curious non-Muslims to their premises, and physical and verbal attacks on Muslims. This dynamic was observed in the emergence of each new event,[4] when the imaginary of Islam in Brazil was re-energized, updating orientalist rhetoric and producing contradictory effects of aversion, violence, but also of renewed interest. One of the main targets of these reactions is Muslim women, recognized for their religious attire, particularly the hijab, the scarf that covers their head and neck.

These events prompted many Islamic organizations to prepare a response based on positive visibility strategies aimed at combating what they perceived as a

[1]Muslims are divided into Sunni and Shia; Sunnis follow the Sunnah (the traditions and practices of the Prophet Muhammad, and the compilation of these traditions, the Hadiths), following his successor Abu Bakr. Shiites follow another lineage of succession via Muhammad's cousin and son-in-law, Ali. Alawite Muslims consider themselves Shiites, although many Muslims consider them a sect. The Druze, despite their Ishmaelite origin, do not consider themselves Muslims.

[2]On the morning of September 11, 2001, nineteen men hijacked four American commercial airliners bound for California, crashing into the twin towers of the World Trade Center in New York City and the Pentagon in Washington D.C.

[3]Islamophobia can be characterized as "an exaggerated fear, hatred and hostility towards Islam and Muslims, perpetuated by negative stereotypes resulting in bias, discrimination, marginalization and exclusion of Muslims from social, political and civic life" (Ali et al. 2011).

[4]Similar to the attacks on the London Underground in 2005 (https://pt.wikipedia.org/wiki/Atentados_de_7_de_julho_de_2005_em_Londres#:~:text=No%20centro%20de%20Londres%2C%20houve,a%20ocorr%C3%AAncia%20de%2037%20deaths. Accessed 10/05/21) and the Charlie Hebdo headquarters in Paris, 2015 (https://pt.wikipedia.org/wiki/Massacre_do_Charlie_Hebdo. Accessed 10/05/21).

stereotypical perception of Islam. These initiatives involved producing outreach material, participating in public interfaith events, establishing partnerships with politicians, and creating a legal framework to defend victims of attacks. In these actions, which aimed to disassociate the image of Islam from the multiple forms of violence and oppression, the narrative of "human rights" emerges as a key element. In this chapter, I will analyze Islamic institutional initiatives that, through this language, aim to control the proliferation of negative images (Latour 2004) about Islam. Its objective is to normalize them based on parameters determined by them, circulating information about the religion, to project a positive public image of Islam in Brazil.

The empirical approach will focus on three Sunni Islamic organizations and a case of Islamophobia: (1) *União Nacional das Entidades Islâmicas*—UNI (the National Union of Islamic Entities), which brings together numerous Sunni Islamic entities and has a communication sector designed to develop projects to disseminate Islam, in addition to a team of lawyers to provide legal support for victims of Islamophobic attacks; (2) the World Assembly of Muslim Youth—WAMY and (3) *Centro de Divulgação do Islã para a América Latina*—CDIAL (the Islam Dissemination Center for Latin America), two international organizations that promote policies of positive visibility, using outreach materials and communication channels for the external public; (4) A case of Islamophobia that triggered, at the same time, this institutional network, its discursive strategies, Brazilian civil organizations, bills and Brazilian politicians, showing the extent of reach that visibility strategies can achieve.

The aim of this clipping is to understand the uses of the human rights narrative in strategies that produce information and visibility about Islam for a non-Islamic public. I will show how the articulations around what we can call "policy-visibility" create a dynamic of networked action by Muslim organizations, and the formation of coalitions with politicians, other religious leaders and civil associations. We will consider the hypothesis that the category of human rights and its various narratives constitute a kind of "lingua franca" that enables actors to speak and circulate through this network. Thus, the appropriation of this language becomes an inescapable strategy in policy-visibility. Its "correct" use enables actors to speak, circulate and participate in different spaces, as well as form partnerships and connections. We hope to frame Islam in Brazil—along with other religious denominations in this book—makes use of the language of rights to establish itself as a public religion.

In the first part, I introduce the institutions, their structures and political and institutional strategies to deal with the repercussions of 9/11, in particular, the negative media visibility and attacks on Islam and the community. In the second part, I will analyze human rights in the sheikhs' speeches, institutional materials and in a case of Islamophobia that show, simultaneously, the use of human rights, and the extent of reach of the organizations' policy-visibility.

2 Islamic Migration in Brazil and Islamic Institutional Organizations

Muslim populations that are found in the Americas today were formed through large migratory processes, from the end of the nineteenth century and throughout the entire twentieth century, coming especially from Lebanon, Syria and Palestine. The reasons that motivated these migrations point to the population impacts of decolonization processes in Asia and Africa, labor and educational issues, escape from poverty and war zones (Hajjar 1985). The Muslim population currently residing in Brazil is made up of migrants, refugees of different nationalities, second and third generation Arabs, and Brazilian converts. In the last National Demographic Census, carried out in 2010, there were approximately 34 thousand people, which contrasts with the number estimated by Muslim organizations, around 1.5 million.

Since then, dozens of new mosques, Islamic organizations and associations—commercial and cultural—have been formed throughout Brazil. According to Pinto (2010), the first Muslim institutions date back to 1929. *Sociedade Beneficente Muçulmana* (the Muslim Beneficent Society), in São Paulo, was one of the first organizations to provide support to Muslims to perform Islamic rituals,[5] while the Brazil Mosque was being built, financed by donations from the Egyptian monarchy. Other charitable societies were organized in the 1950s, in Rio de Janeiro and Paraná, aiming to create spaces for sociability for Arab families and keeping generations born in Brazil within the religion. In the 1970s, immigrants from the Middle East arrived in Brazil, fleeing the Lebanese Civil War (1975–1990), the Arab-Israeli wars, the growing Israeli occupation of the Palestinian territories and southern Lebanon. This new Islamic presence was marked by building mosques[6] and creating Muslim associations in Paraná, São Paulo, Minas Gerais, Goiás and the Federal District, most of them Sunni-oriented. The Shia population also grew, albeit to a lesser extent, resulting in building the *mesquita xiita do Brás* (Shiite Brás mosque) (São Paulo), in Foz do Iguaçu, and in Curitiba, the latter also frequented by Sunnis.

These organizations have always operated in a network and until 2001 remained focused on the internal needs of the communities,[7] without dedicating themselves, at least systematically, to proselytizing activities. Hilu explains that this was partly due to the perception that the sheikhs (from Saudi Arabia, Egypt and Lebanon) had of the Brazilian population, perceived as marked by sensuality and hedonism, and therefore not susceptible to receiving the message of Islam. This scenario already began to show some changes during the 1990s, when the first Arab sheikhs who had a command of Portuguese were introduced, and there was a small movement of

[5]The five daily prayers, and the feasts at the end of Ramadan (*'Eid al-Fitr*) and sacrifice (*'Eid al-Adha*).

[6]The mosques and entities were financed by Saudi Arabia and Iran, countries that dispute the spaces of influence of Muslim communities.

[7]Concept of collective unity used by my interlocutors, it comprises Arab families and their descendants in a closer connection, and Brazilian reverts, in a looser way.

Brazilians converting to Islam. At that time, the media coverage of Arab and Muslim peoples would attract people's interest in the religion, although on a much smaller scale than what was seen in 2001. These new elements will be precursors of the transformation that Muslim communities would undergo after the events of 11th September.

The 2001 events would be the great turning point for communities, changing the dynamics of the communities' relationship with the non-Islamic public. This is a topic extensively addressed by anthropologists of Islam in Brazil (Pinto 2005, 2010, 2011; Montenegro 2002; Chagas 2009, 2010; Castro 2007; Ferreira 2009, 2010, 2013; Marques 2010, 2011; Manfrinato 2015). This literature was concerned with understanding how the event impacted Islamic communities in Brazil, both negatively and positively, losing their anonymity.[8] At this time, the need for communities to defend themselves and religion publicly grew, mainly through the fight against negative stereotypes propagated by the media.

Islamic organizations became the privileged spaces for this to happen, especially those that already had institutional structures for the dissemination of Islam in Brazil, such as WAMY and CDIAL. UNI was the first organization created especially for this purpose, with a media and communication project and lawyers specialized in cases of religious intolerance. Next, we will describe this "policy-visibility", which includes institutional strategies of these organizations, their ways of mobilizing religious and non-religious knowledge (Vianna 2015) in the formation of a public Islam.

3 WAMY, CDIAL and UNI: Human Rights and Institutional Strategies

WAMY is an international Sunni Islamic organization founded in 1973 in Saudi Arabia. It has 66 branches and representatives in more than 500 member organizations that work in an international cooperation network aimed at Muslim youth living in diasporic contexts. Its main purpose is to strengthen Muslim youth, inform the population about Islam, establish religious dialogue, and, secondarily, promote human rights, environmental, educational and development projects, combat crime, immoral behavior, violence and drug use. It is characterized as an international cooperation organization, participating in international agencies such as the UN

[8] Other elements have "positively" influenced the image of Islam in Brazil. The *telenovela* (soap opera) *O Clone* (2001), for example, presented a group of Moroccan Muslims as one of its main nuclei. The construction of the characters and situations had a caricatural and orientalist tone, but brought a positive image of Islam, which was hugely successful among Brazilians, including expressions in Arabic, belly dancing, and the jewelry of the characters that were popularized (Ferreira 2015). Sheikh Jihad Hammadeh, who we will talk about later and who provided consultancy to the *telenovela*, told me that, despite the distortions, the telenovela brought a milder tone to the journalistic coverage of Islam at that time.

Department of Public Information (DPI), the International Federation of NGOs for Prevention of Drug and Substance Abuse (IFNGO), and the International Arab Federation of NGOs, among other organizations.

In 2012, WAMY Brasil, in São Bernardo do Campo, became the head office of all branches in Latin America, and started to develop projects for Brazil, but also for the Muslim communities of Argentina, Mexico, Ecuador and Venezuela. WAMY responds to the Saudi headquarters, the country responsible for most of their funding, but builds their projects based on local reality and demands. I learned about the organization that year, after arranging a conversation with its president, the then Sheikh Jihad Hammadeh.[9] Originally from Syria, he came to Brazil at the age of eight. He did part of his religious training in Islamic jurisprudence in Saudi Arabia, at the Islamic University of Madinah and, before joining the ranks of Islamic organizations, he was a volunteer sheikh at the São Bernardo do Campo mosque.

On this occasion, he explained that the organization was responsible for training "promoters of Islam and young leaders". In Islam, the word for disclosure is *da'wa* and must be performed by all Muslims. The publicists prioritized by the entity are the sheikhs, then the young people, the volunteers, and, finally, the external partners. Leadership training was conducted in Arabic, justifying that this would facilitate communication with sheikhs who came from other countries to teach in Brazil. Muslim youth is the primary focus of the institution in its role of keeping them involved in the religion and in their own community. The organization encourages young people to organize themselves into associations, whether voluntary or professional, and to engage in the society in which they live.

The organization's profile works for the community, offering religious guidance, but also looks beyond it.

> WAMY's profile is different, because the other entities are articulated with the mosques and with the local community, they are more of a religious service. WAMY has a profile that is not strictly religious, it is more educational and social. It serves, in general, all young people. Most of the volunteers are not Muslims, nor are the final beneficiaries. They carry out activities in the *periferia* (poor neighborhoods), where public power does not reach. Humanitarian aid is an Islamic prescription. The Prophet (SAAS[10]) said that a man went to paradise because he gave a thirsty dog a drink. Muslims must do good for man and the environment. (June 2013)

At the same time, it articulates partnerships with non-Muslim volunteers and carries out social projects aimed at non-Muslim Brazilians in less favored economic situations. It is not uncommon for religious organizations to fulfill non-religious functions, even if they are based on doctrinal principles: in this case, humanitarian aid

[9]The sheikh is a religious leader in Islam.

[10]Abbreviation of the first letters of a request for blessings and peace for the Prophet Mohammad (S.A.A.S.) and his Purified Lineage (A.S.) as defined by the Arresala website. The words are said right after the mention of the name of the Prophet Mohammed. The letters "S.A.A.S." used after the Prophet Muhammad's name are abbreviations for the words "*Salla Allahu 'Alaihi Wa Sallam*," meaning "may the blessing and the peace of Allah be upon him". In: https://www.arresala.org.br/biblioteca/dicionario-de-termos-islamicos. Accessed on 10/05/2021.

appears to be based on the notion of Muslim "civic responsibility" and Islamic charity. As Morawsca Vianna (2010, 2015) shows, in her research on the Catholic International Development Charity (CAFOD), a Catholic international cooperation organization in the United Kingdom that works with community groups in Recife and Olinda, there are many religious organizations around the world that mobilize knowledge, techniques and languages, both doctrinal and technical-bureaucratic, and that help to expand their reach, partnerships and field of action.

From the Brazilian Islamic organizations, WAMY was one of the first to dedicate itself, after 9/11, to creating new institutional channels with the media and public authorities, as well as a support structure for those who were victims of violence. The organization already had material targeted at the non-Muslim public, but after 9/11 the need to develop a public response by the community developed the policy of disseminating Islam in Brazil.

The press looked to WAMY, as well as other organizations and mosques, for information and reliable sources to publicize official positions on topics related to religion, or mediatized events. They also began to receive many requests for help and guidance from Muslims with reports of Islamophobic attacks. Many Muslim women were being harassed in the street and on public transport with abuse of "go back to your country, terrorist!" or "bomb woman!", situations that often resulted in physical aggression. Thus, WAMY decided to expand its functions, creating a legal sector only to deal with cases of attacks on women and creating guidelines for organizations and worshippers to deal with these situations.

> We had a lawyer for WAMY administrative matters only and we began to realize that many members of the Islamic community complained of [suffering] prejudice and we did not have legal guidance and support. (...) due to lack of knowledge, lack of access, lack of financial conditions, they could not react to these situations of religious discrimination, and women, who suffer more attacks because they are more visible. (...) Now we have volunteers from the community itself, and from outside as well, who take care of these cases. In addition, we have some religious intolerance commissions, within some bodies, such as the OAB (Order of Attorneys of Brazil), within the government and human rights secretariat.

Due to an external demand, from the press, and an internal demand from the community, it ended up creating a second legal sector aiming to encompass legal knowledge in matters of religious discrimination. In addition, it began to appropriate the spaces of public power and civil organizations aimed at religious organizations, forming fronts to combat religious intolerance, racism and xenophobia. The expansion of these institutional channels was possible from the mobilization of technical-bureaucratic knowledge and the formulation of a language that would translate religion outside the community.

At the same time, it focused on networking that leveraged the capacity to amplify the institutional sound box, using existing structures in the community. WAMY's sister organization, CDIAL is a valuable partnership in this regard. It is one of the largest distribution centers for dissemination materials and Islamic educational and social projects in Brazil. CDIAL is located a few meters from WAMY, in São Bernardo do Campo, a city where Arabs from different migratory waves live, as well as a significant number of Muslim converts. Next to CDIAL is the Sunni *Abu*

Bakr Assidik mosque, which has a separate office in the city exclusively for certifying *halal* meat, called *Cdial Halal.*[11]

CDIAL plays an important role both in the scope of international relations between religious leaders and in theological education, and is an information center that produces and disseminates material to non-Muslims. Both WAMY and CDIAL are organizations created in Saudi Arabia that have gone international. Like many of the Arab and Sunni Muslim associations in the country, CDIAL was established in Brazil in 1987, through Ahmad Ali Saifi, aiming to "keep the practices and principles of Islam alive in the Muslim community, especially for young people".[12]

Nowadays, the institution also has social projects, both in the country, such as the Udhiya 2020 Project,[13] which distributed meat in several Brazilian cities to mitigate the economic impacts of the Covid-19 pandemic, and abroad, with the shipment of groceries to Lebanon after the explosion in the port region of Beirut in 2020.[14] The guiding principle of social projects, according to its institutional website, is voluntary Islamic charity, which should help the most vulnerable, "regardless of their profession of faith".

CDIAL also financed the translation of the Quran into Portuguese with free distribution to Brazilian Islamic centers, and other dissemination materials in Portuguese, "that bring direct and indirect benefit to the Muslim community", to be distributed in Brazil, but "in other Lusophone countries, such as Mozambique, Angola, Portugal, Guinea-Bissau, East Timor, Equatorial Guinea, Macau, Cape Verde and São Tomé and Príncipe. In addition, every year CDIAL organizes trips to Mecca, Saudi Arabia, during the period of Islamic pilgrimages, Hajj and Umrah, for Muslims who cannot pay.

There is an online channel available on its website, especially for the press. The organization also promotes events, lectures, training courses and international congresses, such as the International Congress for Muslims in Latin America and the Caribbean, with political themes relevant to Latin American communities. In 2015, the event brought together religious leaders from several countries to talk about how "extremism" has impacted "Muslim minorities". Furthermore, it must be emphasized that the organization is a node in a large network of Muslim institutions in Latin America and Muslim countries. Sheikhs, Muslims, doctrinal materials and resources circulate through this network.

The experience accumulated by these organizations helped to create a unified national organization, which materialized in 2008, in the formation of the National

[11] According to the website, its mission is to "benefit Halal products, guaranteeing and supplying specialized labor for the production process of this type of food, making them healthy and legal for consumption by Muslims and non-Muslims in the world" and its objective, "to achieve quality and excellence in Halal production and contribute to the growth of the Islamic community through joint activities with Islamic institutions and advising companies interested in operating in the Islamic world market." (HALAL CERTIFICATION SYSTEM, Cdial Halal online, 2004)

[12] http://www.islambr.com.br/?p=154. Accessed on 05/10/2021.

[13] http://www.islambr.com.br/?p=6888. Accessed on 05/10/2021.

[14] http://www.islambr.com.br/?p=6908. Accessed on 05/10/2021.

Union of Islamic Entities (UNI). Sheikh Jihad explained that the decision to create it came from the need to organize a collective form of defense and "representation of religion", in the sense of concentrating forces that were previously dispersed:

> [...] the institutions defended themselves individually. An organization was needed to respond jointly. And this role is played by UNI, which represents the unity of Islamic institutions.

The headquarters of UNI are in the Pari neighborhood of São Paulo, in a building that includes the Pari Mosque, on the first floor, the Islamic League, an association linked to the mosque, and the UNI, each occupying a room on the second floor. It has a communication sector aimed at developing projects and producing content for the site, as well as serving the press and researchers. The legal sector is not only geared towards the defense of individual Muslims, but of the religious collectivity called the community, and more broadly, Muslim peoples and Islam. In addition to the communication work with the press, the entity started to think about and coordinate public awareness campaigns, to produce videos addressing issues that appeared in the media, to collect signatures on public petitions, to participate in discussion forums and interreligious meetings to debate the issue of religious intolerance. A narrative line was adopted for interviews and events and made available on the UNI website, bringing political explanations to narratives considered biased, pro-imperialist, considering US interests in the region, or denouncing the prejudice ingrained in Western countries against Islam.

UNI has the task of representing Islam publicly, orchestrating coordinated actions and officially answering for the community in all cases where this opinion is publicly requested. It is an outward looking organization while the other organizations are geared towards training and internal community support. Both—UNI and WAMY—can produce alliances and conventions, local and central institutional networks that constantly intertwine and intersect, according to the need that each position in this network evokes. The circulation of sheikhs is fundamental in this network dynamics and in the circulation of messages that the organization intends.

> I have two different cards for each situation. When I speak on behalf of the Islamic community, I introduce myself as UNI and in situations related to WAMY, I speak as a member of WAMY, which basically are those aimed at the community itself: lectures, camps for young people and WAMY projects...when I'm invited to be responsible for a specific institution in a certain segment, I speak on behalf of WAMY. When I am invited as a representative or speak on behalf of entities or the community, I introduce myself as a member of UNI.

The institutional structures producing content for the dissemination and knowledge of Islam were taken advantage of, while new functions were created to meet the growing demands of the post-9/11 period. These organizations mix religious and non-religious knowledge that help to make bonds inside and outside the religious community. Its main focus seems to be to defend the religion and religious leaders, in intense dialogue with the national media. We will see below how the public speeches of organizations in the media, through their religious leaders, reveal the emergence of a lingua franca that will be widely used in discursive contexts involving Islam.

4 Sheikhs in the Public Sphere: Religion in Focus

All over the world, particularly in the US and European countries, even before, but especially after 9/11, an attitude of suspicion prevails about Islam and Muslim peoples. After the attacks, American and European newspapers used a generalized narrative strategy with an emphasis on the relationship between the villains, "Muslim terrorists", and the victims, the US representing the West (Moreira 2004). In the Brazilian press, Moreira (2009) analyzed the articles published immediately after 9/11 in the Veja, Isto É and Época magazines, all of which were widely circulated in the country, and found that they propagated the North American discourse of the "Islamic enemy" representing the "baddie", against which the US should fight with the "goodie". From categorical assertions such as "fundamentalists want to rule the world in the name of Allah" and generalizations about Islam and Muslims, the narratives created the illusion that all Muslims were directly responsible for the attacks.

This attitude is observed in countless examples given by my interlocutors or in interviews granted by them at the time. On September 13, 2001, the then president of WAMY, Sheikh Ali Mohamad Abdouni, was asked to comment on the religious motivations behind the September 11 attacks by the newspaper Estadão, even before his authorship was assumed:

> There are fanatics in all faiths. Killing innocent people goes against the Quran. Even so, Islamists are pointed out as suspects whenever attacks happen. (...) One cannot generalize. If a Muslim promotes a terrorist act, he/she must be punished, but not his/her religion or his/her country of origin. When an American was blamed for the Oklahoma bombing, there was no talk of his religion or the American people as terrorists.[15]

What he says answer the journalist's question about the authorship of the attacks and the possible religious motivations behind the action. The sheikh is offended by the media's immediate reaction of associating terrorist actions with Islam and Muslims, a common discursive practice, in his opinion. The explanation, which separates Islam from terrorist acts—killing innocent people is against the Quran—comes with a critique of media generalizations and stereotypes. In this short article in the São Paulo newspaper, a historian also makes a statement saying that the pillars of the Islamic religion do not incite any "holy war", indicating, as a matter of concern, possible military retaliation by the USA.

This was one of the first public statements made by a religious leader after 9/11. Many of the official speeches will focus on the charismatic figures of the sheikhs,

[15] In: http://internacional.estadao.com.br/noticias/geral,sheik-islamico-diz-que-ha-fanaticos-em-todas-as-religioes,20010913p26772. Accessed on 10/05/21.

such as Jihad Hammadeh, who has become, over the years, very well-known both inside and outside the community. He began giving statements to the media as a "volunteer sheikh" at the mosque in 2001, and is now in high demand, appearing on many television channels to explain the history, concepts and principles of Islam. In an article published in October of the same year,[16] his interviewer emphasizes the sheikh's charisma and confidence in front of the cameras, and his ability to deal with difficult questions, being lighthearted and good humored, which would become a trademark. The content of his speeches in the media follows the line announced by Sheikh Abdouni: he separates religion from terrorist acts, showing that the Quran forbids the killing of innocent people, and that Islam is a religion that seeks, above all, peace in the world. Although he did not present himself as a representative of Islamic organizations at the time, his charismatic approach in front of the cameras quickly placed him as one of the main contacts with the media in the community.[17]

The sheikh's speeches, as well as his interviewers' questions, show repetitions to everyone: accusatory interpellations that place organizations and the community in a defensive position

> We would like to be doing a job and we have to keep explaining ourselves, it's unfortunate. I say: it is visible from the material, form and content of disclosure that there is an attempt for Muslims to explain and justify themselves all the time. (...) people were traumatized, this is a trauma. And that trauma brought low self-esteem. Because a person who has to explain him/herself without having done anything wrong feels victimized, wronged, and this creates discomfort, a problem. Any gaze ends up being accusatory. The work of the entities comes in this direction. We have an individual and collective duty to show who we are. And it takes thorough work in the medium and long term. And it distracts us from the focus, because we have to keep doing this work of defending Islam.

There is an institutional perception that the media narrative constructions place them in the position of defendants in the form of an inquisitorial discursive regime. They are asked to talk about the "barbaric" aspects of religion, and to justify attacks that have taken place in other parts of the world. The condition of possibility of his speech is not that of self-representation: it is overdetermined by the reiterated need to corroborate or try to deny the representation produced by others. And with each media event, a new ripple effect provoked more interpellations and attacks, generating a reactive dynamic between organizations and the media.

From 2011 to 2012, UNI filed two lawsuits, the first in June 2011 against Editora Abril and journalist Leonardo Coutinho, author of an article denouncing the existence of a terrorist network in southern Brazil in Veja magazine, and the second,

---

[16] https://www.terra.com.br/istoegente/115/reportagem/xeque_jihad.htm. Accessed on 05/10/2021.

[17] Having started out as a volunteer at the mosque, he became an important reference for the media, which began to invite him as a consultant on more than one Globo soap opera, as an interviewee on high-rated programs, such as *Fantástico*, and as an Islamic leader. in the program "*Sagrado*" on the Futura channel. During this period, he built up a wide network of connections with famous actors and actresses, NGO representatives, directors, journalists, among others, and startede his own Youtube channel: https://www.youtube.com/user/kifak1417. Accessd on 10/05/2021.

against Google, for publishing the short film *A Inocência dos Muçulmanos*[18][19] *(*Innocence of Muslims*)* on the YouTube platform. That year, it also provided assistance in the case of the Realengo Massacre, which was immediately associated with Islam, especially on social networks and the blogosphere. The perpetrator, Wellington Menezes de Oliveira, a boy who opened fire on classmates and teachers at a school in Rio de Janeiro, was not a Muslim, but some news reports said he was, prompting organizations to issue statements at the same time. The official UNI statement that circulated on the websites of other Islamic organizations read:

> THE ISLAMIC COMMUNITY, through its representative entities, publicly condemns the attitude of the citizen Wellington Menezes de Oliveira, who this morning, in the city of Rio de Janeiro, committed the insane and inexplicable act of injuring and killing several children, at the Tasso da Silveira school.
>
> Regarding the first statements made by the murderer's relatives of a possible link between this citizen and the Islamic religion, later denied by them, we reaffirm that he is not Muslim and has no connection with the Mosques and Charitable Societies maintained by the community throughout Brazil.
>
> It should also be clarified that the principles of ISLAM, dictated by the HOLY BOOK OF THE QURAN, preach the peaceful conduct of its adherents and demand from their followers an absolutely different posture from what some people want to hastily attribute to religion and its adherents.
>
> WHOEVER KILLS AN INNOCENT PERSON IT IS AS IF HE HAS KILLED ALL OF HUMANITY (Holy Quran)

In addition, Sheikh Jihad attended the ecumenical act in honor of the victims and in solidarity with their relatives in Rio de Janeiro, reinforcing the statement:

> "We must not forget the lesson so that facts like this do not happen again," said Hammadeh, who also asked people not to make judgments based on religions, but "by their nature and character.[20]"

In order to control the proliferation of negative narratives and images, the organization thus develops various narrative strategies: it condemns, on behalf of the Islamic community, the unjustified violent act of a citizen, indicating that the act was done by choice of free will and not by collective induction. Furthermore, it categorically denies its connection with the activities of the mosque and organization, and, consequently, with the Islamic community in Brazil or with Islam. Finally, it disassociates the doctrine from the stimulus to violence, citing the *surah* "whoever kills an innocent person it is as if he has killed all of humanity". This *surah* will

[18] Produced in the United States, the film generated intense reactions in countries such as Indonesia, Egypt, Libya and Afghanistan, where Google ended up blocking access to the videos, triggering a whole controversy around the issue of freedom of expression and the way Islam is often portrayed in global media.

[19] The first alleged that the magazine offended the religious sentiment of the Islamic community, which UNI represented, by associating Islam with terrorism, characterizing moral damage in the collective moral sphere. The second also invoked the religious sentiment of the Islamic collective by depicting the Prophet Mohammed in an offensive way.

[20] https://m.folha.uol.com.br/cotidiano/2011/04/902067-policial-participa-de-culto-e-pede-uniao-para-superar-massacre.shtml. Accessed on 05/10/2021.

appear in other speeches and clarification notes, indicating that the religion condemns the murder as an attack on all humanity.

Aligning with other religions in the repudiation of the act was also an important strategy to neutralize the perception of extremism associated with Islam. To that end, UNI joined representatives of other religions in condemning the attack. The official declaration and participation in the public act in this solidarity coalition in support of the victims and families represented, therefore, an important part of the political strategies of defense of Islam. However, narratives that showed empathy were also produced. In an interview with the program *Sem Censura* (No Censorship), Sheikh Jihad gave a personal testimony when he told that his wife had been assaulted days after the Realengo Massacre. According to him, after being identified as a Muslim by her clothes, she was verbally assaulted in traffic by a driver, who shouted that she "had to die". The sheikh cited this example as the result of irresponsible media coverage of the event:

> The media needs to make it clear that this tragedy had nothing to do with any religion. Or else you will be collaborating with the world movement of deconstructing the Muslim religion

In order to offer public responses to the intense coverage given by the national and international media to the acts of violence associated with Islam, but also to the renewed interest in the religion they aroused, UNI gradually gave more dynamism to its press sector. In an interview carried out in 2020 with one of the employees of this sector, Dalila, she says that the intensity of the news in 2012 ended up establishing the organization as the spokesperson for Islam: "a Muslim passed by in the soap opera, they called UNI, there was an attack, call UNI". According to her, the expansion of the sector resulted from a "natural growth" that strengthened the relations between the work of the consultancy and the contact network of some sheikhs, such as Hammadeh, who were more engaged in talking to the public outside the community, giving interviews, giving advice to "thematic" soap operas, going to inter-religious events. Previously, UNI was only called upon to respond to attacks and negative situations, it was rarely or never consulted about any positive point about the religion or the Arab peoples.

Among the sheikhs who make up the organization is Sheikh Mohamed Al-Bukai, of Syrian origin. He moved to Brazil in 2007, visiting the Sunni mosques of Santo Amaro, Pari and Brazil. He was also part (at different times) of the UNI and the Islamic League, both located in the Pari neighborhood. Similar to Sheikh Jihad, Sheikh Bukai has given many interviews, participated in interfaith events held by and for migrants and refugees, the World Social Forum, public rallies for religious freedom or in support of humanitarian agendas in the Middle East. Since 2011, he has been engaged in the reception of refugees from the Syrian conflict, particularly in humanitarian actions and the distribution of resources and accommodation for newcomers.

In addition to ensuring, like Jihad, that Islam is a peaceful religion that is not linked to violent actions, the focus of Sheikh Bukai's narratives relates to social justice and human rights. In one of his interviews, invited by the philosopher Luís

Felipe Pondé,[21] who directs the television program *Religião no Contemporâneo* (Religion in the Contemporary World), he spoke about the attacks committed against Muslims in New Zealand and other topics on religion and politics, gender and the media. The questions revolved around sensitive topics such as the relationship between democracy, politics and gender in Islam, and Sheikh Bukai sought, in his answers, to show that there would be no incompatibility between these terms:

> There is no political form, nor in the Quran anything like "how to govern". There are values, yes, that Islam demands from a government: justice, equality. They are human rights.

In his opinion, religion would guide the actions of the faithful, offering them notions of right and wrong, contributing to their search for justice, divinely inspired and immutable, bringing benefits to society as a whole. His narrative seeks to situate religion as a body of rules and prescriptions that teaches respect for life and plural coexistence, as it would transmit to Muslims the notion of civic responsibility and respect for difference. Touching on sensitive points about tolerance and coexistence in democratic societies, his objective seems to be to assure his interlocutor that Islam is not to be feared.

The topic of tolerance is recurrent in journalistic approaches, which become an opportunity for sheikhs to talk about Brazilians' adherence to Islam. In 2016, newspapers publicized the Hashtag operation carried out just before the Olympics began in the country. The operation, coordinated between the Brazilian Intelligence Agency (Abin in Portuguese), the Federal Police and the Armed Forces, led to the arrest of 15 Brazilian and Arab Muslims on charges of terrorism, whose regulation had been sanctioned that same year. In an interview given by Sheikh Jihad to the magazine called Istoé,[22] he comments that the convicted individuals were people known in the community, but who had never shown "signs of radicalism". He complains about the need for "fact finding", but says that if they are guilty, they should be punished "according to the law." He notes, however, that the new anti-terrorism law enacted to ensure the security of sporting events, by strengthening police security protocols, could induce people to discriminate against Muslims:

> Recently the Brazilian Intelligence Agency (Abin) released a poster showing how to recognize a terrorist, saying that people with strange clothes are suspicious persons. Any Muslim can fit that description. There was an uproar in the Islamic community. The Brazilian government itself is creating fear and discrimination. The legacy that is left can be very bad for Brazilian society.

The vague indication of "strange clothes" and "suspicious persons" appears as a reference to the clothes used by the *black blocs* (black blocks), hooded protesters who participated in the 2013 demonstrations, forming a human shield ahead of the acts aimed at ensuring the protection of other protesters who make the security line

---

[21] https://faustomag.com/mohamad-al-bukai-o-isla-e-garantia-de-felicidade-para-a-vida-toda/. Accessed on 05/10/2021.

[22] https://istoe.com.br/esta-dificil-ser-muculmano-aonde-voce-vai-vira-alvo/. Accessed on 05/10/2021.

of the acts. The black blocks were portrayed by the media as directly responsible for the acts of vandalism to private property committed in the acts.

Next, the sheikh describes examples of discrimination at airports that indicate a judgment based on Islamic clothing. He reports the case of a Muslim lady who was coerced to remove her hijab at the boarding line, not only showing discrimination, but also the desire to humiliate, revealing the woman before everyone. He also gives a personal testimony, reporting that a passenger refused to stay on the flight he was on with a Saudi sheikh friend, dressed in his religious robes. According to the sheikh, many experiences prove that there is a suspicious attitude towards Muslims:

> The Muslim feels wronged, silent. Discrimination evokes that feeling. People around you start looking in a different way. Wherever you go, you become the target of whispers, of looks. It's especially unpleasant when people start to back off if you reach into your pocket for anything, like a wallet or cell phone.

Their clothing or diacritical marks, like the Arabic language, are shown as triggers that activate fear in people, which cause visible and embarrassing reactions for Muslims. The sheikh still compares Catholic religious clothing, saying that "if they were nuns, they would not cause the same reaction", showing the difficulty of accepting Muslims when compared to a Christian religion in Brazil. This ambiguous reading of Islamic religious dress in Brazil will be the focus of a case analyzed later. Next, we will describe the doctrinal elaborations of human rights that support the positions of the organizations analyzed here and that have become one of the main ways of talking to the non-Muslim public.

5 Human Rights in Islam

One of the main messages conveyed to the press is that Islam is a religion of peace, *Salam*, and that respects human life. These messages are used to decouple Islam from the ideology that associates the religion with a "culture of death" (Asad 2006). This message is englobed in a body of *surahs*, or Islamic verses, under the name of "human rights in Islam", an articulation between the legal knowledge of human rights and Islamic doctrinal knowledge.

This message or body of verses helped create a language for speaking to non-Muslims, and it was widely used with a view to dismantling ideas perceived as distorted ideas about religion. The target audience, Sheikh Jihad explained to me, was not Muslims, who learned these values "gradually during their lifetime", but "non-Muslims", because it was necessary to give "a visibility to Islam that was understandable to Westerners" and to show that Muslims "are also civilized and not savage brutes as the media claims".

Organizations present these messages in brochures and leaflets at organization receptions, mosques, and are also sent for distribution in other Islamic centers and schools. They are also available in e-book format on the institutional website, where there is a place for questions, videos and news and thematic articles. Most of the printed materials I saw were translated from English versions or reprints of Lusophone versions prior to September 11, whose contents were developed aiming to provide clarification, as shown in the preface to the booklet *Islão em Foco*, on which much of the outreach material will be based. In the following excerpt, we clearly see the objective of dialoguing with the media coverage of Islam:

> [...] television channels, news and magazine articles, films and even textbooks, everything seems to deform Islamic doctrine and not always innocently.

The first English edition of the book is from 1975, it was translated into Portuguese in 1978, sponsored by WAMY and CDIAL. Its author, Hammudah Abdalati decided to write this book during his experience in Islamic communities in Canada. After graduating from the Al Azhar University in Egypt, he was sent to the country as a sheikh to guide Canadian communities. In addition, Hammudah was a Professor of Sociology at Syracuse University in the US, which made him aware of the specific cultural issues that young Muslims face in the West. The intention was to produce enlightening material for non-Islamic audiences, but also to strengthen and provide religious education for Muslim communities in the diaspora, which was growing under the influence of local culture and proselytizing. Some of the materials that still circulate in organizations and mosques are reprints from the 1980s and 1990s, when Islamic organizations became concerned with the formation and experience of Islam by Muslims born in a diasporic context.

Simply by searching the Internet, one can find several documents on human rights and Islam from that period, such as the Arab Charter on Human Rights (1994), the Cairo Declaration on Human Rights in Islam (1990) and the Universal Islamic Declaration of Human Rights (1981). The elaboration of the documents almost always coincided with major political processes in the Middle East, such as the Gulf War (1990) and the Iranian Revolution (1979). In addition to media coverage, this phenomenon is also the result of contemporary trends in the international system, led by the United Nations (UN), the US and other international human rights agencies, but also within the Islamic States themselves (Halliday 1996 *apud* Mendes 2008).

The content of this material presents and explains the main precepts of the religion, and some points related to "human rights in Islam", or sub-topics, such as "women's rights in Islam", "rights of non-Muslims living in Islamic countries".

The decision to translate *Islam em Foco* into Portuguese came from an agreement signed at the Congress of Islamic Communities organized by the Islamic University of Madinah (Saudi Arabia) in February 1977. In addition to the five pillars of religion: the shahada or profession of faith, which means the utterance of the words 'there is no God but Allah and Mohammad is his messenger (S.A.A.S.)', the profession of faith, the five daily prayers, fasting during the month of Ramadan, *zakat* (charity), and pilgrimage to Mecca. Among concepts such as Piety, Faith, Prophecy and Sin are the concepts of (1) Freedom, which Islam understands as inalienable for Muslims and non-Muslims: "every human being is born free from subjugation, sin, inferiority"; and "his right of freedom is sacred as long as he does not deliberately violate the law of God or desecrate the right of others"; (2) Equality, where "all men are born equal before God, and there cannot be any kind of subjugation of one man or race by another"; a (3) Fraternity that is based on the concept of "the oneness of God and humanity (...) where all men are brothers". The concept of Peace follows, emphasizing that peace, *Salam*, is the way a Muslim addresses God, how he/she addresses his brothers/sisters, how he/she identifies him/herself—Muslim (peaceful)—whose objective is to build lasting peace in this world.

Other material produced by WAMY is a series of leaflets, even more simplified and divided into themes such as "The Five Pillars of Islam", "What is said about Islam", "Mary, Mother of Jesus", and "Women in Islam". One of them is entitled "Human Rights in Islam" and evokes God as the guarantor of the dignity and honor of all human beings, whose uniqueness imposes the concept of fraternity and unification of humanity. The leaflet states that "human blood is sacred in any case and cannot be spilled without justification. And if anyone violates this sanctity by killing a soul without justification, the Holy Quran equates it to the killing of entire mankind." It also states that it is not permissible to harm "women, children, the elderly, the sick or the wounded", and that "a hungry person must be fed, a naked person must be clothed, and a wounded or sick person must be medicated, whether they belong to the Islamic community or belong to your enemies."

"Human rights in Islam" are divinely centered, from which their universality and immutability emanate, and therefore, according to the institutional pamphlet, cannot be revoked, changed or disrespected. It would be a principle of the faith, to be practiced by all Muslims, and not just used for "display and show" or applied to "nobody" as in the constitutional charters, but "applicable to every believer". The concept of the believer here relates to the children of God, all humans created by him, as opposed to the disembodied abstraction of Western Human Rights Bills. They must also guarantee 1. The Security of Life and Property; 2. The Protection of Honor; 3. Sanctity and Security of Private Life; 4. The Security of Personal Freedom; 5. The Right to Protest against Tyranny; 6. Freedom of Speech; 7. Freedom of Association; 8. Freedom of Conscience and Conviction; 9. Protection of Religious Sentiments; 10. Protection from Arbitrary Imprisonment; 11. The right to Basic Necessities of Life; 12. Equality before Law; 13. Rulers not Above the Law; 14. The Right to Participate in the Affairs of the State.[23]

These two texts show that human rights in Islam are based on the concept of the oneness of God and the creation of humanity, which would also give him this oneness and universality. Thus, people would naturally be born believers, or Muslims, insofar as all would be children of God, from which derives the concept of "reverted", the Muslim who returns to this "natural condition". This definition of the believer as the holder of the rights conferred by God contrasts with the disembodied abstraction of Western Human Rights Charters, synthesized in the concept of "nobody" just above. The reference to "display and show" is related to the political uses of human rights, especially in relation to Muslims, as opposed to being a

[23] "Os Direitos Humanos no Islam", Site: www.wamy.org.br. Accessed on 05/10/2021.

principle of faith, a religious obligation of every believer. The other principles listed describe other aspects of human rights, such as freedom of conscience, security of life, private property and political freedom and participation.

The document sought to cover human rights and their counterparts within Islamic doctrine beyond a study of jurisprudence, simplifying both in language and format—brochures and leaflets—focusing on the broad readership, positioning stands at each mosque entrance, Islamic organization and center. Thus, these formulations, whose genesis and place of emergence occurred elsewhere, appear as part of a strategy of positive visibility and dissemination of information by these organizations.

Next, we will see a case of prejudice that triggered, at the same time, this institutional network, its discursive strategies, Brazilian civil organizations, bills and federal deputies, showing the extent of the reach that policy-visibility can achieve. We will see how a case of prejudice against a Muslim woman and her hijab from this Islamophobic imagery triggered a public response that caused a small publicity phenomenon, placing the victim in a public position of spokesperson for Muslim women.

6 From Abjection to Rights

In early 2015, I was in Brasília to celebrate the National Day of Islam, in the Chamber of Deputies. The day was proposed as a Bill by the former Muslim deputy from São Paulo, Haifa Madi in 2009.

It was on that occasion that I personally met Charlyane Souza, a young Brazilian Muslim woman who, 2 months earlier, had suffered embarrassment during the Order of Attorneys of Brazil (OAB) examination. She was being requested, at the moment, by religious community lawyers, deputies interest in religious freedom agenda and religious leader arranging meetings and taking pictures from newspapers as the face of empowerment of Muslim women. This notoriety was due to the repercussion of the episode of Islamophobia suffered by her during the OAB examination. Before starting the test, the inspector asked her to leave the room and was asked if she "was an Arab, why was she dressed like that and if she had a document proving that she was Muslim". The inspector told her that, according to the rules of the public notice, no candidate could wear any "headcovering accessory" that would hide her identity. Charlyane's response "this is not an accessory and I can't take it off" was not enough for her to continue taking the exam and she had to finish it without a hijab, in a separate room. The request for a document proving her religiosity was required of her, as anyone could "dress up as a Muslim".

A public exam supposes that the candidate follows the rules in a public notice. In this specific one, there was no rule that prevented the candidate from wearing any religious clothing. However, the presence of a woman wearing a hijab constituted an unusual case with which the inspector felt challenged to deal with as unusual behavior. First, the inspector asked whether Charlyane was an Arab, which would give her the necessary authenticity to justify the hijab, while establishing a suspicious attitude towards her. On receiving a negative response and seeing that she was talking to a Brazilian woman, the perception that that veiled presence was an artificiality increased. The inspector insisted more than once that Charlyane remove her hijab and, in the end, took her out of the room so that she could continue the test in a separate room. After the test, Charlyane denounced the episode judicially and in the media as an act of "religious intolerance" and "xenophobia", due to the position of the inspector in relation to the hijab and Arab women.

The complaint had huge public repercussions on social networks, and in newspaper articles (television and press), leading to a proliferation of public notes in support of it, an official apology from the OAB and the promise to change future notices to contain the right to wear religious clothing. The OAB emphasized the importance of ensuring the fundamental right to religious freedom, constitutionally guaranteed and one of the cornerstones of secular States. They also presented a formal invitation to Charlyane to compose the Special Commission on Religious Law and Freedom of the OAB, as a representative of the Muslim community of São Paulo. Inspired by her case, federal deputy Wadson Ribeiro proposed *PL* (Bill) 979/15, which ensures the use of religious clothing in public places in Brazil. On the occasion of the commemoration of the National Day of Islam, pamphlets with the proposed law were distributed and the speeches made in the plenary invited those present to form political coalitions on the fight against religious intolerance. The Bill proposes to criminalize discrimination for the use of religious clothing to those who:

> I - Prefer, prevent, impede, deny or prevent the issuance of identification documents by using religious clothing or attire such as veils, headscarves, skullcaps, taqiyah caps, kippahs, turbans, necklaces or guides, among others.
>
> II - Refuse, deny or prevent the use of religious clothing or vestments, such as veils, headscarves, skullcaps, taqiyah caps, kippahs, turbans, necklaces or guides, among others, in public events or in any other similar situation.
>
> III - Prefer, prevent, impede, deny or prevent access, stay, embarkation or disembarkation for reasons of religious clothing or attire, such as veils, headscarves, skullcaps, taqiyah caps, kippahs, turbans, necklaces or guides, among others.

In the justification, the author says that the project aims to reinforce the secularity of the Brazilian State, but that it shelters in its territory a diversity of religious and cultural manifestations that cannot be curtailed in its right of public expression. The author emphasizes that the purpose of the Bill is to ensure that the aforementioned clothing are not confused as mere headcovering accessories, ensuring the right to use them in identity documents, driving licenses, passports, among others. This elaboration of the hijab as something that cannot be confused with an accessory is the result of conversations Wadson had with Muslim women, especially Charlyane. If the hijab is not coded the way it should due to a lack of knowledge in society, the Bill creates a guarantee that religious people are not discriminated against, and still makes religious groups visible as legitimate citizens. Ensuring its existence and free expression—argues the author of the Bill—reinforces the Brazilian culture of tolerance, strengthening democracy by consolidating republican principles defended by Brazil in its Magna Carta.

The justification, based on the concept of pluralism,[24] says that it is not up to the State to question or interfere in the life of religious citizens in their public activities and religious practices. If it does, it will be hurting the dignity of the religious person. The case of photographs in official documents is an example in which the state ban would produce in the religious "a distorted image of him/herself, since his/her image (photo) is a constitutive part of his/her personal, community and religious identity" (PL (Bill) 979/15). Photos in official documents are an especially sensitive case for Muslim women who wear hijabs. In addition to personal embarrassment, they end up facing embarrassing situations when traveling to Muslim-majority countries—a common practice among many religious people[25]—and they have to present their passports at airports.

The "distortion of the image" that the photo without a hijab promotes in Muslim women is imposed by a secular ideal of female corporeality, which limits the possibilities of self-presentation of religious subjects, making them "abject". Charlyane's case shows that the problem of wearing a hijab in public is linked not only to the predominance of prejudice against Islam in Brazilian society, but also reveals how institutions play a fundamental role in regulating and normalizing the conduct of religious people. Thus, Charlyane, as a recently graduated lawyer, sought her defense in the very laws that regulate religion in Brazil:

> The hijab is part of women's protection in relation to society as a whole and also in the eyes of men. Taking them away in public spaces hurts the dignity of Muslim women. (...) As an operator of the law and a citizen who has the full right to exercise my right, I don't want any Muslim woman to go through the embarrassment I went through.

7 Conclusion

The dynamics of producing visibility and the political action of these religious subjects is indelibly marked by stereotyped media frames that create negative images about Islam. Historically brought to Brazil by Arab and African populations, Islam seems to be marked by a non-Christian and foreign ethnic identity, which helped to mark its difference in terms of the Brazilian nation.

Islam as a public religion in Brazil is built as a "minority" professed by an Arab migrant population (Hilu 2010), but as a growing engagement of Brazilians (Ferreira 2009) in a predominantly Christian-Catholic country. If we compare the Brazilian reality with that of European countries, we notice significant differences. Europe has a long and ancient relationship with Muslim populations and has built its identity and concept of Christianity and civilization in relation to non-white Muslim "others".

[24] Pluralism—one of the defining characteristics of a democratic system—guarantees the existence of several parties with equal right to exercise power. Thus, it needs clearly defined rules and procedures to guarantee the coexistence of various opinions.

[25] Many Muslims, both Arabs and Brazilians, regularly travel to Muslim countries to study religion, get married or visit family.

Part of his "myth", as Talal Asad (2003) calls it, resides in denying the multiple cultural exchanges with these people, placing himself as homogeneous and more evolved. The author states that it is impossible to integrate Muslims into the identity concept of Europe, except as something to be overcome and feared. Unlike Europe, Islam is not seen in Latin American societies as the main threat to the Catholic world, which is mainly represented by evangelicals.

As a country of Catholic Christian formation, Brazil went through the process of separation of church and state without creating—like many European states—an anticlerical tradition, but in a secular civic culture (Montero and Dullo 2014; Giumbelli 2002, 2008; Oro and Camurça 2018). From the 1980s onwards, the authors state that there was an increase in evangelical converts and a gradual process of denaturalization of Catholicism as a central element of national identity towards a Christian plan that includes an enormous religious diversity.

What we intend to show in this article is how Islam is perceived in Brazil not only as a minority, but as a minority professed by non-Christian foreigners, a characteristic that holds a potential accusation of non-belonging and even expulsion from the body of the nation.

The 11th September attacks placed Muslims under the spotlight of public opinion. Curious journalists flocked to mosques and civil organizations showing the need to organize a massive response from Muslim communities. The organizations, which already had an apparatus for disseminating Islam, re-edited materials, updated messages and modes of public presentation to deal with the new demand. They created new institutional channels to receive interested Brazilians, many of them becoming new converts, while contacts with journalists enabled the emergence of a speaking position in mainstream media.

The speeches focusing on a message of presenting Islam to the general public were constructed from the lingua franca of human rights, in order to detach the associations between Islam and the multiple forms of violence and oppression, and at the same time serve as a way of denouncing forms of intolerance and religious discrimination. The way in which Charlyane triggered her defense, resorting to the universe of law, reallocates the hijab within the secular landscape of the society in which she is inserted, in an attempt to widen the perception of common sense regarding the public presence of the religious body, in which Muslim women occupy a representative and modeling role. At the same time, in this case, she chooses to activate her rights as a religious presence in public spaces and institutions to broaden collective understanding of the right to difference and even prevent other women from having the same problem.

The accounts, speeches and situations described here show how the critical judgment of Islam passes through the public presentation of religious bodies, deciphered in a key of suspicion. The response found in doctrinal and human rights texts, incorporated in legal defense actions and political participation, show the development of a complex institutional communication apparatus that supported the expansion of the public voice of Islam in Brazil.

References

Ali W, Clifton E, Duss M, Fang L, Keyes S, Shakir F, Fear, Inc (2011) The roots of the Islamophobia Network in America. https://cdn.americanprogress.org/wp-content/uploads/issues/2011/08/pdf/islamophobia.pdf?_ga=2.52409961.1338061803.1627262411-1395118733.1627262411

Appadurai A (1996) Modernity at large: cultural dimensions of globalization. University of Minnesota Press

Asad T (2006) On suicide bombing. Arab Stud J 15/16(2/1) (Fall 2007/Spring 2008):123–130 (8 pages)

Asad T (2003) Formations of the secular: Christianity, Islam, Modernity. Stanford University Press

Castro ICS de. Orientalismo na imprensa brasileira. A representação de árabes e mulçumanos nos jornais 'Folha de São Paulo' e 'O Estado de São Paulo' antes e depois de 11 de setembro de 2001. 2007. Dissertação (Mestrado em Língua, Literatura e Cultura Árabe) - Faculdade de Filosofia, Letras e Ciências Humanas, Universidade de São Paulo, São Paulo, 2007. https://doi.org/10.11606/D.8.2007.tde-01092011-102913. Acesso em: 2023-08-27.

Chagas GF (2009) Identidades religiosas e fronteiras étnicas: um estudo do ritual da oração na comunidade muçulmana do Rio de Janeiro. Religião & Sociedade 29:152–176

Chagas GF (2010) A pedagogia do Islã: aprendendo a ser muçulmano no Rio de Janeiro. In: FERREIRA, Francirosy Campos B. (Org.). Olhares Femininos sobre o Islã: etnografias, metodologias e imagens. Hucitec, São Paulo

Ferreira FCB (2009) Redes Islâmicas em São Paulo: "Nascidos muçulmanos" e "revertidos". Dossiê Estudos Árabes & Islâmicos, Revista Litteris

Ferreira FCB (Org.) (2010) Olhares Femininos sobre o Islã: etnografias, metodologias e imagens. São Paulo: Hucitec.

Ferreira FCB (2013) Diálogos sobre o uso do véu (Hijab): empoderamento, identidade e religiosidade. Perspectivas, São Paulo, 43:183-198, jan./jun

Ferreira FCB (2015) Telenovela e Islã: dos estereótipos à visibilidade. Horizonte, Belo Horizonte 13(38):771–802

Giumbelli E (2002) O fim da religião: dilemas da liberdade religiosa no Brasil e na França. Attar Editorial, São Paulo

Giumbelli E (2008) A presença do religioso no espaço público: modalidades no Brasil. Relig Soc 28(2):80–101

Hajjar C (1985) Imigração árabe: 100 anos de reflexão. Ícone, São Paulo

Halliday F (1996) Islam & the myth of confrontation. I. B. Tauris, London, p 1996

Latour B (2004) Não congelarás a imagem, ou: como não desentender o debate entre ciência-religião. Revista Mana 10(2):349–376

Manfrinato H (2015) Islã, mídia e direitos humanos: políticas de representação e visibilidade a partir do agenciamento de uma rede de instituições islâmicas no pós-onze de setembro. dissertação defendida em 2015, no PPGAS-USP

Marques VLM (2010) Convertidos ao Islã: brasileiros e portugueses (Converted to Islam: Brazilians and Portuguese) - DOI: 10.5752/P.2175-5841.2010v8n17p125 HORIZONTE 8(17). https://doi.org/10.5752/P.2175-5841.2010v8n17p125

Marques VLM (2011) Os Muçulmanos no Brasil, vol 15. Etnográfica, Lisboa, pp 31–50

Mendes NR (2008) Islã e direitos humanos: uma questão de (in)compatibilidade? Bol Tempo Presente (UFRJ) 31:1–12

Montenegro S (2002) Discursos e contradiscursos: o olhar da mídia sobre o Islã no Brasil. Mana, Rio de Janeiro, 8(1)

Montero P, Dullo E (2014) Ateísmo no Brasil: da invisibilidade à crença fundamentalista. Novos estudos CEBRAP:57–79

Moreira JM (2009) Islã e Terror: estratégias de construção na mídia impressa. Tese em Comunicação e Semiótica, Pontifícia Católica de São Paulo, São Paulo, p 169 f

Moreira JM (2004) 11 de setembro de 2001: construção de uma catástrofe nas primeiras páginas de jornais impressos. Dissertação em Comunicação e Semiótica Pontifícia Católica de São Paulo, São Paulo, p 122

Oro AP, Camurça MA (2018) Da secularização ao espaço público: meandros e mediações frente ao esquema de separação entre secular e religioso. Horiz Antropol 24(52):7–20

Pinto PGHR (2005) Ritual, etnicidade e identidade religiosa nas comunidades muçulmanas no Brasil. Revista USP, (67), 228-249. https://doi.org/10.11606/issn.2316-9036.v0i67p228-249

Pinto PGHR (2010) Islã: religião e civilização: uma abordagem antropológica. Editora Santuário (Cultura e Religião), Aparecida

Pinto PGHR (2011) El Islam en Brasil: elementos para una antropología histórica. Revista de Historia Internacional 12(45):3-21

Vianna CM (2010) Os enleios da tarrafa: etnografia de uma parceria transnacional entre ONGs através de emaranhados institucionais de combate à pobreza. Tese de Doutorado, Faculdade de Filosofia, Letras e Ciências Humanas, Universidade de São Paulo, São Paulo. https://doi.org/10.11606/T.8.2010.tde-17092010-144221. Recuperado em 2023-08-27, de www.teses.usp.br

Vianna CM (2015) Cooperação internacional católica: entre a política dos movimentos sociais e o ativismo da fé em ação Dossiê "Religião e política em outros termos". Religião & Sociedade.

Human Rights and Works of the Imagination: An Ethnography of the First Ordained Transgender Reverend in Latin America

Aramis Luis Silva, Olivia A. Barbosa, and Renata Nagamine

Abstract This text is articulated around the ethnography of the clerical ordination of Alexya Salvador, the first transgender Latin American pastor. Interested in describing and reflecting on possible contemporary ways of correlating the categories of religion and human rights, this analysis focuses on the production of iconic scenes and communication artifacts that inscribe living pictures into networks oriented to redefine the meanings of these categories based on concrete and communicable experiences. In this framework, human rights can be understood as a language in action that allows agents who designate themselves and are recognized as religious to give form and expression to their imagination, which are unmarked by stabilized borders among the political, the religious, and, in this case, the erotic.

1 Introduction

In this chapter, we analyze some contemporary ways of correlating the categories religion and human rights. Other chapters in this volume look at how these same categories are related. In our chapter, we do this through an ethnography of the ordination ceremony of Alexya Salvador as "the first Latin-American transgender pastor", who is affiliated with the Metropolitan Community Church of São Paulo, a religious denomination that emerged in the United States in the 1960s, has spread around the world, and that claims to be the "human rights church".[1] In addition to her

[1]In the field of "inclusive churches", an emic classification that encompasses the set of religious institutions formed by associated actors concerning gender identity and sexual practices in tension with the heteronorm, ICM can be mentioned as it puts into practice what it enunciates to be "radical inclusion", welcoming people who would be segregated due to social prejudices. Founded in Los

A. L. Silva (✉)
Federal University of São Paulo, São Paulo, Brazil

O. A. Barbosa
University of São Paulo, São Paulo, Brazil

R. Nagamine
Brazilian Center of Analysis and Planning, São Paulo, Brazil

P. Montero et al. (eds.), *Religious Pluralism and Law in Contemporary Brazil*, Law and Religion in a Global Context 4, https://doi.org/10.1007/978-3-031-41981-2_10

ecclesiastical position and gender identity, Alexya Salvador's other identities are "black woman", "married woman", and "transgender mother". She has engaged with these identities according to the context and differently on the public scene.

On January 26, 2020, a ritual event brought together leaders from different religious denominations and representatives from various social movements at the altar of a church in the center of São Paulo. This event provides scenes that supports the central argument of this chapter: that human rights is, among other things, a language that actors use to perform in the public space and that goes therefore well beyond its regulatory dimension. We argue that this language enables actors who identify as religious to communicate their imaginations regardless of established boundaries between politics, religion, and, in this ethnographic case, eroticism.

The three authors of this chapter look at the ethnographic scenes from two different points of view. Two of the authors were not in Brazil at the time the event took place and accessed it through the Metropolitan Community Church of São Paulo's Facebook page. The other author watched the event from the audience. The reason why we share this is to draw attention to two articulated dimensions of the phenomenon. The first is that Alexya Salvador's ordination ritual can be read as a dramaturgical writing. In this writing human rights metamorphose into a liturgical drama thus making intelligible the trajectories of a new public persona: the "transgender pastor".

Our ethnography entertains a double anthropological dialogue. The first is with Turner (1986), who reconsiders the notion of drama considering Dewey and Dilthey in their essay on the anthropology of experience. The second is with Clifford Geertz, who encourages us to think about the liturgy on stage along the lines of a thick description (Geertz 1989). A second dimension of the phenomenon, which is articulated with the previous one, concerns the circulation of video recordings of the ceremony through electronic media. This highlights the materiality of the liturgy when apprehended and codified in scenes that can be transferred by different communication devices. It is in this context that the iconic scenes, taken as artifacts of social communication that inscribe *tableaux vivants*, i.e., living pictures, on multiple digital communication platforms, make sense.

We are aware that our approach covers one possible way that actors use language performatively (Butler 2015), that is, to perform in public as "the human of human rights". When Alexya Salvador rises as "the first transgender reverend in Latin America", however, numerous national and international actors had for decades shaped what we can describe as the arena of human rights. We are aware, moreover, that the following ethnographic scenes unfold in a broader communicational circuit whose rules are in constant mutation and dispute.

Angeles, United States, in 1968, ICM can be found in more than 30 countries and was implemented in Brazil in the 2000s. It is now fully operational in small groups in Fortaleza (CE), Teresina (PI), Rio de Janeiro (RJ), Belo Horizonte (MG), São Paulo (SP), Cabedelo (PB), Salvador (BA), Vitória (ES) and Maringá (PR).

Human rights have been a common language for building and regulating social relations inside and outside domestic borders, grounded in the belief that humans share a common humanity. To take human right as language implies looking at the interstice between structure and action. Chapters by Nicácio and Manfrinato of this volume also take seriously the linguistic aspect of human rights. Regarding this ethnography, we understand that if human rights persist as linguistic formulas, it is because they make sense in particular social imaginations. These derive from situated historical experiences, as the studies by Hunt (2009) and Sliwinski (2006, 2009, 2015) show.

Hunt's work (2009) on the modern origins of human rights shows how the circulation of certain media, such as books, in pre-1789 France allowed for the urban and suburban Frenchmen to perceive the suffering of distant others as their own. According to Hunt, the shaping of this social sensibility in the 18th century created favorable conditions for the emergence of the idea of "rights of man". Sliwinski (2006, 2009, 2015), in turn, follows an image trail to tells human rights' history through images. In pieces published in the arc of a decade, she analyzes how encounters aesthetically mediated by photography, lithography, and other artifacts have contributed to the emergence of the idea of humanity, without which that of "rights of man" would hardly have been imagined. The process would have prepared the terrain for Hunt's actors, among others, shape some of the forms that have made "humans", "humanity", and "human dignity", that is, the unity, the totality, and the substance of the human rights discourse, intelligible.

The idea that sensibilities impact on the social life of rights has heuristic value in other empirical fields, as shown in the chapter by Nicácio of this book. In this ethnography specifically, the dialogue with Hunt's and Sliwinski's studies helps us to clarify our emphasis on iconic scenes when analyzing Alexya's ordination ceremony. From a communicational viewpoint, the iconic scenes work metonymically conveying the meaning of the transgender pastor's ordination. But the circulation of scenes such as these also contributes to reshape human rights' place and role in social life.

Besides Turner's and Geertz's, our look is influenced by the writings of Birgit Meyer (2010, 2019). Meyer proposes to shift the analysis from the the cosmological and ideological contents of religious discourses to how religions are made. In order to do, she has famously developed a material approach to religion, according to which religions are seen as "aesthetic formations" that become tangible and intelligible by conforming an aesthetic materialized in buildings, objects, and instruments of worship, as well as in bodily performances and the media. Understood as models of shared experiences, in which "subjects are forged by modulating their senses, by inducing experiences, by molding their bodies and by producing meanings" (Meyer 2019, p. 54), aesthetic formations are inducers of collectivity. Though Meyer's ideas are not intermingled with our description, they allow us to frame the groups on the ethnographic scenes alongside the São Paulo Metropolitan Community Church as means of mediation that affect bodily senses and mobilize sensations, producing thus situational gatherings. On another level, Meyer also encourages us analytically approach the public presence of religion and media uses in relation to each other:

in our case, this means looking at audiovisual media, which reshape religious messages and create ways of mobilizing and connecting people. It is worth remembering that two authors of this chapter have experienced the ceremony through a screen.

Meyer's proposal can benefit, however, from the perspective of a pragmatic sociology. She doesn't work with it, but bringing them together enables us to consider the arena in which human rights come to life as a space of visibility and communicative interaction in which plausible speakers are constituted according to their ability to form audiences (Cefaï 1996, 2017). So, we can look at how the different actors who are visible in the ethnographic scenes aim to project themselves in such arena to mobilize and persuade people, gathering audiences and, insofar as it lasts, forming communities.

When reading the scenes of this *sui generis* ordination ceremony, we demonstrate that human rights is a language that participate in social life in acts of communication. Though human rights are written in the Constitution of the Republic of Brazil ("1988 Constitution"), actors dispute and define their meanings in specific circumstances by using them from different positions in public. This language enables the Metropolitan Community Church of São Paulo to communicate its experience with the divine to an audience far beyond its regular congregation. On another level, we will show, however, that religious leaders and the public can only come together if using historically established codes, ways, and formulas. On the one hand, this touches the problem of the fossilization of communication and visibility strategies in aesthetic forms that underlie the whole ethnographic discussion. On the other, these aesthetic forms provide frameworks that lend meaning to content publicly produced within a procedural structure. By using human rights in different contexts and temporalities, the Metropolitan Community Church in São Paulo cast them as universal and timeless. In the context of ethnography, these rhetorical and aesthetic forms, such as the declaration and the oath, are experienced in stage acts by actors who incarnate human dignity in a ritual ceremony claimed from the institutions. Thus, the rhetorical formulas of human rights, such as the one inscribed in the article I of the Universal Declaration of 1948, according to which "all human beings are born free and equal in dignity and rights", point to an imagined world of the reign of God on earth, here and now.

The following section brings a description of the scenario and the characters on stage, as well as some of the alliances that place them in the social networks (family, activism, and religiosity) converging to the ceremony. Looking at these elements allow us to analyze the composition of the *tableaux vivants*, the living pictures, which we understand as communication devices that bring to life the "dead letter of human rights' documents". These living pictures to some extent result from a liturgical program that aims to make a human rights church visible to two distinct audiences: one that attends the ceremony in person and those accessing it on digital platforms. Next, we describe the ritual cycle as an integrated text, highlighting three moments of the liturgical script: the Liturgy of the Word, Anointing, and Eucharistic Liturgy to show that discourses can be better understood when viewed as social actors in action.

2 The First Ordained 'Transgender Reverend' in Latin America

On the afternoon of January 26th, which is Trans Visibility Month in Brazil, the doors of the *Paróquia da Santíssima Trindade* (Holy Trinity Parish), in *Praça Olavo Bilac* (Olavo Bilac square), located in Santa Cecília, a central district in the city of São Paulo. The doors of the church welcomed guests who packed the central aisle of the *Igreja Episcopal Anglicana do Brasil* (Anglican Episcopal Church of Brazil) for the ordination ceremony of Alexya Salvador, who was later recognized by various media sources to be the first transgender pastor in Latin America. In addition to holding the services for the Anglican community and being available for wedding rentals, the brick-faced church and reinforced concrete, simulating the praying hand position, were provided at reasonable prices to perform the Metropolitan Community Church liturgy. The amount charged covered electricity costs and other expenses of the architectural complex, such as the banquet hall, where a reception was held with snacks, cake, and soft drinks for the guests.

The venue was not chosen at random. In terms of intentionality, it solved the practical problem for a local religious association that, despite being associated with a transnational network and having growing media coverage, at the time only had a small and simple mezzanine on *Avenida Duque de Caxias* to physically gather its congregation. There wouldn't be enough room for so many guests. In terms of the desire for expression, the Metropolitan Community Church of São Paulo, which values and practices not having religious conventions, found a scenographic venue characterized by conventional features to design in liturgical form what its leaders think of as honor and pomp. In the ceremony, the altar and pulpit demarcate spaces for speaking and listening and positions in the ecclesiastical hierarchy. The A-acoustic structure amplifies the aesthetic effects of the praises sung by the Metropolitan Community Church singers and the music played on an electronic organ. The spatial arrangement allows processions down the central aisle, lined with a red carpet that connects the street (the world) to the altar (the sacred) and arranges the congregation profiled on church pews on the rectangular Italian stage. The Metropolitan Community Church is a community organization that promotes itself as a church from the margins, seeking to redefine religious norms. By choosing a model church, they publicly validated their project to produce non-traditional leadership.

However, having a capacity to seat 250 people, the discreet and elegant Anglican church designed in 1950 by the architect Jacob Maurício Ruchti would give the event much more than a new aesthetic for worship at the Metropolitan Community Church. With a high peaked ceiling that diverts one's eyes upwards, and the stained-glass windows designed by the artist Maria Leontina, which fill the Holy Trinity Parish with warm colors, the church housed the event: Alexya's ordination, a special Metropolitan Community Church service, would serve as a liturgy to publicize alliances, reach more people and, perhaps, create new communities.

In the pulpit and in the congregation, there were representatives of various social networks. People arrived quietly and looked for where their people were to sit in groups. The Anglican hosts were there, a religious group that states on its website that it is a community "marked by the diversity of age, ethnicity, sexual orientation, and denominational origins".[2] Anglican church members who were part of the administrative staff helped organize the event, for example, managing the sound system. Other members of the community, including pastors and leaders, attended the service, gathering to the left of those looking at the church altar divided into two blocks. Surrounding them were Alexya's relatives and friends, the Metropolitan Community Church members, other churches and civil society organizations, and a film crew for the documentary called *Deus é Mulher* (God is a Woman). Throughout the entire ceremony, in addition to the Metropolitan Community Church cameras that captured the images which can now be viewed on Facebook, the producer's lenses swept the church in search of the best shots, showing, here and there, someone who looked shy as they knew that they could be from then on, definitively inscribed in the scene, and, until that moment, without knowing how and where it would circulate. At the end of the service, the congregation was informed about how the images would be recorded and shared.

The diversity of the congregation, of those who watched the ceremony from the pews, was mirrored by those who were called to the altar and empowered by the ritualization of the naming. Being at the altar, which means, to be in a sacred space, also meant having and publicly displaying an identity (a name that designates and gives a position in a classification system), representing a group and/or a cause. In the case of the ceremony, the appearance at the altar was a public acknowledgment of the dignity of these names and causes.

In the background of the scene, serving as the institutional backdrop for the event, were local leaders from other cities in Brazil within the Metropolitan Community Church, as well as two international ecclesial authorities: Ines-Paul, a non-binary transgender religious authority from Germany, and Bishop Nancy Maxwell, a lesbian from the USA. In the corner, just behind the right pulpit, a group of trans women and drag queens from the church were sitting down, elegantly dressed in golden liturgical robes, along with the other guests of honor. As we will see later, the story that unfolded at Holy Trinity Parish was largely centered around feminine identities, including trans women, lesbian women, and cisgender women.

Among the guests were celebrities who showed evidence of the Metropolitan Community Church alliances within civil society, such as the actress Renata Carvalho, who gained national recognition with the controversial play called *O Evangelho Segundo Jesus, Rainha do Céu* (The Gospel According to Jesus, Queen of Heaven), in which the son of God was incarnated as a trans woman. The play had already been performed on the altar at the Anglican parish. Renata's position within the activism field was marked by the words stamped on her basic white T-shirt: 'Fight like a transvestite.' As the president of the National Association of Transvestites and Transexuals, she is a prominent figure in the community. Along with Renata were Maitê Schneider, founder of *Transempregos*, an electronic platform that

[2]Full text available at http://www.trindade.org/drupal/node/753.

connects companies and trans people looking for work; trans activist Renata Peron; Erica Malunguinho (Erica da Silva), educator and plastic artist who was elected in 2018 as the first transsexual woman in the Legislative Assembly of São Paulo by the *Partido Socialismo e Liberdade*—PSOL (Socialism and Freedom Party), the party for which Alexya ran for the same legislative position, having obtained the 10,486 votes in the election that accredited her as a substitute. In the 2020 municipal elections, Alexya returned to institutional politics. First, as a pre-candidate for deputy-mayor in the PSOL elections alongside federal deputy Sâmia Bomfim, in which she was beaten by Guilherme Boulos and Luiza Erundina running together as a ticket. Later, she appeared as an unelected candidate for the São Paulo City Council. At the altar of the Protestant church, Erica, Alexya's political party colleague, declared her adherence to Afro-origin religions. This declaration honored an important achievement for trans people: the right to practice their faith, even from a position of ecclesiastical authority.

The ordination scene of the Metropolitan Community Church reflects alliances based on religion as a facet of identity. In this context, as we will see below, relationships are established between actors and groups in which human rights serve as a basis for sustaining a new ecumenism. This new ecumenism is marked by the idea of inclusion of those marginalized by issues of gender identity and sexuality, and liberation from oppression and prejudices linked to social taboos. From this perspective, we can identify a confluence of actors in events concerning sexual diversity and gender. These actors include Tábata Tesser from Católicas pelo Direito de Decidir, Jean Tetsuji from the Honganji Buddhist temple Nambei, and representatives from various collectives and entities such as the *Coordenação Nacional dos Comitês Islâmicos de Solidariedade, Coletivo de Inclusão Luterana, Evangélicos pela Diversidade, Ordem Anglicana Missionária, Grupo de Ação da Diversidade Católica, Movimento Inadequados e Coletivo LGBT Ferraz de Vasconcellos.* Batista da Silva (2019) had previously documented the coalition logic of this new ecumenism in other public events involving the ICM, although the church participated as an invited ally rather than as a leader of the coalition.

To conclude, the altar is complemented by another iconic element that is fundamental to the storyline of the event: Alexya's family, positioned in the right corner of the scene, just behind where she would remain until the time of her ordination liturgy. The pastor's mother and father, sitting shoulder to shoulder, highlighted one of the central themes of the Metropolitan Community Church and other 'inclusive churches': the importance of family acceptance for LGBTQ individuals. Roberto, the pastor's husband, appeared with the parents and the couple's three adopted children, two of them trans girls.

The family history will be narrated during the religious service through a report and a testimony that blend together to form one story. This story is about a *sui generis* family that consists of a transgender woman, a cisgender man who identifies as gay, a cisgender boy, and two transgender girls. The story will show how this family's formation has both political and theological significance and how it can be understood as a single narrative. It is a configuration that confronts the pattern of the "natural family" defended by those who will be called 'conservatives' and 'fundamentalists' on the stage. However, the actors at this event diverge from the typical strategy of the LGBT movement, which aims to use secular institutions as a protective barrier against religious leaders. Instead, these actors position themselves as a novel facet of the LGBT community, claiming ownership of this religious moment by bringing it to life through ritual performance. This is done not only to reaffirm the value of the family as an institution but also to show performatively that a family formed by actors who carry identities outside the norm expresses the intersection of secular political projects with divine purposes. Alexya, who is being put on par with the Virgin Mary during the ceremony, has already been recognized by the media as the first trans woman to adopt children. At the event, she will be iconized as a symbol of the revolution in customs and as an embodiment of God's love.

Now that the arrangement of the stage, which served as a public representation of the Metropolitan Community Church's religious beliefs and practices, has been presented, we will analyze the events that unfolded during the ceremony. To do this, we will follow the liturgical script defined by the church itself and scrutinize key moments of worship, paying attention to one fact: discursive content to be broadcast and circulated publicly must have a form. We will now analyze the scenes.

3 Liturgy of the Word

After the Penitential Act, there was a communal atmosphere in the Holy Trinity Parish. Trans women associated with civil society organizations and members of the Metropolitan Community Church sang praises in the background. Then, actress Renata Carvalho from the National Association of Transvestites and Transsexuals was called to the microphone and stood at the altar to read the first reading of the afternoon. Renata opened the liturgical section, which was suggestively called the Liturgy of the Word, with the Metropolitan Community Church Statement of Faith. The reading, like the entire event, was translated into Brazilian Sign Language (Libras).

Trans women, drag queens, and religious leaders formed a *tableau vivant* against the backdrop of a large gray concrete panel depicting three crosses on the altar. The crosses included a wooden one without the crucified Christ from the Anglican church and two Celtic crosses from the Metropolitan Community Church, displayed on banners. The banner on the left, with the acronym of the denomination in English, "MCC" (Metropolitan Community Church), showed the Celtic cross in pink and blue, referring to the flag of the trans movement. The banner on the right, adorned with the colors of the rainbow, alluded to the LGBT movement. Renata then proceeded to read the following:

> (Preamble)
>
> The Metropolitan Community Church is a chapter in the history of the Church, the Body of Christ. We are people on a journey, learning to live into our spirituality while affirming our bodies, our genders, and our sexualities. We don't all believe exactly the same things.

> And yet amid diversity, we build community, grounded in God's radically inclusive love for all people. We are part of an ongoing conversation on matters of belief and faith, shaped by scripture and the historic creeds, building on those who have come before us. Our chapter begins when God says to us, "Come, taste, and see."
>
> (Our statement of faith)
>
> "Come, taste and see!". Jesus Christ, You invite all people to Your open table. You make us Your people, a beloved community. You restore the joy of our relationship with God, even amid loneliness, despair, and degradation. We are each unique and we all belong to a priesthood of all believers. Baptized and filled with Your Holy Spirit, You empower us to be Your healing presence in a hurting world. We expect to see Your reign on earth as it is in heaven, and we work toward a world where everyone has enough, wars cease and all creation lives in harmony. We believe that, having put our faith in God, we are filled with God's spirit, and that this means actively putting our faith into action, and seeking God's reign on earth. Therefore, we will actively resist systems and structures which are destroying Your creation. With all of creation, we worship You – every tribe, every language, every people, every nation. We know You by different names, Triune God, beyond comprehension, revealed to us in Jesus Christ, who invites us to the feast.[3]

The Metropolitan Community Church Statement of Faith is rooted in a historical tradition of enunciating and inscribing rights in constitutional and international orders. This tradition is of modern, revolutionary, and utopian origin, and calls for action to transform the world. As in the Universal Declaration of Rights, the Metropolitan Community Church Statement of Faith has a preamble. Preambles are an enunciation of principles that prepare the public for the announcement of specific rights. Examples of iconic preambles include those of the United States Declaration of Independence and the Universal Declaration of Human Rights[3], which was proclaimed in 1776 and 1948 respectively. Preambles appeal to people's values and emotions, giving meaning and guidance to their beliefs. This appeal is made through the enunciation of shared values or memories, expressing that one belongs to a community that the very enunciation encourages one to imagine, as is clear, for example, when the 1948 Declaration recalls, in its preamble, that

> [The] disregard and contempt for human rights have resulted in barbarous acts which have outraged the conscience of mankind, and the advent of a world in which human beings shall enjoy freedom of speech and belief and freedom from fear and want has been proclaimed as the highest aspiration of the common people.

It is therefore significant that the initial act of the ceremony is the reading of a declaration that includes a preamble and an affirmation of faith. The document assumes, after all, a form conceived to be read in public and consecrated as a rhetorical device by modern revolutions to announce principles of organization of political power and rights. Uniting theological and political aspects by evoking personal experiences of suffering (relationship with God "amid loneliness, despair, and degradation"), it announces the Metropolitan Community Church's principles, which can be summarized as resistance to systems and social structures, that are mediated through the recognition of rights. In line with its understanding of religion

[3] Available at https://mccchurch.org/files/2017/01/DECLARAÇÃO-DE-FÉ-DAS-ICM'S.pdf (last accessed on 21 April 2020).

and community, it is clear that the church focuses on social action within a moral framework: to preserve what is considered good (nature, for example) and the transformation of what is bad, as the social structures of oppression.

In another context, the Metropolitan Community Church Statement affirms the prevalence of incarnated religious subjects and emphasizes the "importance of embracing our physical bodies, genders, and sexualities as we learn to live our spirituality". It also recognizes the material, social, and cultural needs of the community as a whole, formed through shared experiences and rituals. These spiritual needs are universal (observable in every tribe, language, people, nation) and can be addressed in various ways, reflecting the church's religious universalism that acknowledges God by different names and welcomes diversity. This opens up space for the new LGBT ecumenism, which promotes peaceful coexistence with other religious affiliations and is expressed through various rituals during the service. For example, during the communion, everyone, regardless of their religious affiliation or identity, is invited to partake in the bread and wine. This act of 'radical inclusion' is a central aspect of the Metropolitan Community Church's beliefs.

After activist Renata Peron sings Salm 50, which calls for divine intervention to create a pure and guilt-free heart, feminist Tábata Tesser from Catholics for the Right to Decide takes the microphone. Her mission is to show the audience that trans people hold significant positions in the production of the religious subject of the Metropolitan Community Church. This institution, formed mostly by cisgender homosexual people, has its subject closely associated with militancy, as Tábata's speech clearly shows. To demonstrate this, Tábata reads a text that describes the life trajectory of trans and black activist Sylvia Rivera, immortalized for her role on the front line of the Stonewall riots and deaconess of the New York Metropolitan Community Church. The legend that Sylvia attacked the policemen who humiliated people that participated in the Stonewall riots on the night of June 28, 1969, has become celebrated as the birth of the sexual and gender diversity movement in the LGBT world. Tábata reminds the audience that Sylvia worked tirelessly on behalf of marginalized members of the gay movement, especially those facing poverty, racism, and transphobia. Just hours before her death, Sylvia asked the New York Metropolitan Community Church pastor to set up a place for the community's youth to spend the night. Consequently, Sylvia's Place, a social project by New York Metropolitan Community Church, was opened to meet her request.

Tábata's story describes Alexya's journey as an individual on the margins of conventional ideas, blurring the boundaries between politics and religion. While focusing on Alexya's unique experiences, the story also turns her into a living symbol of the "battle flag" of the Metropolitan Community Church in Brazil, which was prominently displayed at the 2017 national retreat. This retreat brings together the church's leaders and members periodically. At the 2017 retreat, Alexya, who was already a mother to a son and in the process of adopting her first daughter, played a prominent role in the opening religious service and gave a lecture titled "Christrans". In her speech, she boldly proclaimed that "gender will be the last human revolution to be made".

In 2017, due to her increasing popularity, Alexya was invited to Cuba by the newly opened local Metropolitan Community Church. As a religious leader and spokesperson for the trans cause, she began to represent the church more and more prominently. She appeared in various media outlets, defending not only her gender identity and that of her daughters but also advocating for trans family rights, given the new configuration of her family. Her appearances showcased a unique alliance between transgender individuals and the religious community.

During the ordination ceremony, the alliance between religion and transgenderism reaches its boldest metaphorical expression, giving an unprecedented theological dimension to the trans experience. This alliance is established during the Liturgy of the Word, through the successive presentation of different feminine forms. First, Maitê Schneider, from the Transemprego platform, recites the *Magnificat* (Luke 1: 46–55[4]), also known as Mary's Song, which is a common song in the Catholic liturgy that Mary, the mother of Jesus, would have sung during her visit to her cousin Isabel, who was pregnant with John the Baptist. Then, Bishop Nancy Maxwell of the Council of Bishops and the Metropolitan Community Church Bishops takes the microphone from center stage, displaying her hierarchical position encoded in liturgical attire. Her words are translated by her Brazilian girlfriend, who a few days later would become a Metropolitan Community Church reverend in Belo Horizonte.

The female bishop explained that Alexya was given the opportunity to choose the scripture passage for the liturgy of the word, and as a former Catholic, she chose the *Magnificat*. The bishop believed that this was the right choice and proceeded to perform an exegesis of the text. She explains that the *Magnificat* describes how Mary, a poor virgin girl, found support from an unlikely source, Isabel, an older woman who was too old to have children. The bishop believed that this passage was about the encounter between those who were considered unlikely by society's rules. The bishop used Alexya's words to justify her choice of the Magnificat and suggested that, like Mary, Alexya's motherhood and life context were also unlikely. Therefore, the bishop drew an equivalence between the maternity positions of biblical women and Alexya's experience. However, the bishop also pointed out a difference in her reading from what Alexya had done. She concluded that God uses people because of, rather than in spite of, their gender, age, and social context. The bishop then addressed Alexya directly and stated that during her ordination, God calls her for who she is, including her gender, social context, courage, true heart,

[4]My soul proclaims the greatness of the Lord, my spirit rejoices in God my Savior, for He has looked with favor on His humble servant. From this day all generations will call me blessed, the Almighty has done great things for me, and holy is His Name. He has mercy on those who fear Him in every generation. He has shown the strength of his arm, He has scattered the proud in their conceit. He has cast down the mighty from their thrones, and has lifted up the humble. He has filled the hungry with good things, and the rich He has sent away empty. He has come to the help of His servant Israel for He has remembered his promise of mercy, the promise He made to our fathers, to Abraham and his children forever. Glory to the Father, and to the Son, and to the Holy Spirit, as it was in the beginning, is now, and will be forever. Amen.

unfailing love for the Saint, authenticity, vision, motherhood, unshakable knowledge of her identity, and her claim to be recognized as loved by God.

4 Anointing

As Alexya's story intertwines with others, her public biography and the celebration of diversity, which are central to her process of becoming a subject, are constructed. In this narrative process, the Metropolitan Community Church aims to be recognized as a privileged institution for the formation of a diverse and militant Christian subjectivity. This aspect of the church becomes evident when, following the ceremony, Reverend Cristiano Valério, the founding pastor of the Metropolitan Community Church of São Paulo and leader of the Metropolitan Community Church Network in Brazil, begins the anointing liturgy by narrating Alexya's biography.

In a narrative turn, assuming that divine designs can be discerned in human trajectories, Cristiano Valério, who has followed Alexya's gender transition process as both pastor and friend, recounts her life story. He tells us that she was born into a Catholic household and, at 18 years old, founded *Comunidade Rainha da Paz* in Mairiporã, a city in Greater São Paulo, to provide social support for the homeless. Pastor Cristiano Valério also informs the audience that she entered the Diocesan Seminary of Bragança Paulista, in the state of São Paulo, where she began her theological studies as a seminarian, suggesting a coherence in her path that could only be understood by expanding our understanding of what religion constitutes. However, Cristiano highlights the tension between faith, sexuality, and gender identity that led Alexya to renounce her vocation. In exchange for the priesthood, she pursued a career in education and obtained degrees in Language and Literature.

The pastor's narrative continues to make room for the theme of conjugal love, which works as a turning point in a newly-formed path towards the intelligibility of a subject. When Alexya's love story was shared from the church pulpit, it became an iconic moment. According to the pastor, in 2009, Alexya happened to meet her future husband, Roberto Salvador, on the São Paulo subway. In February 2010, while still identifying as a man, Alexya and Roberto attended the Metropolitan Community Church in São Paulo, hoping to find a church that would accept and celebrate their love story.

According to the leader of the Metropolitan Community Church, in 2011, just a month after the Supreme Federal Court recognized same-sex unions as a family, Alexya and Roberto were among the couples who made their relationship official in a collective marriage ceremony held by the Metropolitan Community Church at the University of São Paulo Law School's noble hall. This part of the pastor's narrative pays tribute to another iconic event previously organized by the Metropolitan Community Church, where Alexya had already emerged as a central figure. The church, which sees itself as a cradle for creating new activists for LGBT rights, hosted a combined civic and religious marriage ceremony at one of the country's top law schools, thereby sparking an idea of religious citizenship.

Cristiano explains that sometime after the wedding, Alexya became a deaconess in the local community and, in October of that same year, she underwent her gender transition. According to the reverend, since then, Alexya's life has been completely transformed. Being true to herself, Alexya began to experience her new life in God. She became the first trans woman to adopt a child in Brazil and was later installed as a lay pastoral assistant at the Metropolitan Community Church of São Paulo, where she exercised her pastoral ministry for 2 years.

The reverend goes on to recount Alexya's journey until she found the Metropolitan Community Church, highlighting the obstacles she faced as a gay and then trans woman, a Christian, and as someone who also discovered her blackness. The reverend further points out to the congregation that Alexya's ministry and her public figure extend beyond national borders and religion. He mentions that Alexya gave lectures and advocated for human rights causes in other countries, and is now vice-president of the Brazilian Association of Homotransaffective Families (ABRAFH): "she is a human rights activist, a transfeminist, and is passionate about adoption, people with disabilities, public education, and social struggles".

From this account, we can see that Alexya's struggle to find acceptance for being on the margins of Catholicism, gender, and family social conventions is a key aspect of her identity as a human rights subject. In this new community, the Metropolitan Community Church, her Christian practices are part of a broader action for social justice and the transformation of the conditions in which marginalized and destitute individuals inhabit the world. According to the reverend, he also speaks from the margins of Christianity, but there is a place for him, a gay and black cis man, for Alexya, a trans woman, and for the use of human rights to create the reign of God in the world, here and now.

Continuing with the ceremony, Cristiano Valério then invites Bishop Ines-Paul, a non-binary transgender reverend of the Metropolitan Community Church, who traveled from Germany specifically to preside over the anointing of Alexya. The most solemn and photographed moment of the ceremony is when a trans woman and a non-binary person are the main protagonists. Wearing a white tunic with pink and blue sashes and crimson pumps, Alexya walks to the center and stands in front of the altar, in the aisle between the front row pews, where Ines-Paul awaits. Seated next to Bishop Nancy Maxwell behind the altar, Ines-Paul stands up and walks to the center of the scene, where Alexya prostrates herself at the cross. Wearing liturgical robes over black clothes and boots of the same color, the bishop sprinkles Alexya with anointed water. After about a minute of prostration, Alexya kneels before the bishop. Both hold open a black folder, in which Ines-Paul begins to read, in English, Alexya's tasks as a minister. In front of religious leaders and activists, the congregation, and attentive cameras, Ines-Paul says that Alexya's tasks are to "proclaim the Gospel," "announce the good news of Jesus, who opposes injustice, segregation, and death," and "declare the unconditional love of God." After the same reading is translated into Portuguese, the bishop proceeds with a series of questions and answers. Alexya confirms her calling, publicly submits to accountability, and makes church commitments her own.

During the ceremony, Alexya's responses—"yes, I will do that"—reveal the formal nature of the game being played: an oath. This rhetorical form has the power to create connections between the liturgy of the Metropolitan Community Church and other solemn declarations that are already ingrained in their imaginations, such as oaths taken in court, professional oaths, and pledges to the flag. The use of this rhetorical form serves as a model that supposedly illustrates how the 'sacred' and the 'legal' intersect and come together.

In Alexya's oath, she pledges to spread the gospel of Jesus Christ through her words and actions, oppose injustice and segregation, love and serve all people equally, and "continue to fight against all 'religious fundamentalism' that segregates, excludes, and kills." Ines-Paul emphasizes that the Metropolitan Community Church does not tolerate social injustice or demonic forces that seek to destroy God's creation. He/She asks Alexya if she is even more committed to fighting for human rights and building the "reign of God" here and now. The oath thus concludes with human rights at the center of the anointing.

On one hand, these religious actors view human rights as a form of action in the world, a means to build the kingdom of God on earth, which they understand requires the pursuit of social justice, including the transformation of the world into a more accepting place for diverse expressions of gender, sexuality, and religiosity. On the other hand, the oath emphasizes "the struggle for human rights," acknowledging that these rights are innate, as is often reiterated in documents and speeches. By gathering femininities and masculinities in a solemn moment outside of nature to reaffirm their commitment to fighting for human rights, they remind us that the formal recognition of rights and subjects is a result of the narratives of suffering that the world imposes on those who belong to groups put at risk. This recognition can be achieved through social action that transforms societal conventions and through affirming the dignity of these individuals through their actions, bodies, and speeches that create shared sensibilities and make it possible to imagine their inscription in legal forms.

The Metropolitan Community Church places a strong emphasis on community, which it defines not only as those who physically attend its services, but also includes those who are reached by its commitment to justice and imagination. This community-oriented approach is highlighted when Ines-Paul emphasizes the church's focus on ecumenism and interreligiousness, and invites all religious leaders and the entire congregation gathered to lay hands on Alexya. Everyone comes together to pray in a show of unity:

> Creator God of all life and human diversity, we ask that through your Son, Jesus Christ, you send your Holy Spirit, holy Ruah, upon our sister Alexya Salvador, filling her with your grace and power so that she may fulfill the role of an ordained cleric in the Church. We pray that our sister, Alexya Salvador, will also exalt you, Lord, among your marginalized and excluded people, fearlessly proclaiming the Gospel of liberation to all and administering the sacraments with her life. Make Alexya a faithful shepherd, a patient teacher, and a wise counselor. We ask all this through your Son, Jesus Christ, in his many names. Amen.

Throughout the prayer, the scene is full of emotion and repeatedly lit up by guests' cell phones and camera flashes as they rise from the pews to record the moment. The tense movement of the cameraman filming the documentary “Deus é Mulher” can also be seen, as he searches for the best angles to capture the meeting of the leaders. Through their equipment and bodily movements throughout the church, the cameraman and production staff demonstrate that for some, prayer extends beyond the present moment and becomes a scene that they create. Meanwhile, Inês-Paul, through her preaching, guides Christianity towards a world that must be transformed by principles of social justice, including the materiality and diversity of life. However, discussing these principles can also be seen as a discontinuity in relation to certain interpretations of Christianity, as it displaces the idea of equality in God and places diversity at the center, which finds its condition of possibility in the equal love of God.

Finally, Alexya is ordained with sacred golden vestments, which are brought to her and placed by her ordination “godmother”, Ana Ester, a theologian and future reverend of the Metropolitan Community Church of Belo Horizonte. Months later, she would move to the United States and marry the American Metropolitan Community Church bishop who was in the pulpit. Inês-Paul introduces Alexya as the new cleric of the Metropolitan Community Church, the Reverend Alexya Salvador. The entire assembly stands up and applauds effusively. Alexya greets the assembly, then turns to the altar and takes her place on the other side next to the leaders. The offertory liturgy begins, in which the Reverend Márcio Retamero, leader of the Metropolitan Community Church of Rio de Janeiro who had moved to São Paulo, reiterates that members of the Metropolitan Community Church are encouraged not to deny their bodies, but to embrace them as holy and from the Lord. Actress Renata Carvalho and Alexya’s three children, including two trans girls, enter the church and bring offerings and gifts of bread and wine.

5 Eucharistic Liturgy

After being ordained as a reverend, Alexya receives the offerings and consecrates the bread and wine, which are symbols in the Christian tradition representing the body and blood of Christ, and begins the Eucharist, a sacramental liturgy that refers to the sacrifice of the son of God on the cross, which is made present and updated in each Christian service. Holding a silver thurible, she solemnly circulates the altar, purifying it. Then, she turns to the congregation and speaks for the first time:

> I arrived at the Metropolitan Community Church 10 years ago and when I climbed those steps, I didn’t know who I was. When I got to those steps, I was pretty sure that God didn’t love me. I was sure I was God's mistake. And when I arrived at the Metropolitan Community Church, I, who came from a Catholic tradition, learned that I couldn't get near the altar because I was in sin. Only a few people were invited to the supper and these few people had to wear a badge. And I walked in, and I remember that Reverend Cristiano said that night that this table is not of the Church, that the table in the Metropolitan Community Church is Jesus Christ’s table. Jesus didn’t turn away Judas, even though He knew he would betray Him. Jesus didn’t turn away Peter, even though He knew he would deny Him three times. Jesus broke bread that last night for all the people present, regardless of their sexual

orientation or gender identity. He wasn't concerned with whom they slept with or what their political views were. He simply broke bread.

And when I heard that message it was transformative, because I had heard the opposite my whole life. I had to be part of the club, I had to get my stuff together. I had to catch up with sound doctrine. And that night Jesus embraced me fully. Me and my husband. When I arrived at the Metropolitan Community Church I couldn't imagine everything that God had already thought out for me. I couldn't imagine all that God had already planned out about my life. This is why I chose today's gospel: The Magnificat. Because just as God did wonders for Mary's life, today I can tell you that the Lord has done wonders for me. And Holy is His name. The wonders of God are in this transvestite body, in this transgressive body, because, for God, it doesn't matter what genital organs we have or what our ideal bodies look like. For God, what matters is that we have an open heart, a willing heart, and a welcoming mind.

Her first speech as a reverend shares the story of her encounter with the Metropolitan Community Church and her own journey as a trans-Christian woman through the church. To retell the story of her successive encounters, Alexya draws from her Catholic past, her sense of inadequacy and non-belonging, and then highlights her transformative encounter with her new church which she qualifies as "transformer". She remembers climbing the steps, feeling lost and unsure of who she was. The image of the path is not arbitrary. It combines with the narrow door of the Metropolitan Community Church and the Gospel according to Matthew, which is the way that leads to life. Access to the Metropolitan Community Church put Alexya in contact with readings that reinterpret the Bible to reshape traditional meanings, especially regarding the exclusivity of the truth of faith and moral constructions related to the uses of the body for erotic and affective purposes.

The transformative character of her encounter with the Metropolitan Community Church lies in the fact that religious agency is inscribed in the history of Christianity even though it may exist on the margins of traditional interpretations. To the sound of the gospel praise "Because He lives" and raising her voice, Alexya consecrates the bread and wine, starting the Eucharistic supper. As she leaves, she thanks God and asks for the lives of all transvestites, all trans women, all trans men, all non-binary people, the "misfits", those who, like her, "are out of the box". She records in her ordination memory two trans human rights activists, Marsha Johnson and Sylvia Rivera, "examples of faith." She gives thanks to all the lives of activists who "fell to the ground" and recalls that Brazil is the country that kills the most transvestites in the world. She asks the Lord to unite her in communion with all transvestite sisters, trans male brothers, transgender sisters, all misfits, all LGBTs, gays, lesbians, pansexuals, asexuals, bisexuals, all human beings who in the past paved the way for that ceremony to take place.

If we are able to walk the streets today, despite the violence, and if we have gained some rights, it is because many people gave their lives for us to walk in the street today. Our place is not only on the street corners, my dear ones, but wherever we choose to be. Our place is where God calls us. And it is this God who is a transvestite, yes. This God who is gay, yes. To this God who is a lesbian, yes. To this God who is a man, yes. To this God who is a woman, yes. To this God who is a person. This God loved the world so much that he chose to be born as a man through Mary. So, my dear ones, when you hear people say that Jesus is a transvestite, before being shocked, think a little. You are not exclusive to God, we are all exclusive to God. Men, women, white people, and black people. We are the Lord's chosen people.

In the final act of consecration, Alexya sings gospel praise into the microphone with her hands raised and eyes closed. Having broken the "bread of justice", "bread of equality", she finally invites everyone to communion, which she offers alongside Cristiano Valério and and two international ecclesiastical authorities from the Metropolitan Community Church, Nancy Maxwell and Ines-Paul, who are seated to her left. Those present gradually line up, without crowding, and communion takes place slowly, to the rhythm of the *Magnificat*.

In Alexya's speech, she references human rights, which she suggests were won through struggles and sacrifices of countless individuals. The scene illustrates how communion, surrounded by a belief in "radical inclusion," embodies these values. It is imagined that those seeking to build the reign of God share a belief in human rights. In the recording of the scene, many express these values through their bodies as a means of communication and religious community, either situational or aspiring to permanence. Additionally, the Metropolitan Community Church supper provides a space for several alliances to gain body and social forms: (i) the LGBT attendees who present themselves to the church as gays, lesbians, bisexuals, transvestites, or Christian trans people; (ii) the Metropolitan Community Church community itself, which articulates alliances to form a global network of inclusive communities; and (iii) alliances between religious leaders themselves and between then and activist leaders.

Alexya uses her voice to draw our attention to another powerful symbol—the transformation of the altar into a table, an instrument, and a space of communion. It is from the table that the experience of the meeting is possible, the possibility of everyone coming together around it as "the great truth of faith". In the religious practices of the Metropolitan Community Church, the Eucharist serves as a powerful form of radical inclusion, and it takes the form of a drama centered around an invitation that encourages the exercise of free will. This is precisely how Alexya addresses everyone in her first Eucharistic liturgy:

> For those of you attending a Metropolitan Community Church service for the first time, I want to share with you what I've learned, because I received it for free, I want to transmit it for free. The great truth of faith: that this table is not mine, and these elements are not mine. You don't even have to be a Christian to join us here. Look around, there are so many beautiful people from other faiths who are here today, and that's because the Metropolitan Community Church values the truth - the truth that no one can erase. We are not a new church. Rather, we are a chapter in the history of Christianity that cannot be stopped. If you feel moved to join us in our supper and communion, you are welcome to do so. However, if you prefer not to participate, that's okay too. God's principle is freedom, respect, and human dignity.

The story unfolds in two parts. Firstly, the person's gesture of standing up and walking towards the center of the church, thereby exposing themselves with all their differences. Then, the act of communion, where the community comes together and experiences an aesthetic formation that can be circumstantially experienced. And there, in the Eucharistic liturgy of the Holy Trinity Parish, receiving communion was also an opportunity to assume a new position in the congregation. It allowed for the exchange of passive listening for actively participating in a polyphonic invitation and aligning oneself publicly with a cause expressed through both religious and political grammar. The act of coming together at the table represents the refusal of any form of exclusion, including on the basis of one's faith or lack thereof, and emphasizes the centrality of community. Alexya's use of the table in her speech, in which she refers to it as "the great truth of faith," is reminiscent of Arendt's reflection on public space as an intersubjective space in which actors appear to one another. According to Arendt (1992), the table simultaneously brings people together and sets them apart, enabling equal individuals to exchange ideas through words. The meeting around the table facilitates the communication of ideas and the revelation of one's true self. Building on Arendt's reading, we can see that in the reverend's speech at the table, she establishes a regime of equality and visibility, which fosters the construction of alliances through open exchange and sharing of bread in front of everyone.

The Eucharistic liturgy led by Alexya prompts us to reflect on the iconic images of religion. The live image resulting from the pastor's worship, which is now also shared in the form of photographs and videos, contests the traditional depictions that portrayed the liturgy of the consubstantiation of the body and blood of Christ in a masculinized manner. As a trans woman, Alexya not only challenges the norm by assuming the role of conducting the first sacramental ritual, where Jesus first performed the sacrificial act of offering his body and blood to his followers in the form of bread and wine, but also rejects the erasure of femininity in this scene, which is evident in Leonardo da Vinci's painting, The Last Supper, one of the most renowned depictions of the first ritual. By allowing herself to be portrayed as an icon in the ordination liturgy, Alexya feminizes the ritual on stage and proclaims through her actions: "God is a transvestite, yes! God is gay, yes!... God is all people," concludes the newest reverend in Brazil.

6 Final Considerations

To analyze specific social ways of correlating religion and human rights categories based on the ethnography of Alexya Salvador's ordination ceremony, this chapter took on the challenge of demonstrating that human rights can be seen as a language in action. Religion, assumed in common sense as a self-referred concept to an ontological totality, transmutes into an operating code of a dramatic and liturgical plot.

Following this path and paying attention to capturing what we call iconic scenes, human rights and religion were approached as sensitive and intelligible experiences that build arenas of interlocution and proposition in public acts, and the circulation of meanings. As we have shown in the previous pages, it is in this operation that subjects and their multiple groups of belongings are modeled pari passu.

By taking human rights beyond their regulatory dimension and religion as a linguistic construct, this chapter also situated these two categories beyond horizons that restrict communication processes to verbal discursive exchanges. Reading the living frames exposed on the church's altar as a specific aesthetic-political regime, we were able to glimpse how the communicative power of religion and human rights categories is linked to particular social imaginations, which are susceptible to ethnographic scrutiny.

Taking the liberty of furthering our own chapter, it's important to note that imagination involves making the absent present. This requires creating an image that lies between sensibility and understanding, which not only doesn't have the real as a model, but is a schema for it. As proposed by Hannah Arendt (1992), this schema provides (i) a synthesis of the infinite multiplicity of the world of appearances, allowing the apprehension of the sensible, and (ii) an image for concepts, making the world an object accessible to thought. As these schemas are shared, sensitivity and understanding transform the world into an object of communication, making knowledge and understanding possible. Thanks to them, we can build a common world, communicate about it, and work together to transform it. The shared nature of these schemas leads us to believe that our interactions involve the formation of sensitivities and an imaginary, understood as a set of forms created by the imagination that make the sensitive intelligible.

Human rights documents, with their widely shared rhetorical formulas, play a critical role in the modern imagination by providing people with an image of a fairer world and offering ways to achieve it. As we saw in the ethnographic scene described, human rights are not just discourses relegated to the legal field, but are iconized in scenic acts that incite the congregation to experience them through a liturgy. The liturgy provides aesthetic means for audiences to internalize abstract ideas of rights through the narrative of a unique life trajectory, that of the trans pastor. From this perspective, the problem of the strategy of public visibility moves beyond the dispute over the naming of the figure 'trans pastor' to its inscription in a broader social imaginary.

To understand the dynamics of this operation in the ethnographic scene, we had to explain that the language of human rights belongs to an imaginary that precedes and overflows the Metropolitan Community Church in time and in its modes of use. This language gives substance to an imaginary through codes such as love, family, dignity, suffering, and overcoming, as well as ritualized rhetorical forms and formulas such as oaths, declarations, proclamations, and calls.

It is the transversality of human rights understood in this specific sense that makes it possible for the imagination of visitors and, above all, leaders of the Metropolitan Community Church, shaped in Alexya's liturgy of ordination ceremony, to form alliances with leaders of different religious communities and social movements. The situational meeting around imaginaries is experienced together from a shared language, forming a coalition. The materialization of this situational confluence finds resources in the traditions of law and Christianity.

As mentioned before, Hunt and Sliwinski have written about how books and images have contributed to the emergence and spread of the idea of human rights. They argue that the circulation of certain artifacts has shaped people's sensitivities and created conditions for the recognition of human dignity as a central idea in the history of human rights. In analyzing Alexya's ordination ceremony, we focus on iconic scenes recorded metonymically in social media. These scenes convey the meaning of the liturgy and contribute to the conformation of a new sensitivity to human rights.

Paraphrasing Ernst Gombrich (1995), there is no religion; instead, it's the religious leaders who shape it. In line with this view, we aim to draw attention to a particular type of religious actor: one who employs human rights to make the divine immanent in public life, while simultaneously committing themselves to political causes and establishing themselves as transcendent public figures.

Birgit Meyer has developed a material approach to religion, arguing that religions become tangible and intelligible by conforming an aesthetic materialized in the structure of space, objects, and instruments of worship. This inspired us to create a diversity of religious groups that comprise the ethnographic scene alongside the Metropolitan Community Church of São Paulo. Meyer's propositions become denser from the perspective of a pragmatic sociology, which enables us to consider the arena in which human rights come to life as a space of visibility and communicative interaction in which plausible speakers are constituted based on their ability to form an audience. The different actors in the ethnographic scene aim to mobilize and persuade people through specific aesthetic-political regimes.

This process, anchored in a language that has become a global language of justice, links and coordinates two imaginations that the church's congregations conceive as autonomous: the political and theological imagination. It is this ability to coordinate these two imaginaries that underpins the communicative power of the church. This can be observed in the scenes of the service, which reveal that the religious agency's capacity to link and coordinate imaginations is proportional to its ability to form coalitions expressed through iconized public scenes that interest everyone who is part of the living framework that embodies a system of alliances.

The altar of the Holy Trinity Parish thus becomes a stage for affirming the identities and causes of social movements or a platform for proclamations and oaths. Despite recurrently showing the religious under the weight of convention, the altar also embodies the new LGBT ecumenism, with trans women, drag queens, lesbians, gay men, non-binary people, and leaders of religious collectives and social movements expressing themselves. The altar becomes a setting for a ritual that transcends time and space, captured in an audiovisual piece with unrestricted access, connecting the church and its characters to new networks and imaginations.

References

Arendt H (1992) Lectures on Kant's political philosophy. University of Chicago Press, Chicago

Butler J (2015) Notes toward a performative theory of assembly. Harvard University Press, London

Cefaï D (1996) La Construction des Problèmes Publics: Définitions de Situations dans des Arènes Publiques. Réseaux Commun Technol Soc 14(75):43–66

Cefaï D (2017) Públicos, Problemas Públicos, Arenas Públicas. . .: O que nos ensina o pragmatismo (Parte 1). Novos Estudos CEBRAP 36(1):187–213

Geertz C (1989) A interpretação das culturas. Guanabara Koogan, Rio de Janeiro

Gombrich EH (1995) The story of art. Phaidon, London

Hunt L (2009) A invenção dos direitos humanos: uma história. Companhia das Letras, São Paulo

ICM. Igreja da Comunidade Metropolitana de São Paulo. Culto de ordenação clerical de Alexya Salvador. Available at https://www.facebook.com/icmsp/videos/2611996965521927. Accessed 19 Apr 2020

Meyer B (2010) Aesthetics of Persuasion: global christianity and pentecostalism's sensational forms. South Atl Q 109(4):741–763

Meyer B (2019) Como as Coisas Importam: Uma Abordagem Material da Religião – Textos de Birgit Meyer. In: Giumbelli E, Rickli J, Toniol R (eds) Editora da UFRGS. UFRGS, Porto Alegre

Silva JB (2019) Um lugar à mesa: estudo sobre a produção pastoral do ativismo "católico LGBT" brasileiro. Dissertação, Universidade de Campinas

Sliwinski S (2006) The childhood of human rights: The Kodak on the Congo. J Vis Cult 5(3): 333–363

Sliwinski S (2009) The aesthetics of human rights. Cult Theory Crit 50(1):23–39

Sliwinski S (2015) Inventing human dignity. In: McClennen Slennen S, Schultheis A (eds) The Routledge companion to literature and human rights. Routledge, London, pp 173–183

Turner V (1986) Dewey, Dilthey, and drama: an essay in the anthropology of experience. In: Turner V, Bruner E (eds) The anthropology of experience. University Illinois Press, Urbana, pp 33–44

MIX
Papier aus verantwortungsvollen Quellen
Paper from responsible sources
FSC® C105338
FSC
www.fsc.org

If you have any concerns about our products,
you can contact us on
ProductSafety@springernature.com

In case Publisher is established outside the EU,
the EU authorized representative is:
Springer Nature Customer Service Center GmbH
Europaplatz 3, 69115 Heidelberg, Germany

Printed by Libri Plureos GmbH
in Hamburg, Germany